HERRING
A HISTORY OF THE
SILVER DARLINGS

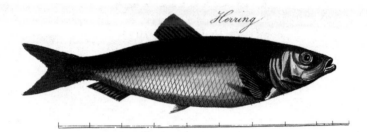

Herring

HERRING
A HISTORY OF THE
SILVER DARLINGS

MIKE SMYLIE

TEMPUS

To Petros for introducing me to Karya...
and Moe for sharing it.

First published 2004

Tempus Publishing Limited
The Mill, Brimscombe Port,
Stroud, Gloucestershire, GL5 2QG
www.tempus-publishing.com

© Mike Smylie, 2004

The right of Mike Smylie to be identified as the Author
of this work has been asserted in accordance with the
Copyrights, Designs and Patents Act 1988.

British Library Cataloguing in Publication Data.
A catalogue record for this book is available from the British Library.

ISBN 0 7524 2988 4

Typesetting and origination by Tempus Publishing Limited
Printed in Great Britain by Midway Colour Print, Wiltshire

Contents

Acknowledgements

This book has been more than ten years in waiting. Over that time I have travelled widely about Britain with the Herring Exhibition that has seemingly acted as a magnet to folk with a story to tell about their nostalgic days herring fishing. To all those who spent a few minutes or much longer, thank you for your time. To those fishermen who allowed me time on their boats, thank you for putting up with questions while you worked. A personal thanks, in no particular order, goes to: Angus Martin, Lachie Patterson, Neville Orton, Robert Prescott, Robert and Pearl Simper, Denise Owens, Alex West, Michael Craine, Roy Mildon, David Linkie, Alexis and Petros Kounouklas, Billy Stevenson, Charles Payton, to Maria Strömsholm for proof-reading and to Campbell McCutcheon at Tempus. Also, a word of thanks to the Scottish Fisheries Museum at Anstruther for use of their library. The museum is the only one in Britain that fully portrays the herring fishery and is to be recommended. At the end of the book is a bibliography of books concerning the herring fishery and I thank those authors, whether dead or alive. Only because of the work they undertook many years ago is it now possible to recount images from the great era of the herring industry. And great it was. Wherever I go I hear stories of how the harbours were crowded with fishing boats. How many times I have heard that the harbour could be crossed on the boats, I don't know! It is a common recollection and, although I doubt it occurred in some of the places I've visited, it must have been a reality in a very many others. This book can only be dedicated to the generations of people that made it happen – the fishers, apprentices, curers, herring lassies, coopers, labourers, fishery officers, merchants, boatbuilders, net-makers, sail-makers, rope-makers etc.

The passage from George Campbell Hay's poem *Seeker Reaper* is published by kind permission from the Trustees of the Lorimer Trust, while Angus Martin's poem *Tonight the Fleets* is published with the author's kind permission.

The Author

Mike Smylie – otherwise known as 'Kipperman' – is a naval architect, maritime historian, fisheries ethnologist, maritime archaeologist and herring smoker. He runs the Centre for Maritime Vernacular Culture and has recently completed two years' research at the Scottish Institute of Maritime Studies at St Andrew's University, where he gained an MPhil. He is the author of four previous books on fishing and fishing boats and has written widely on maritime matters in various magazines and in *Fishing News*. In 1995 he co-founded the 40+ Fishing Boat Association, Britain's only organisation dedicated to all types of fishing boats, and he edits their magazine *Fishing Boats*. Since 1996, he has been travelling around Britain to maritime festivals each summer with the Herring Exhibition. He alternates living between Wales and Greece.

By the same author:
The Herring Fishers and other Vignettes (London, 1995)
The Herring Fishers of Wales (Llanrwst, 1998)
The Traditional Fishing Boats of Britain and Ireland
    (Shrewsbury, 1999)
Anglesey and its Coastal Tradition (Llanrwst, 2000)
Kipperman and the Red Herring (Llangaffo, 2000)

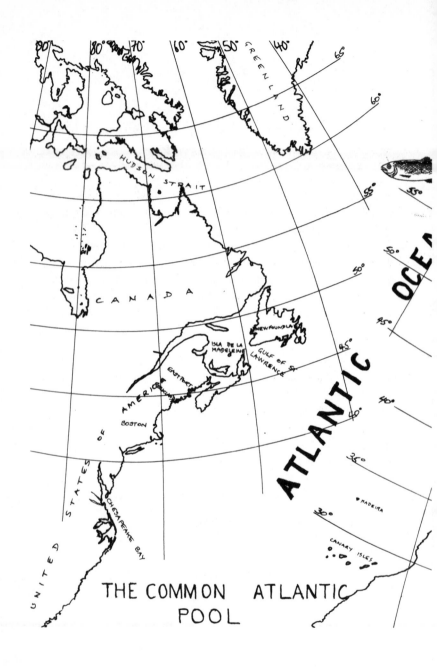

THE COMMON ATLANTIC
POOL

Introduction

'Herring for Health 6½d'

'Herring for Health 6½d': A title that reflects two of the finest qualities of the meagre herring – its healthy aspect and its cheapness. The title actually came from a government information film from the late 1940s when herring was deemed sufficiently available to feed the war-weary population at a time when rationing was still in force. I have adopted it for this introduction, which makes no apologies for suggesting that re-introducing these wholesome plentiful fish into our national diet could make a real impact upon the country's health. At the time of writing, one of the uppermost debates in Britain concerns the National Health Service and its ability – or inability – to cope with the demands and needs of a cutting-edge society. As life is prolonged due to advancement in medical technology, and with pressure in over-worked hospitals that struggle with a surge in drug- and alcohol-related problems, preventive medicine would seem the way forward. However, instead of extolling the virtues of a balanced diet, society seems to advocate an intake of burgers and other nutritionless foods whose taste comes more from a few droplets of manufactured liquid than from nature's own larder. The beneficial aspects of food are often overlooked due to the mercenary multinational institutions' intent on profit rather than human decency. This is also reflected in the increasing rise in obesity among the British population, half of whom, it has been suggested, are overweight.

Herring are rich in the omega-3 fatty acids that are found in all oily fish. Herring contain, on average, about ten per cent oil. These polyunsaturated fatty acids are much more beneficial than the harder fats found in meat. Herring are also full of Vitamins A and D. Omega-3 fatty acids have been proven to help reduce heart disease and arthritis and improve brain function and behaviour. One Orkney-based doctor's surgery has even gone as far as giving out prescriptions for herring instead of conventional medicines. Now comes the news that herring and other oily fish help to reduce the risk of women having premature babies, or babies born underweight.

Its protein content is high when compared to many other foods, according to the Herring Industry Board of old. One pound in weight of meat has 685 calories, while the same amount of eggs has 635, potatoes 370 and milk 310. Herring, at the other end of the scale, has 755 calories per pound. It is also mineral rich, especially as a source of iodine. The only danger is mercury content, although many scientists point out that the average Briton does not eat enough fish for this to matter.

Herring is undoubtedly plentiful, although stocks were dangerously close to a total collapse in the 1970s before the North Sea Fishery was closed down for several years. It re-opened in 1981, as we shall see in Chapter Fourteen, and supplies have remained relatively buoyant since then. However, much of today's herring is caught by industrial fishing vessels which send the entire catch to factories to be processed for fish meal, pig food and even for electricity generating. Much of this is taken as a by-catch – in other words it is taken by vessels fishing for other species – some even being found to have by-catches of up to ninety-seven per cent herring. Only a small percentage goes for human consumption which, to many people, is regarded as both wasteful and unnecessary.

The trouble with herring is that it doesn't have a good public image. It was regarded once as the food of the poor, who hated it, although they often had nothing else to eat. Fresh herring is considered to be bony and therefore unpalatable. Kippers are smelly and also full of bones, although both of these descriptions are unfair. Kippers gained a bad reputation when dyes were first added in the Second World War to quicken the smoking process, but most today are free of these colourings. The bones are easy to remove and modern cooking techniques reduce the smell about the kitchen. Canning techniques now enable all sorts of sauces to add taste to the fish, and sales of these are perhaps minutely on the increase now that they often appear on the supermarket shelves, especially those German stores whose numbers have recently exploded. I have just eaten a tin of herring fillets in mango and pepper sauce as I write this. A quick snack with a huge punch!

Cured herring can usually be found in the large shops and fish stalls, as can kippers under the label 'Manx' or 'Loch Fyne', both of which are widely respected. However, most of the herring itself comes from the North Sea these days and is smoked locally, although small amounts are being landed in the Isle of Man after many years of dearth.

Landings by long-shore fishermen are on the increase as well, as are the North Sea and Northern Atlantic catches. Fraserburgh has the largest fleet of pelagic trawlers in Britain, but much of this herring is landed outside the country. Here history is repeating itself, for the Scottish herring industry of the nineteenth and twentieth centuries relied more upon the export market than home consumption for its growth. However, if the British public could be persuaded to eat two herring a week, and a ban was imposed on the industrial fishing of herring, then we would most certainly see an improvement in the nation's health. Both actions, though, would mean government involvement, an action on their part that, at the present, seems unlikely. On the one hand, clearing away vast tracts of the rainforest to breed cattle for burgers is acceptable in some quarters, not least those multinationals who are increasing their number of outlets across the world, selling food that is exactly the same wherever it is bought; and on the other, industrial fishing is profitable and unlikely to be outlawed, especially in European politics. The wranglings over the National Health Service look set to continue, I suppose, until the accepted view is a form of privatisation. The past failings of the Common Fisheries Policy of the European Union are ignored while cod stocks plummet further. Those voices of concern are all too often smothered by the avarice of big business and the intransigence of government.

Herring, though, remains relatively cheap, even within its small market. Scientists are beginning to realise that healthy stocks of the fish are building up. The price would presumably decrease through a higher uptake in the retail sector. If half of the population of Britain ate two a week, the yearly landing to supply this market would be less than half a million tons, the sustainable level it was at before the advent of the purse-seine net in the mid-twentieth century. This is, then, realistic. The only stumbling block is the lack of impetus. Thus, if this book has any purpose, it is to document the historical importance of the herring, and to highlight its versatility. May the herring be recommended in its rightful place in the daily diet of the people.

PART ONE

The Common Atlantic Pool

The herring – who finds in the shining waves
Board, lodging and washing free –
Though small is, of all kind Neptune's gifts,
The sweetest by far to me.
He wanders about, through the roaring main,
With his sisters, and cousins, and aunts,
In shoals so tremendous, to count 'em were vain,
And what's more – nobody wants.
He won't make you squeamish when recently caught,
And is not to be sneezed at when high-cured and 'saut';
On the table of Dives he's lavishly spread,
And sweetens for Hodge his poor crust of bread.
For this bounteous gift dear old Ocean we thank,
And draughts e'en miraculous draw on his bank.

From *De laudibus divinae sapientiae* by Friar Neckham (died 1227)

Kipper Soup

Ingredients:
1lb of fresh kipper fillets, skinned
2 cans of chopped tomatoes
2 cloves of crushed garlic
2 tablespoonfuls of tomato purée
¼ pint of milk
Pepper
Natural yogurt, to serve

Method:
Jug the kippers for 5 minutes. Drain and reserve the liquid. Flake the fish
into a food processor. Add the tomatoes, garlic and puree. Blend until
smooth. Pour the mixture into a large saucepan and add a pint of the
reserved liquid together with the milk. Bring to simmering point and simmer
for 5 minutes and season. Serve hot with a whirl of natural yogurt.

CHAPTER ONE

Henry Sutton's Finest

The midday sun is tepid, yet across the dusty square my neighbours sit under the shade of their vine, aghast as we continue working, clearing fertiliser-bagfuls of rubbish from the house during this, the siesta hour. Downstairs, the cellar is dark and dank, having no window large enough to let in more than a smidgen of the spring sun's rays. The house, last inhabited in 1963, needs company to let it hum once again.

It is a new acquisition, this house. This is the first sortie after weeks of negotiation and paperwork to secure the sale. Two weeks to prepare for major works to transform the place from unlived in, near dereliction to paradisiacal home. Clearing out the old, breathing in some new; keeping, of course, the tangible elements of the house's past and the atmosphere of originality.

So out go the old bags of fermenting wheat from below ancient wooden store bins, as does firewood infested with huge wormholes, and lime plaster that has fallen away from high walls. We sort through boxes containing relics of a past life – rusting tins, battered aluminium pans, nails, hinges. There's a wooden loom in various pieces and a hollowed-out tree trunk that was once a grain hopper. A box full of sheets of paper appears from beneath this. I lift it, and another similar but empty box and take them to the light to investigate. They seem to be ledger accounts, sums of money owed by individual names. There are pages of them, I notice as I flick through. One has '1924' written at the top, another '1931'.

The boxes themselves are wooden, with red and blue stencilling on their outer sides. I shriek because I cannot believe what I am reading. For this house, as you may have guessed, is not in Britain. No, it is high up in a mountain village in central Greece.

'Hey, look at what I've found,' I cry out to a friend working above, 'You won't believe this!' In red there's a huge 'HS' surrounded by

'HENRY SUTTON, GT. YARMOUTH' and below, in bold letters, **'FINEST SELECTED CURED HERRING'**. In smaller writing, 'CURED & PACKED UNDER THE MOST MODERN HYGIENIC CONDITIONS'. Inside there's a triangular stamp with a crown and the word 'SOMMEN' with 'SWEDEN' below. Obviously the boxes are of Swedish origin, being filled in England and exported to Greece. Later I learnt that Suttons exported almost exclusively to Mediterranean countries. Fate had surely delivered me to these boxes.

John Mowson began working for Suttons in the 1950s. Henry Sutton himself had started the business by pushing a loaded narrow troll-cart (sometimes called a row-cart after the 'rows' within which the fishermen lived) selling herring at ½d each. That was way back in the 1870s. His son, also Henry, later took over and developed the business, smoking herring and exporting it, especially to Egypt, Cyprus and Greece. He built himself a house on the front at Yarmouth, where the Prince of Wales was a regular visitor. Percy, his son, in turn took over, further expanding markets in West Africa, South Africa, America, Australia, the Middle East and Italy, where silver herring – those smoked for only twenty-four to forty-eight hours – were eaten in the fields. John travelled extensively attending to these markets during his time with the company and remembers over 500 people being employed by them. 'Yarmouth was alive with smokehouses in those days,' he told me.

By chance I met Aleko the evening following the find of the boxes. A group of us were in a bar and he came over, recognising my Greek friends. It was Aleko from whom I'd bought the house, but I'd not met him as the whole transaction had been dealt with through Petros, my Greek friend, and his father, Alekis. It was Aleko's parents who had died in 1963, thus leaving the house empty for almost forty years. After the first ten years of tending it, the family had begun to forget. But not enough for him to be unable to fill me in on the history.

Alongside the main house was a former taverna, its roof now totally collapsed, walls in a sorry state. This was the original structure, inside of which his father had opened a small store in 1923, selling produce and, of course, herring. He bought his boxes from a merchant in Athens, some 100 miles to the south. How he had got there he wasn't sure, for the village was only accessible by using a steep mountain path that wound its way up from the coast some 2,500ft below, although the mountain base was only half a mile from the sea. Donkeys were

The Place to make Red Herrings, *by S. V. Meulen (1792).*

the only mode of transport then. Today, tractors and 4x4s wind their way up the six miles of road from the town below – a town that only grew up after the 1960s.

Herring in Greek are 'regga' (ρέγγα), perhaps a reflection of their regal status! Or perhaps this produces 'to regale' – to entertain lavishly; to feast. Maybe this denotes food fit for kings, or the fact that herring really are the kings of the sea. However, the point is that once I'd come across these boxes – and let's face it, there cannot be many people who would get excited about such a discovery – I began to ask specific questions about this source of food.

Given the diverse food available in Greece (although the critics say the food is boring, it is so only for the tourists and not for the natives) – it is perhaps natural to wonder why herring were imported all the way across Europe into these remote tiny villages. The reason, though, is the same as it was in British villages and towns, it was cheap and nutritious. Herring was regarded as winter food, so that supplies packed in Great Yarmouth during the autumnal fishery could arrive in

Greece by the beginning of the winter period. Thus they were caught in the North Sea, cured and smoked in Great Yarmouth, packed into Swedish boxes, loaded onto vessels and shipped to Athens and many other ports in the Mediterranean. Once there, they would last for up to six months.

The herring were surrounded in paper in their pretty boxes. They were heavily smoked, whole with their guts in. They were golden herring, similar in looks to red herring, although not exactly the same. A company called AJK also exported golden herring mainly to Greece and Italy, according to Reggie Reynolds. They were cured in big concrete tanks in the ground before being slowly smoked for up to two weeks. Reggie described them as being 'salty as hell'! Aleko's father sold them individually from his little shop, from where they were carried home to be baked over the fire. The women of the house saw to this, turning them over frequently as they heated. Then olive oil and lemon was poured over the top – oodles of oil fresh from the trees at that time of year – and they were traditionally served with the local green vegetable 'horta', which literally translates as 'grass' and resembles spinach. This grows wild on the mountains and is still widely eaten these days, being very tasty. And, this being Greece, the fish was washed down with liberal amounts of 'retsina', always homemade just as it is today, and tasting strongly of the pine resin that makes this white wine unique.

In 1932 they built my house, and the shop doubled up as a taverna. Here herring was served. It is said that the taverna owners used to always bake the herring because this made it even saltier. The fish themselves were a lovely golden colour and full of salt. Making the fish more salty allowed them the luxury of drinking more retsina! Then, in 1942, the Germans came to the village and took over the top floor of the house. Aleko's parents were forced to live downstairs, where they stayed for nearly twenty years after the Germans had gone. War must be abysmal for those who experience it, but for those of us who haven't it is merely sad. In my village, Karya, war came in the form of reprisal after Greek resistance fighters ambushed and killed twelve German soldiers. The houses were set alight and the villagers fled into the mountains. My house, the German barracks, survived, so that now it is the oldest in the village. After the war, Aleko's parents stayed below and the taverna never reopened, such were the scars of battle. But the two wooden boxes from Henry Sutton remained with them among their meagre possessions.

One evening we went to Georgios' workshop where he restores furniture. Work had ceased and a table had been laid out on a board supported by two saw benches. The board was covered in a tablecloth and the cloth in turn by plates of salad and grilled lamb. Retsina came from plastic bottles. Feta cheese was sprinkled with oregano from the mountains. Petros got some fried chicken. An impromptu feast was about to begin. Kostas sat opposite me. He was probably in his late sixties, with hair as white as the cheese and a face that reflected all that is good about Greece. He had been a carpenter, an expert of the wood, I was told. However, once the subject of herring came up, he recalled his first job of the day when he had been serving his apprenticeship in Athens. He made wooden skewers so that he and his fellow workers could roast the herring over the workshop fire for their breakfast. Herring, he said, were the food of the poor man in Greece, and they only ate them in winter. Later that evening he sang, while Vasilis played guitar and Yanis the bouzouki. The music was 'rebetiko', traditional folk music that came to Athens in 1927 after the Turks had forced Greek people out of their homes in the eastern part of the Aegean; what was then part of Greece but is now Turkey. With the poignant music came memories. Yanis recalled that the poor folk of Athens, usually those with no work, gathered in open-air cinemas to watch films. While watching, they wrapped their herring in newspaper and set them alight to cook them. Sometimes the dusty arena was alive with these shimmering fires, and one can imagine the sweet scent of herring mixing with the nocturnal smells of the city. We experimented with a herring I'd bought earlier that day. Today's newspapers don't burn as well as they used to, but the herring really was salty!

One taverna in Athens, Kostas told me through Petros, who always interpreted (for rarely does anyone in this part of Greece speak English), only sold herring and copious amounts of retsina to wash it down. 'It was always a crowded place,' he recalled. Vasilis remembered eating herring at home with onions. Someone else told me that another traditional fare was herring with bean stew. Butterbean stew is well known throughout Greece, even to tourists. Yanis still eats at least one herring a week. 'It helps to keep the weight down,' he said with a wry smile.

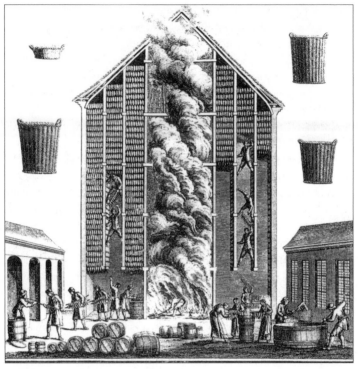

Making Red Herrings, *by Du Hamel du Monceau (1769).*

Today's herring still comes in wooden boxes. I found one such boxful on the island of Skiathos, in a tiny market shop that sold everything one could possibly need to eat. Marketed under the brand 'Komo', this came from Comeau's Seafoods Ltd of Saulnierville, Nova Scotia, Canada. Inside were double-smoked herring. The price was €3.20 per kilo – about £2. The fish I bought cost €0.54 – about 30p. With fresh herring at over £2.50 per kilo in Britain, one does have to query the price difference. How can it be cheaper to cure, smoke and pack the fish, and then send it several thousands of miles, than it is to land it into Britain and transport it to a supermarket?

Filleted herring is popular in Greece these days. This is normally marinated in olive oil and lemon. It is particularly popular served with ouzo. Here I discovered something new in Greece – homemade ouzo.

This is not the manufactured variety that turns milky on the addition of water, but a clear fiery liquid that needs no water. Perfect for the fillets of herring, although some say they prefer beer, I'm told!

I did meet an English-speaking Greek. This was another Kostas who was playing his baglamas (a tiny bouzouki) and singing in a bar. He was an ex-naval officer who suggested that people were perhaps reticent to talk about their herring experiences because of their shyness in not wanting to admit they ate 'poor food'. Iceland, he told me, had been the source of herring for the country at one time, although Canada seems to have captured the main market these days. 'You eat herring then?' he asked my friend, Moe, sitting next to me, after she had told him she had good eyesight. 'Yes', she replied, 'and lots of other fish.'

'That's because of the fish, then. Greek fishermen have perfect eyesight. It comes from the phosphorescence in the water. The fish glow. The farmers, they only eat meat. They can't see at all well'.

'Does that mean the fishermen don't touch meat? Are they vegetarian?' Moe asked him. I'd had years of experience in trying to make Greek people understand that being a vegetarian meant that you can't even taste a tiny bit of the meat.

'Well, yes they do, but they prefer fish'.

'So why are their eyes better than his?' She was referring to me, of course, short-sighted as I have been since a teenager. Thus began a discussion about the pros and cons of eating meat. We seemed to be drifting off the subject at hand. As they spoke, I considered the meagre herring. Its influence stretched across a continent, and an ocean. Canned herring can be found on any supermarket shelf. It has history, I thought, and it has made history. It was time for a thorough appraisal of the King of the Sea.

Bloater or Herring Paste

Ingredients:
1 ½ lbs of bloaters or red herring (weighed after cleaning)
½ lb fresh butter
1 teaspoonful of anchovy essence
Salt & pepper

Method:
Clean the herring and cook in boiling water for about 20 minutes, changing the water if necessary. Remove bones and skin and mince the flesh finely by passing through a mincing machine. Put into a bowl with the butter and anchovy essence and mix thoroughly. Season to taste. Put into small jars, pour some melted butter on top and tie down when cold. Store in a cool place.
Note: kipper paste can be made in the same way.

CHAPTER TWO

A Hundred Herring
Baked in a Pie

They were the favoured food of kings and queens and, at the same time, the fodder forced upon marching armies. They were almost force-fed to the slaves of the Caribbean plantations in their undignified bondage. Early prehistoric man ate them, as did the Romans, then the Saxons, and the Vikings after them. Mediaeval communities caught them and ate them. All out of choice. The Industrial Revolution progressed on the back of the meagre herring. From the Lancashire cotton mills to the South Wales coal pits, herring were the staple food of the workers. Samuel Johnson ate them for breakfast, as did thousands of others. Hundreds of thousands ate them for tea. Today, though, we shun this tasty, precious little fish. While our north European neighbours still regard herring as a source of nutrition, and here a few seek the scarce supply of a decent kipper, to the majority the herring is dead. How far from the truth they are, for the King of the Sea is about to stage a spectacular comeback.

Much of the evidence for man's early consumption of herring comes from middens, where large amounts of their bones have been found among other kitchen rubbish. To the archaeologist, a midden is a worthy paradise, for it enables him to formulate a picture of the different layers in that heap of what, to most, is just ancient household refuse.

We know the Romans were keen on herring, as the remains of their bones have been found in their encampments, among, of course, all the other fish bones and shells. For the sea was an easy and nutritious source of food; archaeological excavations have proved this beyond doubt. Nothing, indeed, has been documented concerning these little fishes before the seventh century, so all reliable information has been discovered through these various digs around our coasts, although some of the stories are based on local tradition. We know from the Bible that fishers have been skilful in their work from man's very early days on earth, but it makes no mention in particular of the herring. This isn't surprising, given that the herring is a fish of the northern latitudes and is rarely found south of a line drawn across the Atlantic between Brittany on the European side and Chesapeake Bay on the other. This particular species is the *Clupea harengus* and is the herring we know in Europe. In the Pacific Ocean another branch of the species is to be found and this goes under the name of *Clupea pallasi*. Both of the species are subdivided into smaller groups, as we shall discover in time.

It is probable that man's first fishing experiences were quite by chance. Many of us have walked along beaches and seen rock pools. In the days when fish was plentiful – before man had begun his assault on the seas to denude them of all living creatures – these rock pools would have stranded fish once the tide had ebbed away. All early man had to do was get to the rock pools before the seabirds did and carry the fish home. He then learnt to increase the size of the pools by adding stones around. Thus he discovered the secret of the fish weir. We know, from archaeological evidence, that early man was doing this 6,000 years ago. He learnt to build his own weirs in suitable situations on beaches, sometimes using stone to build up the walls, and some-times wooden posts intertwined with hazel or willow. These passive structures simply filled up and emptied with the tide, leaving fish trapped behind the walls. Later he used the tide to take the fish into the structures and prevent them from escaping as it ebbed. These active fish weirs were deadly. He used nets instead of solid walls, and then thought about setting nets on their own. He set lines with hooks attached on the beach. These, he thought, would be better in the open sea, as would the nets. And so he developed his fishing boat and ven-tured out to become a true hunter-gatherer, a warrior of the sea. Fishing, for the first time, became more than a simple search for food. It became a skill and a fight with the most basic of elements – the sea.

The Romans are said to have learnt about herring on the East Anglian coast. Of course, it wasn't known as East Anglia when the soldiers at the Garianonum encampment, a few miles west of what is now Great Yarmouth, caught and ate the fish. It was a huge estuary with sandbanks stretching over what we today call the Norfolk Broads with Breydon water being all that remains of this marshy area, the name probably

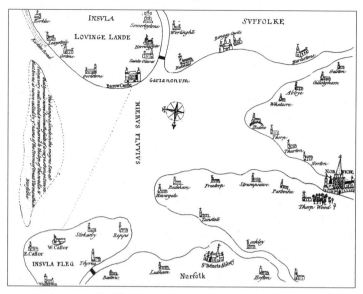

Map of what is now the Norfolk Broads dating from AD 1000, with Herringfleet clearly shown by John Ives (1774).

originating from the Viking period. But the Romans began a tradition of herring fishing along this coast that lasted well into the twentieth century. To the south of Burgh Castle, close by this Roman fort, lies the village of Herringfleet, a sign surely of an industry of importance.

Once the Romans had departed in the fifth century, along came the Saxons from across the water. Cerdick the Saxon is said to have arrived with five ships in the year 495 and found an ideal base upon a sandbank. In the next century he and his men built a stronghold here and discovered an abundance of herring. Felix, Bishop of the East Angles, built a church with 'godly men placed in it to pray for the health and success of fishermen that came to Yarmouth in the herring season'. That was in AD 647.

Two documented citations of herring support the belief of a fishery of substance in England before 1066. In the annals of the monastery of Barking in Essex, which was founded in 670, there is a mention of a tax known as 'herring silver' levied upon herring. Meanwhile, from the monastery of Evesham, which was founded in 709, come various references to the herring fishery. With Evesham being many miles away from the sea, it is presumed that herring was widely accepted and valued as an advantageous food. Royalty considered herring pies a delicacy and Yarmouth pledged to furnish the king each year with a hundred herring baked in twenty-four pasties. More than one private estate on the coast was held on the tenure of herring pies!

So what exactly is a herring? The word itself is said to come from the Teutonic word *heer*, meaning 'army'. This is an apt description indeed, for the fish swim in huge shoals – sometimes three or four miles long and more than two miles wide – containing millions of the silvery fish. That the word comes from the Teutons, an ancient Germanic people living in Jutland in the fourth century BC and moving to France by the second century BC, shows the antiquity of the fishery. However, this is disputed by some that say the word is simply a variation of the Anglo-Saxon word *haering*, although it is probable that that word itself comes from the Teutons.

The herring is delicately shaped for speed and has a beautiful colouring when out of the water. It is about ten inches long, although there are regional variations as in the North Atlantic where they can grow up to fifteen inches. It is pelagic because it comes to the surface of the sea to feed. This is the time when the fishermen have their best chance of catching the fish.

It is at night that the herring rise to the surface to feed. The Vikings must have discovered this when they arrived on these shores in the late eighth century. Some say that the reason they came was that, being fishers and farmers, they needed fertile land and rich inshore waters, neither of which they had back home. It has also been suggested that they were the first traders in herring, judging by the amount of herring bones found in South Uist in the Outer Hebrides, for the suggestion is that if there is more fish caught than can be eaten, the fishers must be trading the surplus to other groups of people. The Vikings settled all around northern Britain, from the Thames estuary right round to the Severn estuary and over to the Irish coast, so it would seem that they might have been catching herring on a large scale. That their influence remained in the fishing field is proved by the design of their boats, which had an enormous – everlasting in fact – impact on boat design all around our coasts.

Before the Norman Conquest, the night waters off Great Yarmouth and other fishing bases along the east coast were packed with fleets of boats from Holland, Flanders and Normandy in the autumn, for it was then that the shoals appeared. Some came from as far away as Norway. Yarmouth was the centre of herring activity according to the Domesday Book (written in 1086) and became the English herring capital. Twenty-four fishermen were based there. Nearby Lowestoft didn't fair as well, its fortunes flagging while those of Yarmouth thrived. Competition between the two towns lasted into the twentieth century. The Domesday Book tells us that the manor of Beccles, a few miles inland of Yarmouth, paid an annual tribute of 30,000 herring to the Abbey of St Edmund, which was later increased to 60,000 herring after the Norman invasion. Beccles, now several miles west of Lowestoft, was then another small herring-fishing harbour on the shore of a shallow estuary that, in reality, was entered through one of two channels either side of Yarmouth. It appears that the sea retreated in the years before the Norman Conquest, creating the town of Yarmouth proper, and that the 'estuary' reached as far inland as Norwich. According to eighteenth-century writer John Ives, these two channels were for:

shippes and fishermen to pass and enter into that arme of the sea for utterance of theire fishe and marchandizes.

Nearby Dunwich became a free burgh on payment of, among other items, an annual tax of 24,000 herring. Sandwich in Kent paid 40,000 herring annually to the monks. Silver was brought into Newcastle-upon-Tyne and exchanged for silver from Bohemia, along with wool, butter, oysters, cheese and cattle.

Yarmouth was the centre of a 'free fair' and the herring fishery was described as 'the noblest fishery for herring in Europe'. The fair lasted from 29 September through until 10 November, a period of forty-three days, and the fishermen themselves and the merchants who bought the catch regulated the entire business. The sixteenth-century historian Damet described the town as having:

great numbers of the fishermen of Fraunce, Flaunders, and of Hollande, Zealande and all the lowe countryes yerelie, from the feaste of Sainte Michaell the Archangell, untylle the feaste of Sainte Martine, about the takinge, sellinge and buyenge of herringes.

The Packing of the Herring into the Barrels, *by S. V. Meulen (1792)*.

The town itself was under the control of the Crown when, in the eleventh century, the king granted the rights for regulating the mediaeval fair to the barons of Hastings, one of the Cinque Ports of the south coast. Later on, these privileges were extended to the other Cinque Ports, much to the dismay of the local merchants and fishermen, especially after Henry I made Yarmouth a burgh in 1108 for an annual payment of ten milliards of herring. However, as this equates to ten billion fish, it does seem a preposterous amount! King John granted another 'most important' charter to the town in 1209 on the proviso that they provided the king with fifty-seven ships for forty days at their own cost. According to De Caux, this number of vessels from the one town was the same number as all the Cinque Ports could muster, which suggests the importance of Yarmouth at the time. Agreement was eventually reached between the town fathers and those in control of the Cinque Ports that the herring fair be equally regulated by the two bodies. But the bitterness continued until, in 1297, twenty-nine vessels belonging to Yarmouth were set alight and 200 fishers killed by boats

The Hooping of Herring Barrels, *by S. V. Meulen (1792).*

from the Cinque Ports. Yet it was almost another 400 years before the latter stopped sending their bailiffs to the fair after their power waned.

The Statutes of Herring were passed in 1357 and again three years later. By the first set of statutes, herring had to be brought into Yarmouth for selling and could not be sold prior to this. Furthermore, people were not allowed to buy herring to hang in their houses 'by covin' at a price above 40s a last. Small boats, called pykers, were forbidden from selling herring in the harbour at Yarmouth between Michaelmas and the feast of St Martin. The second statute removed many of these restrictions on what the fishermen could and could not do to sell their catch.

Whereas much of Yarmouth's herring was exported, that of Scarborough was consumed within the boundaries of Yorkshire. There, too, was a herring fair, lasting for ninety-eight days from 24 June up to the start date of the Yarmouth fair. Although over twice as long, the Scarborough fair wasn't as busy, yet even so hundreds of vessels are said to have landed fish there, including many foreign ships, especially from Flanders and northern France. This peaked in 1304 with 355 lasts of herring being landed by foreigners, a last being a 100 Hundreds and the latter being, at that time, 100 fish (nowadays this is between 123 and 132 depending on the region). The same source tells us that there were 5,237 foreign landings and that this market was valued at £444. The average vessel landed between 5,000 and 15,000 fish, which were valued between 10s and 60s. Small fishing boats started to be charged a 2d landing fee while the larger fishing ships were already paying 4d fifty years previously to finance the building of a new quay.

At about the same time, Edward III gave the 'good men of Tenby' in south-west Wales the rights to raise money to build the town's first quay. This was completed in 1328. Previous to this, boats had to draw up the tidal river Ritec into Pill Lake to beach in the mud and unload. The fishermen paid tithes of herring and oysters for Mass to be said on their behalf in the tiny St Julian's chapel that was located at the harbour. Herring was landed in substantial quantities all around the Welsh coast at this time. In 1206, in the *Brut y Tywysogion* (Chronicle of the Princes) it is written that:

that year Maelgwn ap Rhys built the castle of Abereinion. And then God gave an abundance of fish in the estuary of the Ystwyth, so much that there was not its like before that.

Judging by the records, this was herring, for fishermen were being fined for selling herring below the high-water mark, thus escaping the payment of market tolls. In 1294, at Llanfaes on the Isle of Anglesey (Ynys Môn), a custom of one penny on every measure of herring landed was charged, as well as every herring boat having to pay another one mease of herring every time they entered or left port. The money raised helped Edward I build the castle at Beaumaris, part of the chain of castles he built around the coast to keep the Welsh in hand! On the north side of the jutting arm of the Lleyn peninsular, the tiny hamlet of what is now called Nefyn possessed sixty-three fishing nets in 1287. Across the St George's Channel, herring were being caught in 1202 by Irish fishermen, who donated them to the Abbey of Connal.

In Scotland very little is known of the Middle Ages' fishery. Tradition has it that the men of Loch Fyne and the Clyde were catching herring on a grand scale long before anyone else. It is also said that the Dutch came in the year 836 to buy salt herring from that area. The Abbey of Holyrood was granted the right 'to fish herring at Renfrew' in the mid-twelfth century. About the same time it is said that English, Scottish and Belgian fishermen followed the herring around the Isle of May in the Firth of Forth. However, herring are referred to as dried, as opposed to smoked, as well as salted in the Scottish Parliamentary Papers of 1240. No taxes appear to have been levied on their capture. At Berwick-upon-Tweed, the mayor in the year 1285, one Robert Durham, ordered herring, among other fish, to be sold 'on the bray' alongside the boat that landed them, and the fishermen were not allowed to carry the fish ashore after dusk. In Fife, it was to the Cistercian Abbey of Balmerino, in north Fife, that the fishermen were required to pay a levy of 100 salted herring from every barrel they landed. In return, the fishermen were given rights to dry their nets on the foreshore and erect and lease booths. Today, the site where the fishermen dried their nets is close by the Scottish Fisheries Museum where the story of the Scottish herring fishery is told.

In France, the first mention of the herring fishery appears in a charter of about 1030 of the Abbey of St Catherine, near Rouen. This allowed for a saltworks near Dieppe to pay the abbey 'five milliards' of herring. In 1169, huge amounts were being caught in the river Meuse, proving that the shoals swam to the French coast. In 1155, Louis VII outlawed the buying of anything but mackerel and salted herring at Etampes and, some thirty years later, Philip II gave a charter to the town of Liège, allowing them to sell fresh and salted herring. Thus herring remained a staple fish for the fishers of ports such as Boulogne and Dieppe right through into the twentieth century.

Likewise, the Hollanders were sending out their fleet of vessels to follow the shoals around the North Sea. But it is to the Swedish southern coast that we must now turn to see Europe's very first great commercial fishery.

Finnish Herring Pie

Ingredients:
4 medium herring
2 large onions, sliced
1oz oil
½oz butter
1½lb. potatoes, sliced
4 tomatoes, peeled and sliced
Salt & pepper
¼ pint milk

Method:
Scale and bone the fish, leaving on the tails, and soak in salted water for several hours before using. Fry the onions lightly in the oil until golden. Grease a fireproof dish with the butter, put in a layer of potatoes, followed by a layer of onions and tomatoes, seasoning each layer. Place the rolled fish on top and surround with more slices of tomatoes and potatoes. Pour in the milk and cook in centre of oven for 1½ hours at 350 degrees Fahrenheit (Gas Mark 4).

CHAPTER THREE

A Refreshing Change
to Salmon

'The herring have disappeared owing to magic, bad men having sunk a copper horse in the sea and thereby driven the herring away from the coast.' So wrote the tenth-century historian Peter Clausson in an attempt to explain why in some years the herring migrated close to the shores of Sweden and Norway and at other times completely deserted them. Such was the fickle nature of the herring! Throughout the last millennium it seems man has been striving to understand the erratic tendency of the shoals to come and go as they please. The effect has been to make or break empires.

The Baltic herring fishery dates back to the eleventh century and probably earlier, although nothing appears to be known about it. If indeed Clausson was writing in the tenth century – this seems to be unclear – then this in itself is proof of its importance at that early time.

The first documented evidence comes from the beginning of the twelfth century when there were vast shoals of herring in the Baltic. By the beginning of the following century it was being caught in quantity off the coast of Pomerania, which today overlays the German/Polish border. It was carried ashore on horseback and a 'horseful', so to speak, sold for the equivalent of about a quarter of today's penny. Along the coast, the Prussians were said to be fishing by 1259. In 1428 the Danish kings imposed a toll on herring boats crossing over the Sound between Denmark and Sweden.

Catholic Europe relied heavily on herring to replace the meat deemed unholy on certain days of the week. Salt curing was the usual way of preserving the fish before it was transported from the north to southern Europe. In Denmark, which in fact controlled most of what we now know as Sweden, the Church insisted that fish be eaten on

Wednesdays, Fridays and Saturdays. This lasted until 1536, when the
Catholic ties were broken. Other Catholic countries consumed huge
amounts of herring, thereby developing a ready and massive market.

The south-western Swedish shores of Skåne saw the biggest expansion in the herring fisheries after about 1200. Along the entire coastline of the region – centred on the towns of Skånor, Falsterbo and
Ellenbogen (the present-day Malmo) – thousands of small boats sal-
lied forth, mainly during the months of August, September and
October, landing fish into the temporary camps set up along the
shore. Some say the fishing lasted from 25 July to 29 September of
each year; others say it lasted into October. However long the season
lasted, the fish was cured on this shore to be transported to the
intended markets by cargo ship. In about 1525 it is said that there were
7,515 vessels active in the fishery, although this figure does seem exces-
sively high. These boats were crewed by between three and six men,
and are said to have been small, stout rowing boats of a Viking nature:
in other words they were double-ended craft, with an excessive sheer-
line and flaring ends. Some probably set small sails. They used an early
form of a drift-net and, annually, caught and landed some 10,000 tons
of herring. However, according to one source, each boat was capable
of carrying between 20 and 40 tons of herring, which would mean
the arithmetic is awry. On the one hand a small rowing boat would be
incapable of staying afloat with so much herring aboard and secondly,
over 7,000 boats catching even ten tons a night over a two-month
period would account for much more than 10,000 tons annually. It is
more likely that each boat landed between 20 and 40 tons a season,
which would reduce the number of boats fishing to a more reasonable
figure of about 3,515 or less.

The Swedes from Skåne used to say that 'Man kan inte gora alla till
lax, sade gud och skapade sillen' ('"one cannot make everyone into
salmon," said God and thus he created herring'). Herring, as such, was
considered the food of the working people, whereas salmon was
deemed good enough for all sections of society. And it was in obvious
abundance!

The merchants from the towns of Lübeck and Bremen were among
the first to realise the benefits of grasping control of this lucrative
trade in herring. They discovered the necessity of salting the fish
to preserve it during its long journey either overland or, more

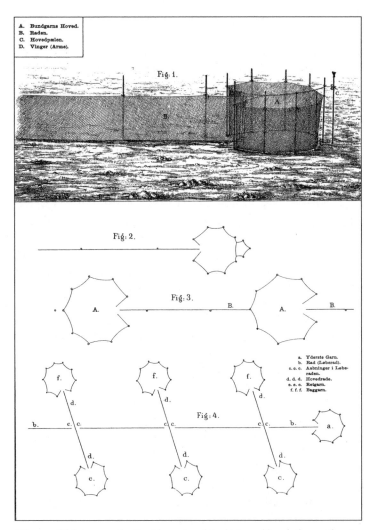

The use of fish traps on the Danish coast predates history, although these with nets drawn by C.F. Drechsel in 1880 are nineteenth-century. One of the oldest fish traps found in Europe is in Denmark.

commonly, by sea. In the twelfth century the town of Kolberg – now
Kolobrzeg – in Poland was famous for its market in salted herring.
The Poles had a poem they sang after a particular victory in 1105:

*They brought us herring and stinking fish, and now our sons are bringing
them to us fresh and quivering.*

Thus emerged the powerful Hanseatic league of merchants mainly,
but not exclusively, out of the regulation and mastery of this herring
fishery. They first obtained a privilege from the Danish king, Waldemar
Seier, in 1203, to fish off the Skåne coast, although some sources point
out that these privileges were not secured until 1343. Herring, at the
time, was in such abundance according to the historian Saxo that 'they
could be caught with the hands, and it was almost impossible for a boat
to make its way through the dense masses of fish'. Large markets were
held at the principal herring town of Skånor and it has been estimated
that some 60,000 to 70,000 people visited this coast during the
autumn fishing months. The Hanseatic merchants learned to control
every aspect of the operation, from the fishing, the landing and the
curing, to the transporting and export. They controlled the salt used to
cure the herring by buying up the saltmines at Luneburg. This salt was
excellent in quality, the impurities having been removed by the addition of blood to the boiling brine and later, of beer to form white
crystals. They traded widely, sending their herring to Flanders, the Low
Countries, France, England, Poland and all around the Baltic, as well as
to the home market in Germany. They had warehouses in Norwich
and Kings Lynn from where they traded herring for wool, corn, hides,
beer and cheese. They traded herring to Russia for timber for ships to
increase their fleet. And so grew their influence around the Continent,
even the globe.

    However, they had to obey certain, if not plenty of, regulations.
Herring could not be salted on board vessels to prevent smuggling,
although the duties were low. The Hanse supplied their own entire
workforce and no foreigners were allowed to salt their herring. On
the other hand no German was allowed to salt herring for the king or
for the Danes. All herring exported through the Sound was free of
duty, although the king had the right of 'royal purchase'. This forced
every fisherman to sell to the Crown 240 herring at half the ruling

price. These were taken to the various curing houses owned by the Crown at Falsterbo, Skånor, Dragor and on the island of Moen. It is through the records of this fish in the first few years of the reign of King Frederick I (1523-1533) that we find that 37,500 persons were employed in the Skånor and Falsterbo fishery and that 7,515 boats were prosecuting the herring. One tunna, equal to a barrel, was worth two florins, according to one report, although another puts it at sixteen Danish marks in 1539. The total catch in 1537 in Falsterbo was 96,000 barrels with the entire number of herring caught in the Danish monarchy at 360,000 barrels. This more than exceeds the previous estimates of 10,000 tons of herring caught annually, and suggests that that figure relates to a much earlier year.

Such was the importance of this fishery that Rome decreed that work could continue on Sundays and other holy days. In England they had warehouses in London as well as Norfolk. The Steelyard was sited on what is now Cannon Street Station, and from here they brought herring and other commodities to trade around western Europe. In fact, so reliable was the currency of herring that the merchants in England demanded payment in 'pounds of easterlings' – later to become 'pounds sterling'.

Lubeck remained the seat of the Hanse towns for over 350 years. Its armorial bearings had three herring upon a plain gold shield and thus the meagre herring was the emblem of this hugely influential trading league.

However, like everything else, all good things come to an end. The reasons for it are varied. Towards the end of the sixteenth century it seems the Hanseatic league lost their commercial supremacy through the north of Europe, first in Scandinavia by 1560 and subsequently throughout the rest of the continent. Some say it was a special agreement between the Danish Crown and the merchants that caused the loss of their privileges to control the herring fishery. Others say it was due to an unnatural increase in rainfall at the same time as very high tides, culminating in the herring deserting the Skåne shores. Perhaps it was a mixture of both, with the herring – being fickle, remember – deserting and thus reasoning the merchants to relinquish their hold on the fisheries. The only certainty is that the Hanseatic league lost much of its political influence and the Swedish fisheries never regained their strength again.

However, that wasn't the end for the Baltic herring. It didn't simply disappear. Whereas the Dutch were the next in the order of things to control the fishery in the North Sea, the fishermen continued to fish on a much smaller scale. Indeed, even today, herring is caught all around the Baltic, from Finland in the north to the east coast of Denmark. It remains high on the list of favoured foods in all the countries that dip their coastlines into this massive inland sea. Whether it be Danish roll-mops, Swedish jellied herring, German herring in a mustard sauce, Polish smoked herring, or Finnish herring with dill, it is still more widely available in those countries than it is here in Britain.

It is to the Bohusland coast we must look to next, that part of the western coast of Sweden that lies to the north of Halland (the province directly north of Skåne) and south of the Norwegian border. Here we find that:

in 1747 and 1748 a large number of herring began to approach the northern portion of the coast of Bohusland; later they went further south, as far as Marstrand, and in 1752 they made their appearance near Gothenburg.

That was in a herring report dated 1758. Little documented fact is known about the fishing prior to this time, although it is pretty obvious it was being caught. It the 1760s it was being found either side of the island of Marstrand and down towards Gothenburg. As this area is roughly parallel to the northern tip of Denmark, it would appear that this was Skagerrak herring that was not keen on entering into the narrower confines of the Kattegat or, still further, into the Sound (Oresund).

Again, it was autumn time when the herring came inshore, proffering the best chances of its capture. The drift-net – often referred to as the 'floating net' – was the preferred method of capture, although fixed nets were sometimes used, these being fastened to the seabed using grapnels. Seine-nets were adopted after the sixteenth century in some parts of the coast. The herring spawned in the spring, as early as March in Skåne and late summer in Bohusland. This could be accounted for by H. Widegren's assertion that two types of herring exist in these waters. Firstly there's the herring proper – the *Clupea harengus* – and the 'stromming' – *Clupea sprattus* – more commonly known as the sprat and often sold immature as anchovy. The herring went by a variety of names – the garssen herring, loff herring, fat herring, Kulla herring, skarp herring, small herring, spiced herring, Norwegian herring, anchovy or Blekinge herring. All in fact relate to the same two types of herring and the name depends purely on the way it is cured.

A word here about the boats in common usage. In Skåne it seems that there is no boat peculiar to that region. They have simply adopted vessels from either the Sound, Bornholm or the Blekinge region. The Sound boats, most of which were built at Viken, north of Helsingborg, were about 30ft long in the nineteenth century with a 20-foot keel length, suggesting long overhangs in true Norse fashion. They were generally cutter-rigged with boomed mainsail and jib, although many set a topsail as well. Similar boats worked across on the Danish side where the *sildebåd* – literally 'herring boat' – worked from harbours such as Hornbaek and Skovshoved.

The common Bornholm boat was between twenty-five and 30ft long and set only one spritsail. These were usual on the east coast of Skåne, closest to Bornholm. In Blekinge the boats were of a similar size, although some were smaller and again a spritsail was the preferred rig, allowing the sail to be dropped in an instant.

In Bohusland the smaller *snipa* was the favoured boat, this resembling the Danish *smakkejolle* which were used for herring fishing in the inland seas around the southern archipelago. They too were rigged with one spritsail and were renowned for their speed. The type remains in use today as a pleasure craft among the islands, where they are often raced.

In 1914 there were only fifty decked boats north of the Blekinge region while on the west coast there were 1,774, over 1,100 of which were based in the Bohusland area. The decking of boats to offer more safety for the crew came about in the late nineteenth century as developments in design of both boat and gear improved. However, these figures serve to point to the fact that, whereas the Bohusland herring fishery survived throughout the nineteenth century, the further east you travelled, the scarcer the fish was. Other fisheries for whitefish, eels and lobster gained ground at the expense of the herring. With the advent of motorisation, and increased mechanisation, the inshore herring decreased. But we have much more ground to cover before we begin to consider those effects that forced an almost total collapse in the European herring fishery.

To sum up this chapter on the Swedish herring, we will digest some of the selected ways that Swedish herring is cured. These come from a paper dated 1874 by H. Widegren entitled 'A Short Introduction to the Proper Care and Management of the Baltic Fishery' in the *United States Commission of Fish and Fisheries Report of the Commissioner for 1878* and translated by Herman Jacobson. These four ways of preparing the herring are deemed the preferred options.

Firstly, to prepare common Baltic herring for home consumption and the German Baltic ports, strong salt such as that from St Ybes or Lisbon should be used, although Cagliari and some looser English and French salts can be used if the fish are intended for speedy consumption. A word about salt at this point. Lisbon salt, from Setubal, south of the city, was reputed for its whiteness and the dryness of the large crystals and deemed perfect for curing. Cagliari was developed as one of the largest saltworks in the Mediterranean through Genoese merchants moving to Sardinia. English salt, in the main, came from the saltmines of Cheshire, while the bulk of French salt was from the Atlantic coast where the sun was hot enough to evaporate the sea.

The herring are gutted and cleaned, leaving in the milt and roe, and then rinsed in clean seawater and left to drain in baskets. Then they are placed loose in tight barrels and sprinkled with dry salt and left for twenty-four hours, at which time they are removed and once more allowed to drain. They are then packed into barrels or tubs, in layers with their backs down, with crushed salt in between every layer until the container is full. A light weight is placed atop to keep the fish in the brine, although it must not be so heavy as to squeeze the fat and juices out of the herring. These are allowed to stand for a few days to shrink, with more fish being added. Once settling has finished, the barrels or tubs are sealed and given a daily rolling and turning upside down to ensure the brine fully penetrates the fish. Just prior to shipping they are once more opened and topped up if necessary. They are then considered fit for market. Using such a method produces a delicately tasting herring.

Secondly, to prepare the so-called 'delicacy-herring' for home consumption. As its name suggests, this herring is not intended for everyday use, and so a looser salt is used such as Liverpool, Luneberg or Cagliari salt. The 'large and fat' Baltic herring is the best fish for the process as, with less salt, it produces a more delicious flavour. There are two ways of curing the fish:

1. The Norwegian method – as soon as the herring are caught they are placed in pure brine while they are being gutted and cleaned. As soon as they have been cleaned they are put in small tubs or kegs, back down, with salt in between and on top. New layers are added as the herring settle until after six days, when an opening is made with a stick between the herring and the side of the tub, which is filled with salt and the top fastened on. Prior to shipping they are topped up if necessary with brine, sometimes a small hole being drilled in the tub and brine poured in this way. They must be often turned and rolled and will then keep fresh for up to six months.

2. The Dutch method – again the fresh herring, as soon as they come out of the water, are placed in small kegs and are stirred for at least an hour in Luneberg salt. They are then gutted and cleaned – and sometimes not cleaned – and placed in barrels with fine Luneberg salt between the layers. Once full, they are closed and examined and filled in the manner of above. This fish will keep fresh for up to one year, although when the fish isn't cleaned it will not keep as long.

Thirdly, to prepare spiced herring. This form of cured herring is normally prepared in small glass jars, and any herring can be used. It is often prepared by 'housewives in order to give some little variety to their meals, but especially to the lunch-table'. To prepare, fresh herring are immediately laid in vinegar, adding one-fourth part water and some salt. After twenty-four hours they are taken out and placed in a tub or keg with the following spices added in the quantities for one *hval* of herring: a pound of dry fine salt, one pound of powdered sugar, one ounce of pepper, one ounce of laurel leaves, one ounce of saltpetre, half an ounce of sandal, quarter of an ounce of ginger, quarter of an ounce of Spanish hops, quarter of an ounce of cloves. The herring should remain in this for a minimum of two months before being eaten. There are different ways and proportions of ingredients, but it is suggested that experiments be made to find the optimum way to suit the particular individual palate.

Potato and Herring Salad

Ingredients:
1lb boiled potatoes
3-4 marinated and pickled herring fillets
1 small green pepper, seeded and finely chopped
1 tablespoonful finely chopped parsley or chives
1 carton soured cream
1 tablespoonful lemon juice
½ teaspoonful paprika
Salt and pepper
1 lettuce

Method:
Cut cooled potatoes into neat dice and the herring into small pieces (soak the herring first in milk if too salty). Add pepper, herbs, sour cream, lemon juice and seasoning to taste. Heap the salad in lettuce cups arranged in pairs and serve with buttered brown bread or sliced cooked bacon or ham.

CHAPTER FOUR

Our Goldmine in the North Sea

The Dutch have a saying that Amsterdam is built upon a foundation of herringbones. Whereas it might seem that herringbones do not make for a substantial footing for any building, it does give an indicator of the importance of the herring fishery to the growth of the country. According to Voltaire, the Dutch 'turned their stinking tons [of fish] into tons of gold'.

Two Dutchmen figure principally in the growth of the herring fishery. The first of these, Willem Van Beukels or Beukelsen – 'literally son of Beukels' – was born, it would seem, in about 1347 into a fishing family living at Biervliet in the province of Zeeland. Presumably he was a herring fisherman, because it soon became apparent to him that the secret behind a thriving herring fishery was to find a better method of preserving the fish. Herring, as we know, don't keep fresh for long and their bright red eyes go dull. Previously, although the curing nature of salt was well known – the Egyptians and Chinese were using it 2,000 years before Christ – herring merely sprinkled with the granules of rock salt didn't last all that long.

So Van Beukels experimented and soon discovered a better way of curing, preserving and barrelling the herring. This single event in 1383, it is widely acclaimed, changed the course of European history. In 1476 the herring fishery was one of the country's principal industries, according to a document delivered to the Grand Council at Malines by the people of Brielle. Like a couple of centuries earlier, the balance of political power in the continent swung towards the Low Countries, for they, almost at once, gained control of the North Sea Fishery. From this commanding position they built a powerful navy that, two centuries later, led to the founding of the Dutch East India Company, otherwise known as the Vereenigde Oostindische Compagnie (VOC). This company opened up the spice routes to the East and put down the first roots of the subsequent western colonisation.

Some writers doubt the importance of Van Beukels' discovery. It has also been suggested that he was in fact a disgruntled Englishman named Belkinson, who, having had his fellow countrymen ignore his find, took it to Holland. From the available evidence though, it seems that Van Beukels did discover the need to gut the fish immediately and immerse the fish in brine rather than simply sprinkling the salt over the fish.

Van Beukels became a national hero after his death when Emperor Charles V visited his grave in 1550 and ordered a monument to be erected in his honour. History, not for the first time it would seem, was altered by one man, although whether history can ever be changed is surely debatable. However, with an ability to cure herring that lasted much longer than previously, the Dutch were able to command a market throughout Europe, sending barrels by ship to the Catholic south where fish was still in demand on meat-free days at least twice a week.

Peter Chivalier, a Yarmouth fish merchant, found a way to cure herring with salt some years before Van Beukels made his discovery, and this he patented. But the difference between the two methods was that Van Beukels thoroughly cleaned the insides of the fish while Chivalier didn't gut his fish prior to salting. It was upon this difference that the balance of power swung.

The second Dutchman responsible for developing the herring fishery in the Low Countries is nameless. However, his discovery was the drift-net as we know it today – a long curtain of netting suspended in the sea just below the surface, held up by floats, and the bottom weighted. This fellow was from Hoorn, on what was then the Zuiderzee, so whether this was designed for herring or the anchovy that occurred in greater numbers in the inland sea is unclear. Presumably, also, the herring fishermen were using some earlier form of net hanging in the water to catch the herring that Van Beukels cured, for the drift-net invention did not happen until, some say, almost thirty years later in 1416. What the new net gave was an increase in size, so that a whole crew was needed to handle it when being hauled. Consequently the size of the catch increased dramatically. But, just as the amount of fish grew, so did the size of the vessel needed to take it on board. And so arose the second great herring fishery.

Yet the fishermen didn't have it all their own way, because the government, keen to protect this offshore goldmine, brought in regulations to control its prosecution. Officers – called *keur-meisters* – ensured compliance. These were probably the first fishery officers seen, a profession that today attempts to administer the misguided policies of the European Union.

Government legislation laid down the date when fishing could commence – five minutes past midnight on the night of 24 June – St John's Day. Masters of vessels leaving Holland to follow the shoals had to swear an oath that they would respect government decrees. Only certain salts were allowed to be used in the curing process, and a law in 1519 prevented the use of Lisbon salt. Later on only that from Spain and Portugal was acceptable while that from France, the West Indies and the Isle of May was not. However, all salt for fish curing was duty-free. The size of the barrel in which the herring were preserved was closely monitored, as were the size and thickness of the staves in its construction. The fish had to be gutted satisfactorily and packed in the same way, and the fish had to remain for at least ten days in the pickle for the home market. Some barrels were branded for export. Foreign herring brought into the country could not be packed in Dutch barrels. To retain their ascendancy in the fishery, quality had to be constant and of the highest degree, and the government were well aware of the importance of the business. The reputation of Dutch herring became unsurpassed and consequently the Netherlands developed into a proud and forceful maritime nation.

The vessels used in the herring fishery in these ancient times were the *zeeschuyt*, two-masted, square-sailed craft that are the earliest form of herring drift-net boats. However, as the boats sailed further afield, bigger boats evolved. Thus, in the second half of the fifteenth century (some say 1416), appeared the *buizen*, or Dutch buss. In 1560 the maritime provinces of Friesland, Holland, Zeeland and Flanders had 700 vessels, each making three voyages during the season and each vessel landing over 800 barrels – each containing up to 1,000 fish – during the season. A barrel was worth £6 and the total value of the catch was something in the region of £300,000. From these figures it has to be assumed that the boats were curing the catch on board, returning simply to off-load prior to filling their holds once again.

Een Pinck ofte Zeeboot

Om kleyne winst en sobre vangst
De Zee-man dickwils is in angst

A Dutch pinck, one of the earliest in-shore fishing boats in the North Sea.

To enable the catching boats to stay at sea for prolonged periods, *jagers* were introduced in the early seventeenth century. These fast, yacht-like craft sailed out to the busses and were loaded up with the cured herring at sea, with which they then raced home. The busses were bulky craft and hence slow, thus they were saved the trouble of the tiresome trip home to unload and so were able to catch even more fish. The *jagers* were able to double up as supply boats, bringing in empty barrels and supplies for the crew, each *jager* serving about ten busses. Thus the busses were able to stay at sea throughout the first part of the fishing season, following the shoals around Shetland and Fair Isle. They then moved southwards down to the East Anglian coast, where they competed with the vastly inferior English fleets. Even so, the seas where they could fish were carefully regulated: Shetland until 25 July, thence off the Scottish coast around Buchan Ness (just south of Peterhead) from that date until 14 September, thence to Yarmouth and finally off the Norfolk coast from 25 November till 1 January. However, jagers were prohibited from tendering the catch after leaving Shetland.

A further advantage the Dutch had over the English and Scots, other than those already mentioned, was that they liked their herring. By that I mean that they were connoisseurs of fresh herring. The population of England and Scotland – although this was before the union – would on the whole only eat smoked herring as a preference, although many coastal dwellers were happy enough with salted herring and potatoes. They had to be, for that was all they had. But the Dutch were particularly fond of their 'Maatjes' and indeed they still are. These are young or 'new herring', sometimes called 'green herring', for which the flags were hung out at the beginning of the season. The town crier would announce their arrival and thus began many a herring festival. In fact, the first batch of herring landed into the country was reserved for the monarch and taken to the royal palace on a horse-drawn carriage decorated with flags and bunting. Those who had caught it were rewarded with the princely sum of 500 florins. It is not surprising, then, that the boats rushed home to get this pole position.

These young herring, gutted and filleted, and cured only briefly, are sweet to the taste. They are eaten by holding the tail between thumb and forefinger and being literally dropped into the mouth, devouring everything but the fin. In earlier times they were unfilleted, and by a careful but firm wrench, half the flesh could be taken off the bone to be consumed and, with another wrench, the other side stripped and devoured. The eating process was an art in itself. I remember several years ago, when at the Vlaardingen Herring Festival, watching herring being consumed in this way, and being amazed at how the Dutch seemed almost to be competing with each other at the smoothness of their hand movement as they raised the fish skywards, and again in their deftness in swallowing it. Some had a look of pure ecstasy as they chewed on this, their panacea of perfect living.

According to Preger, when an escapee from Nazi Holland arrived in London during the Second World War, his unusual accent attracted suspicion, so those interrogating him gave him a herring to eat. When he filleted the herring with the proper Dutch flick of the wrist these suspicions quickly vanished. They were confident that only a true Dutchman was capable of such a feat.

By the dawning of the seventeenth century it has been said that the Dutch fishing fleet numbered something in the region of 20,000 sail boats, more than the entire fleets of England, Scotland, France, Spain,

Portugal, Italy, Denmark, Poland, Sweden and Russia all put together. However, the vast majority of these were small inland craft, and only a tenth were herring busses. That still makes a total of 2,000 in the herring fleet, although it is likely that this figure is inflated. One report states that 2,000 busses were seen anchored off Bressay Sound in Shetland, although this, too, seems highly exaggerated. Almost half a million people were employed in the business, which was worth two million guilders by that time. That Shetland benefited from the fishery, and the trade accompanying it, is clear. Bressay was one of the trading points where booths were set up to sell goods to the fishermen. These were the origins of Lerwick. In 1625 complaints about this trade, and the drunkenness, prostitution, brawling, theft and indeed murder that went hand in hand with it, led to these booths being dismantled.

These busses were, as has already been said, slow cumbersome craft, barge-like in appearance and low in the water. They were rigged with two masts having squaresails, topsails and foresails on running bowsprits. They were between 70 and 100 tons, could carry up to 60 tons of herring and had a crew of fifteen men. However their lifespan was short, it having been said that a buss would only last one season. If this is the case, it must surely be a sign of the profitability of the trade. The nets they set each night were made of the best hemp, or coarse Persian silk, and were half a mile long.

But already there was a feeling of desperation among the English as they watched the Dutch profit from a resource so close to their shores. In 1614 Tobias Gentleman wrote that Holland was no bigger than Norfolk and Suffolk, and had to import everything from timber for shipbuilding to barley, yet she was still able to wage war with Spain and increase her wealth at the same time. Not one of her people was deemed idle, yet 'we are scorned daily by these Hollanders for being so negligent of our profit and careless of our fishing, and they daily flout us that be the poor fishermen of England...' Part of the problem, he reckoned, was that the English fishermen had 'not the right use of making barrelled fish'.

The same feelings were being felt north of the border. In 1534 some Dutch busses were captured and forced to sail into Leith. However the Dutch retaliated by confiscating the property of Scottish merchants in their country. The only result of this stand-off was that neither group of fishermen did much fishing in Scottish waters for almost a decade.

It was James I who, at the union of Scotland and England in 1603, began to formulate plans to create territorial waters around the coast from which foreigners were excluded from entering to fish. The idea of denying the freedom of the sea to everyone was unparalleled in European history, although previous monarchs such as Henry VIII and Elizabeth I had attempted to claim sovereignty over the seas. An ancient understanding had deemed that fishing close inshore was reserved exclusively for the native fishermen, although the Dutch had increasingly encroached upon these grounds. In 1594, when they were granted permission to fish in Scottish waters, it was agreed that this would not be 'within the sight of the shoar, nor in any loughs nor in the seas betwixt islands'.

James set up a commission in 1622 and Dutch vessels were later prohibited from the coasts of Shetland, Ireland and Norway, allegedly because of inferior herring in these parts. Fines of up to 300 florins were imposed by the Dutch authorities for those fishermen flouting the rules. Yet it is supposed that, in reality, this was simply to appease James' complaints. However, even under these restraints, the Dutch still managed to increase their catch. Levies of 2s a last were imposed upon the foreign fishermen who refused to pay until British warships began patrolling and extracting it by force. One British admiral managed to collect 20,000 florins in one year from the fishers.

The Dutch responded to this British insurgency into 'their rightful fishing grounds' by sending in their own naval escorts. Britain, it seems, was largely incapable of policing her own waters. On one occasion, a French privateer attacked a Dutch buss after chasing it right into the harbour at Yarmouth, killing some of the crew who were hiding on the pier and robbing the ship. The town marshal called upon the French to 'desist in the name of the king' and was answered in a typically gesturely manner. However, the next day the French were trapped by two Dutch warships so that they ran their ship ashore at Lowestoft and tried to escape on foot, being captured in the event and imprisoned at Yarmouth. Their fate is unknown.

Oliver Cromwell dealt the first death knell to the Dutch command of the North Sea. In 1651 his Navigation Act prohibited the carrying of fish (and other goods) aboard any other vessel except a British one into, out of, or between British ports. He was offended by the Dutch *fluitboot*, the typical fast Dutch cargo ships, having almost a monopoly

The Dutch fluitboot offended Oliver Cromwell in the seventeenth century and the prohibiting of their fishing in British waters was a catalyst for the Dutch War in 1652.

on this coastal trade. The Dutch, thus angered and financially secure through their fishing, favoured war and so began the first Dutch War (1652-4). In 1653 the whole of the Dutch fishing fleet, amounting to up to 2,000 vessels, stayed at home. During the second Dutch War (1665-7) the fleet was prohibited from fishing and the first feelings of economic hardship were felt. After the third Dutch War (1672-4) and the Peace of Nijmegen in 1678, some semblance of prosperity to the fleets returned. However, the joint enemy was the French and, in 1703, six French warships attacked the Dutch fleet anchored in Bressay Sound, Shetland, sinking the flagship and burning possibly as many as 400 herring busses. By 1736 the Dutch fleet was reduced to 300 vessels and then to 162 in 1779. In 1775 bounties were introduced, but this largely had no effect. The days of the Dutch commanding the North Sea herring fishery were over. It was the turn of the Scots to reap the benefits of what lay just off their own shores.

However, it is worth noting that in the nineteenth century the Dutch herring fishery did make a recovery, but this was mostly after 1857 with the lifting of the Monopoly Act that had previously given the right of fishing solely to square-rigged keel boats, thereby excluding all flat-bottomed beach boats and foreign-owned vessels from catching herring. On the beaches of Scheveningen and Katwijk, from where many of the fishermen who crewed aboard the busses originated, fishing jostled with smuggling as a lucrative pastime. The boats these people used were called *bomschuit*, which were flat-bottomed, squat, rectangular craft with rounded-off corners. They were fishing before 1857 – indeed records at Katwijk note a fish market in the fourteenth century – and they often gutted and cured their herring outside the village to escape detection. They had to be subtle in their catching methods for the same reason.

The *bomschuit* were spectacular craft in many ways, although appearing unstable, which they were not. They looked clumsy and slow, which they were, barely attaining top speeds of 4 knots. They are not unlike the Belgian *scute*, both of which display a certain Scandinavian tradition in their construction. Built locally, they were worked off the beaches, and had a sort of corkscrew affair at one end, enabling one end of the vessel to be lifted so that it pivoted upon the other. So raised, it could be dragged around in a half circle so that it faced the sea after being beached bow-first.

In 1894 a storm on the coast destroyed some twenty-five *bomschuit* from Scheveningen and damaged another 150. Thus a harbour was built which eventually led to their demise, especially after a French lugger – *lougre* – was introduced into the fleet in 1865. This coincided with the adoption of cotton nets that enabled boats to carry more of them. Over the next twenty years some 400 *loggers*, as they became called, were built, mostly in and around Rotterdam, so that the herring fishery once again flourished upon a healthy German export market. This became centred on the town of Vlaardingen, from where the vast majority of the fish was exported. Steam capstans enabled even longer nets to be set, and steam affected the fleets much in the way that we shall see it did throughout the herring fishery of Europe. With Holland neutral in the First World War, they were able to maintain a continuance of supplies throughout, and it wasn't really until the Second World War that they suffered an interruption in their fishing. However, although they achieved another 100 years of herring fishing, it in no way matched their ascendancy of 200 years earlier. Then, of course, came the European Union, which has blighted much of the north European fishery.

Tatties 'n' Herring
(traditional Scottish)

Ingredients:
Herring
Potatoes
Water and salt

Method:
Scrape and clean the potatoes and cover with water in a large pan. Bring to the boil and remove from heat when half cooked. Remove some of the liquid – to about level with the top of the potatoes – and add the gutted, beheaded and cleaned herring. Bring back to the boil and cook in the steam until tender.

CHAPTER FIVE

The Rudiments of the British Empire

Herring was the staple diet in British mediaeval times, even if not wholly liked. It has often been described as the 'potato of the Middle Ages'. In 1429 we even had the Battle of Herrings! On this occasion, when the English army, under the Duke of Suffolk, was besieging Orléans, the Duke of Bedford sent in 500 cartloads of salted herring to replenish supplies. The French, under the Duke of Bourbon, obviously heard about this and attempted to ambush the convoy at Rouvray, although they failed. Thus was nicknamed the famous battle. Later on, the army at Agincourt relied upon herring for sustenance, as did the seamen of the Spanish Armada as it sailed up the English Channel, to be later destroyed through a lack of firepower and, subsequently, by adverse weather on their attempted sail home. Here we find the sketchy beginnings of England's navy, which was later responsible for its global empire building, fed upon herring – backed up by salt cod and corned beef – and crewed by men first experienced at sea through herring fishing.

The question is, where did this herring come from? Most was, obviously, cured. Some, we hear, came from Ireland in the fifteenth century where there was a thriving herring fishery off the east and south coasts up to the early seventeenth century, while some continued to be landed into East Anglia. But, in comparison, it was the Scots who had within their grasp rich herring grounds. They were, in 1491, already exporting herring to Italy, France, Flanders and England, according to Don Pedro de Ayala, the Spanish ambassador to the Scottish court.

However, James IV, it is said, was the first Scotsman really to understand the menace to the country from the foreign fishermen. In 1493 he decreed that boats of at least 20 tons should be built for fishing from the coastal burghs, and that 'stark idill men' were to be pressed into service as crew in these vessels. Not surprisingly, given the lack of experience of the crew, his plan failed to prevent the Dutch from retaining their upper hand in the North Sea.

On the west side of the country the story was different. Herring had been caught in Loch Fyne since time immemorial, according to a string of writers, with most of this being exported to France and Spain. It has been said – admittedly rather tenuously – that it was the Low Country folk who first came here in the ninth century to buy salted herring and that it was the Scots who, in fact, first taught the Dutch to cure their fish.

Part of the catch was paid to the Crown as dues, the rest being taken to Glasgow by boat. Various laws were passed controlling the sale of herring at sea, allowing the native people to purchase the fish before any was exported and, in 1600, prohibiting its export before 11 October, thereby ensuring its availability in the local markets. Herring was, at the time, very common and hardly appreciated, and a staple part of the local diet. None, or at the very least little, seems to have found its way into the English market.

Of Loch Fyne, Hector Boece noted in 1527 that there 'is mair plente of herring than is in any seas of Albion'. In 1555 the Scots' parliament found that the fishermen from the western side of the Clyde had 'resortit to the fisching of Loch Fune and uthers Lochis in the north Ilis for the taking of hering and uthers fischeis'. The difference between these herring and others was their superiority in taste. Bishop Leslie wrote in 1575 of great shoals of herring in autumn and early winter on the west coast, and that those of Loch Fyne were fat and tasty and unlike any others. Sir Walter Raleigh mentioned in 1603 that the Dutch sold herring valued at £1½ million, with the employment of 20,000 Scots and all the herring coming from the Scottish west coast, most notably Loch Fyne. Exactly two centuries later, Dorothy Wordsworth, travelling with her brother William, wrote in the ensuing *A Tour in Scotland* that the fresh herring she ate in Inveraray were 'much superior to the herring we get in the north of England'. The editor of the journal added as a footnote: 'I should rather think so!'

In about 1630 there were 800 small 'slayeing boats' of between 5 and 6 tons each fishing on the west coast at the beginning of the season in July. Numbers rose to 1,500 some years, as the fishing progressed. Over 200 'Cowper boats', of about 12 tons, transported the herring to market. Small boats were said to be favoured because of the deepness and narrowness of the lochs that didn't allow bigger boats access, and the lack of harbours on the entire coast.

In 1674 some 20,000 barrels of herring were exported to La Rochelle. Towards the end of the seventeenth century Greenock was a major herring fishery, probably the largest on the western side of the country, and Glasgow merchants employed Greenock ships to fish and transport the catch to market. However, during the reign of Charles II, the Society of Herring Fishers had particular privileges and use of an enclosed area for curing the fish called the Royal Close. These were bought by the Town Council in 1684 and the business flourished, with up to 900 small boats being actively engaged in the fishing.

The first Association for the Fishing was set up by Charles I, ostensibly to compete with the Dutch, in 1632. This was to be common to the three kingdoms of Britain and was to add 240 vessels of between 30 and 40 tons each to the existing fishing fleet, 200 from England, Ireland and the remainder from Scotland. It was to have a complete monopoly upon the trade of fish and one of its main intentions was to promote the herring fishery off Lewis, although they later realised the locals fished much more effectively with their small craft. In some instances the islanders attacked the foreigners and chased them away! The ultimate success of the Association is shown by the fact that it collapsed eight years later. English, Scottish and Dutch friction again prevented any great development in the fisheries, as we've already seen. In 1642, a vessel skippered by one fisher, William Cobb, was stolen by a group of the Lewismen and the captain and crew kept prisoner for four months. For the realm was entering a period of civil war and the development of the fisheries was, like all trade movement, crippled by uncertain times.

At the end of the civil war, Cromwell brought a period of stability and a desire to expand the fisheries, although in the North Sea this was impossible due to the Dutch Wars. Once the monarchy was re-established, Charles II showed a certain eagerness to invigorate the idea of a Royal Fishery Company. Yet in 1666 London was first devastated by plague, then fire, and once again war. Britain's fortunes were at a low ebb. Throughout these years the society had stumbled along in existence, non-viable and non-profitable. Hardly surprising, then, that at the cessation of war the Royal Fishery Company had simply disappeared, it being finally dissolved by an Act of Parliament in 1690.

In contrast to the west coast, the east was slow to take up coastal fishing. Herring was regarded with suspicion and considered by some to have no commercial value. Caithness fishermen were still using iron hooks in 1767 to catch herring to use as bait for white fish. Presumably those with little concern for the herring fishing were from the inaccessible parts of the country, for one assumes that if people had realised the benefits the Dutch were gaining, they would have been fishing with their nets immediately.

The dawning of the eighteenth century undoubtedly heralded change within the Scottish fisheries. The Dutch influence had waned, while Britannia was beginning to flex her muscles. Westminster controlled the entire island of Great Britain and London politicians began to see advantages in developing a vibrant herring fishery. After all, if spreading their wings meant building a stronger navy, then fishermen had been proved as a store of crew for these fighting ships. Thus, in 1718, came the first universal bounty laws in the time of George I, designed to encourage fishermen to act as entrepreneurs by building and fitting out herring busses. Its true to say that Queen Anne had reorganised the various herring laws in 1704 and decreed the paying of a bounty on exported Scotch herring, yet the system didn't, apparently, work successfully. Fishermen were excused certain import duties on boat-building materials.

The prototype of 1718 was, of course, the Dutch buss system of two centuries before. However, when one considers the method used by the whaler ships of north Europe and later the European cod fishers off Newfoundland, one sees similarities in their use of smaller boats as catcher craft, with the fish being cured aboard the mother ship. In reality this is the only way to work a successful fishery away from the homeport. The main difference with the herring buss method, for the Scots anyway, was that they were often working within sight of land, so that they could just as easily land the catch ashore.

The bounty system gave the owners of herring busses a fixed sum per tonnage of their vessel, initially 30s, which was raised to 50s in 1750. Then, in 1787, came a change in tactic to encourage small boats to fish. The tonnage bounty was reduced to 20s whilst another bounty

The buss fishery was modelled on the Dutch system of the sixteenth century

of 2s 8d was paid on each full barrel of white herring exported, 1s 9d on full red herring and just 1s on spent red herring. 'Red' herring, in this instance, refers to ungutted fish while the 'white' herring refers to fish gutted before being laid in salt.

Throughout the century or more that the bounty system existed there was a vast amount of paperwork for the fishermen to cope with, and for the fishery officers ashore who oversaw the whole business. Salt, taxed for normal use, was duty free for these fishers, although its onboard shipping was very carefully noted. Busses had to be between 20 and 80 tons and could only fish after assembling at specific ports at equally specific times. On the east coast they gathered at Shetland in June and on the west coast at Campbeltown in September. The herring had to be barrelled within twenty-four hours and none was to be taken ashore. The size and extent of nets was regulated, as was the number of boats allowed. In fact, a whole series of Acts of Parliament between 1718 and the repeal of the bounty system in the first half of

LOCH BOISDALE in SOUTH UIST
Sketched without measurement
6 Sept 1784 by SA

EXPLANATIONS

Scale of Miles

HE HEBRIDES

ORKNEY ISLANDS

Europa Pt or Butt of Lewis

THE MINCH

SUTHERLAND SHIRE

CAITHNESS

THE OR WESTERN ISLES

SKYE

ROSS SHIRE

DORNOCH FIRTH

MURRAY FIRTH

CROMARTY

MURRAY SHIRE

BANF SHIRE

ABERDEEN SHIRE

INVERNESS SHIRE

MEARNS

ANGUS SHIRE

PERTH SHIRE

FIFE SHIRE

FIRTH OF TAY

MULL

STIRLING SH.

FIRTH OF FORTH

DUMBARTON SH.

HADDINGTON SHIRE

RENFREW

GLASGOW

LITHGOW

EDINBURGH

BERWICK SHIRE

ARRAN

LANERK SH.

PEEBLES SH.

SELKIRK

ROXBOROUGH SHIRE

A NEW MAP of SCOTLAND;
The Hebrides and Western Coasts,
in particular,
being carefully laid down
from the best Authorities
corrected
by late Observations
1785

Scale of Miles

PART OF IRELAND

WIGTON SHIRE

KIRKCUDBRIGHT SHIRE

DUMFRIES SHIRE

SOLWAY FIRTH

PART OF ENGLAND

the nineteenth century severely regulated, and constrained, the whole British herring fishery.

Much has been written about the fishery after about 1750 when the Society of Free British Fisheries was formed as the last of the royal fishing companies. To elaborate on the abundance of evidence would be repetitious and, more to the point, take up a whole series of volumes. The reader is recommended to the bibliography at the end of this book for further reading.

The Society of Free British Fisheries built two busses – the *Pelham* and *Carteret* – on the river Thames. They were 70 tons each, cost £500 and were crewed by seventeen men, half of whom were engaged in the curing process. However, it appears that most of the crews were either Danes or Dutchmen, such is the conflicting evidence on this. Two more busses were fitted out the following year and they fished off Shetland and the west coast. Yet the Society was inept at making a profit and it collapsed in 1772. One writer suggests this was due to an inability to compete with the Dutch, but evidence tends to support the theory that their control had waned by this time. More likely is the fact that, with only four vessels, they didn't give themselves much of a chance to engage the fishery with success.

The Scots were left to profiteer with their Clyde-based busses. From two craft in 1751, their numbers increased rapidly to 261 in 1766, but then a decline through the American Wars saw a drop in numbers for a few years. They rose again to peak at 153 vessels in 1783.

The twilight years of the eighteenth century were exciting ones for the herring fishery in Scotland as the government really began to take note of the advantage of expanding the fishery. Several travellers were dispatched to see for themselves exactly what was going on. Although Daniel Defoe had passed through in the 1720s and found huge shoals of fish and nothing but 'fishing barks and boats, which are in the season employ'd for catching herring', he didn't make much impact. Thomas Pennant, a Welshman from Flintshire in north-east Wales, journeyed north in 1769 and again in 1772, and his subsequent *Tours in Scotland* are still regarded as the first major accounts of the country

Opposite: *Scotland in the late eighteenth century (from* An Account of the Present State of the Hebrides and Western Coasts of Scotland *by J. Anderson).*

after the Jacobite uprising of 1745. Of Loch Fyne, he noted 600 boats fishing during the season that lasted from September to Christmas. The fishers all worked at night, four men to a boat, setting their nets across the loch. During the day the fishers played bagpipes and danced, and some slept aboard under their sails. Salt, he declared, or lack of it, was a drawback for the curing and export of the herring. He also noted that 300 busses rendezvoused off Kintyre on 12 September for the deep-sea fishery, and that they had to return by 13 January to receive the bounty of 50s per ton of herring. In this he must be confused, as the tonnage bounty, as already stated, is paid on the tonnage of the vessel, not the herring. On the east coast, in his first tour, he noted a small herring fishery at Staxigo, 'the only one on this coast'.

James Anderson published *An Account of the Present State of the Hebrides and Western Coasts of Scotland* in 1785 after submitting it to the Lords of the Treasury. He attempted to explain the circumstances that had repressed the industry of the Scots, and his overall intention was to consider the fisheries and suggest improvements for its promotion. His tome is over 450 pages long, and, as well as suggestions, he provided statistics on the fisheries and observations on infrastructure improvements. Thomas Newte, touring in 1785 in England and Scotland, was another 'English gentleman' who published his thoughts on the fisheries in 1788. Johnson and Boswell journeyed in the same year as Newte, but made few comments on the herring fishery.

Newte gave us a fascinating description of a fishing station in Loch Torridon, the remains of which can still be seen on the south side of the upper loch at Aird Mhor, although the original structure was rebuilt at some stage. The first structure had been built by a Mr Mackenzie, and below it, on the lochside, was a landing place where vessels with a draught of 14ft or less could moor. Above was the store for drying nets (AB) with the salt house (C) leading off this. The curing house (D), seen in section (E) is close by. Further up the rock was another wooden house used as a grain store. Newte suggested that these buildings should be enclosed in stone and lime with a slate roof over – suggestions that must have been carried out at some stage. He noted that other buildings had already been built in stone and used as a cooperage, accommodation for the agent and store for the curers. It is the remains of these that can still be found among the rock and undergrowth.

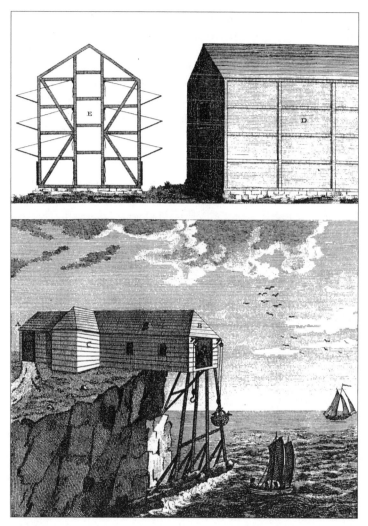

The herring curing station at Aird Mhor, Loch Torridon, *by Thomas Newte (1785).*

John Knox was probably the most influential of all the travellers to the regions. An Edinburgh bookseller, he was sent off to investigate, and his ensuing book, *A View of the British Empire, more especially Scotland, with Some Proposals for the Improvement of that Country, the Extension of the Fisheries and the Relief of the People*, was published in 1784. Although rather grandiose in title, it does fully explain his intentions. Two years later he was off again, and produced *Observations on the Northern Fisheries with a Discourse on the Expediency of Establishing Fishing Stations or Small Towns in the Highlands of Scotland and the Hebride Islands* in 1786 and, the following year, he published *A Tour through the Highlands of Scotland and the Hebride Isles*, the latter being a shortened version of the former. From Knox's observations came, in 1786, the setting up of the British Fisheries Society by various Scotsmen of standing, with the Duke of Argyll as president. Learning from the past errors of the royal fishing companies and fishing societies, they planned to build fishing villages in the Hebrides to support viable fishing communities. After the inland population had been forced under threat of expulsion from their tenanted crofts during the clearances, when absentee landlords favoured sheep rearing to human land cultivation and animal husbandry, the suggestion was that these displaced people – at least those that hadn't been forced over to America or beyond, many dying in the process – would be able to supply the workforce. Settlements were therefore built at Tobermory on Mull, Stein at Lochbay on Skye and Ullapool on Loch Broom: three settlements although Knox had advocated forty.

The same influence persuaded the government to make the major 1787 changes to the bounty system, thus encouraging small boats into the fishery. However, the only barriers still in existence stifling growth in the fishery at this time were the widely despised Salt Laws. Fishermen could catch their herring but then were unable to cure it due to the cost of the salt. Some was smuggled in, and various relaxations allowed fishermen duty-free salt, but such were the restrictions, that the system was unworkable for the majority. It wasn't until they were finally repealed in 1825 that the fishing flourished in the early nineteenth century.

The British Fisheries Society meanwhile bought up land to the south of the river at Wick and built a fishing station there. Pulteneytown, as it was called, was the one major success of the Society, for the west-coast stations (except Ullapool up to a degree) never thrived for long. Wick, as it was universally called, thrived beyond all expectations, becoming the herring capital of Europe within half a century, such was the growth in the herring fishing upon the east coast of Scotland.

Herring, as we have seen, is migratory and its presence fluctuates widely, thus some years there was a glut and others a dearth. But with the opening up of markets for the cured herring and a regulatory system in which fishery officers carefully controlled the quality of the product, its reputation became self-perpetuating. Salted herring was thought great to feed slaves, due to its salt content that replenished lost sweat at work, and vast amounts were exported to the West Indies up to the abolition of slavery in 1833, although this market had already declined after 1807 when Napoleon's Berlin Decree of 1806 prohibited trade between Britain and France and her dependencies.

During the year 1785-6 there were no less than seven reports from the committee appointed to enquire into the state of the British fisheries, and another five during the year 1798-9, giving us all manner of facts and figures for the fishery. On the west coast there were 797 small boats fishing in 1797, and while the east-coast fishery was not worth a mention, that of Shetland was in dire straits. Again we find that it was only upon the west coast that herring was being taken in any quantity, although the inhabitants of the islands and coastal settlements gained very little benefit, other than herring to supplement their meagre diet of potatoes and oats. Control, and the subsequent profit, remained in the hands of the Clyde merchants.

The bounty system was revised again in 1808 with fewer restrictions being imposed on the fishermen. Suddenly the east coast awoke to the possibilities and small boats were obtained and engaged in the fishing from communities all along the coast, from Wick in the north to Berwick-upon-Tweed in the south. New fishing villages appeared on the coast and, although there were few, if any, harbours, the beaches became a hive of activity during the fishing season.

Several writers travelled the country at the turn of the nineteenth century. Thomas Garnett arrived in 1798 as did John Leyden two years later. But it was John McCulloch who, publishing *The Highlands and Western Isles of Scotland* in 1824, was the most observant. His description of the buss fishery at Loch Ranza on Arran really does sum up the activity:

The whole bay formed a beautiful sight when I saw it last, on a fine evening in August, when it happened to be the rendezvous of the herring fleet. The busses that were purchasing fish were at anchor in the loch, each with its flag flying and surrounded by boats in groups delivering their cargoes, while some were running alongside, and others hoisting their sails to stand out again to sea. The dark festoons of the nets hanging over the sides, the white topsails above displayed to dry and the bright yellow hulls of the herring boats, with all their variety of brown and yellow and white sails, and with the smooth green sea below, reflecting every tint, formed combinations of colouring even more exquisite than those produced by the elegant forms of these boats, with their tall masts and pyramidal sails, dispersed and contrasted and grouped in every possible manner. Far away towards the Argyllshire coast, the sea was covered with a swarm of boats of all sizes and kinds, with sails of all shapes and colours, standing away towards Loch Fyne on every possible tack, and gradually diminishing to the sight till they vanished under the distant land. The shore was another scene of life which served to complete the picture. Other boats drawn up on the beach, or ranged along the margin of the water, were delivering cargoes to the country people and to the coopers; the whole green beneath the castle being strewn with fish, and nets, and casks, while horses, and carts, and groups of people in motion, with the hum of their voices, and the hollow sound from the coopering of the casks re-echoing from hill to hill, added to the smokes of numerous fires employed in the cookery or in boiling the oil, rendered the whole scene of confusion, activity and bustle, contrasting strangely with the wild solitude of the mountains around, and the calm repose of the setting sun.

Herring-curing stations such as the one described were to be found in many distant parts of the west coast. Ullapool has already been mentioned, but, to the north of the town, two others were once similar places of activity. On the island of Tanera Mor in the Summer Isles, the remains of stone buildings that were once a curing station can still be seen, while, further south, Isle Martin was base to another fishery at a different time.

Between the mainland and Skye is Loch Hourne, once the base of a thriving herring fishery. Here, hundreds of boats landed their catch, which was cured and then taken by ship to distant markets. What makes these places remarkable is that they were largely within inaccessible regions, where the only way in or out was by sea. Just as McCulloch described Loch Ranza, these places buzzed with activity when the fleets landed during the season, and, just as quickly, when the herring moved on, they reverted to places of silence. For that was the thing about the herring fishery, especially on the west coast: it was limited to short seasons, it thrived for short periods, and then, just as suddenly, it didn't exist. It is as if it never happened.

Herring Mayonnaise

Ingredients:
4 cold cooked herring – boiled, filleted, baked or fried
Green salad with cucumber
4 eggs
White pepper
Dry mustard
2 dessertspoonfuls of white wine vinegar or lemon juice
2 gills of olive oil

Method:
Make the mayonnaise by breaking the eggs and separating the yolks. Free the yolk of the little 'germ' attached, then add two pinches of dry mustard and pepper and whisk it up. Stir in the vinegar and beat again, then drop in slowly the oil, drop by drop, beating it with a wooden spoon. It should be thick as cream when finished. Half cream and half olive oil can be used. When the herring have been masked in the mayonnaise, slice up sufficient cucumber to arrange around. Serve with any kind of green salad. Hard boil the remaining two eggs, cut in quarters, and arrange on the salad to improve its appearance.

CHAPTER SIX

The Influence of the Norwegians

The Revd Marsh's evidence in the 1799 House of Commons report on the British Fisheries (see Appendix Two) provides evidence that there was apparently a vast difference in the quality of cured herring coming from Britain, Norway and Sweden. One must assume that the Germans were among the fussiest of eaters of the product on the Continent. Much of what was being exported to the southern European states was smoked herring, which didn't need as much careful attention to produce the ultimate product.

That the Norwegians were catching herring well before 1800 is obvious given the country's proximity to the rich fishing grounds of the North Atlantic. Ever since the Vikings had uprooted and sailed west in search of fertile lands with which to support their families they had sought to use the sea as a source of food. The *Saga of Olaf Tryggvesson* notes a herring boat going south in about 980 while between 960 and 975 they fished with large herring nets near Christiana. It is probable these coastal communities had been doing the same for centuries before. The only factors in the equation that altered were the ways in which the fish were caught, the amount of fish, and, of course, the curing method. Three centuries later, it was reported that whales could be fished anytime and anywhere except 'the herring-driver during the herring season'. Such was the significance of the herring fishing over the hugely important whale fishery. In 1372 King Magnus the Lawmaker detailed exact rules for catching herring in the first Norwegian national law.

Like much of Scandinavia, Norway was under the control of the Danes for a long time. On 10 November 1587, two herring were caught off the coast and presented to Frederik II of Denmark because marks upon them were deemed to resemble Gothic printed characters. Learned men gathered and declared these to mean that herring would not be fished as well hereabout as in other nations in the future. The king took this to heart – quite literally maybe – and subsequently died. Hence the two herring were then said to have been divine heralds of the king's death.

In Norway it is the spring herring that has been the longest surviving herring fishery. The salting of the herring in barrels or boxes seems to date from about the fifteenth century. According to Friele, between 1567 and 1700 the fishery was severely limited, but developed in the eighteenth century, except between 1784 and 1808. Then, in 1874, the herring deserted the coasts. He suggests that its disappearance from the Norwegian west coast coincided with a thriving fishery off the west coast of Sweden, and when it abandoned the Swedish coast it reappeared off the Norwegian coast. But, as is increasingly apparent with the herring, nothing is certain. Its migration habits can take it almost anywhere! Even today, there is disagreement among scientists concerning the annual cycles of the vast shoals of the fish.

Up to the mid-nineteenth century, the fishing was undertaken either from small open boats, propelled either by oar or sail, or directly off the shore. Their boats largely remained unchanged, especially in building tradition, from the days of the Viking craft. Images of the wild Northmen coming ashore in the late eighth century in these craft at places such as Lindisfarne on Britain's eastern coast fill history books and, consequently, need no description. Built using overlapping wide planks – in other words clinker-built – these craft had enormous influence upon the boat-building techniques of northern Europe. Indeed, as many a study makes clear, a majority of the fishing craft of Britain stem from this Norse supremacy.

However, and this is true for all of the countries bordering the North Sea, the fishermen didn't spend their entire time fishing for herring. As we have seen, it was a seasonal fish, and the Norwegians were as much famed for their cod, as Marsh also noted. With rich reserves of white fish just offshore in the deeper water of the Atlantic, the Norwegians were quick to glean a living from its capture. The export in dried and salted cod was widespread throughout Europe. Even the cod roe was in demand, no less than by the sardine fishers of

France and Spain who used it for throwing into the sea to entice the shoals of that pelagic fish into their seines.

Drift-nets were the tool of the boat fishermen along the entire seaboard of the country, with each boat carrying somewhere between fifteen and twenty-five nets, depending on the area, and a crew of between three and five men. Most of the fishing was practised at night when the herring rose to the surface to feed, but occasional daytime fishing occurred when the herring was being pursued by whales. However, one problem the authorities had was the very serious loss of nets due to the lack of orderliness within the fishing communities. Nets often became entangled with other nets or disappeared because of the strong currents around the shores and fjords. These nets formed floating islands that were big enough to support the weight of a considerable number of people. Therefore they had to be cleared and taken ashore, later to be sold back to the fishermen at public auctions.

During the spring season the fishermen lived away from home, sleeping aboard boats specifically converted for that reason. In the early 1800s the practise of sleeping ashore was more common, often outside in the cold damp air. Dormitory boats allowed a degree of comfort as each fisherman in turn could take his hand to the daily chore of cooking for his group. Once the nets were hauled in, the catch was put aboard one of the many collecting boats and taken to the on-shore curing station. There the gullet was removed prior to the fish being laid in barrels with salt from Cagliari, Setubal or Trapani (i.e. Mediterranean or Portuguese salt) and left to shrink, before being finally sealed and exported.

Seine-fishing involved many more fishermen and the seine was worked from the shore. When the herring were spotted close inshore, the seine-net was cast around the body of the shoal, using one boat to arc it around. Up to thirty men might work one seine, and its efficiency depended on many factors, including the nature of the seabed, the currents and weather conditions, and the skill of the fishermen. Sometimes the herring had to be frightened into staying within the net. To achieve this, the men in the small boats lowered and raised white-painted boards into the sea, making the fish see reflections of themselves. Seines tend to be favoured more to the south of the west coast where the weather is kindlier by comparison to the wild north coast.

Like the drift-net fishery, the herring was carried to the curing station where it was salted. In total, the spring herring fishery was said to
have employed upwards of 6,000 boats, with an annual output of
700,000 barrels in its better years. The vast majority of this was
exported to Sweden, Germany and Russia.

Although the spring herring accounted for the principal exports,
substantial herring was caught in the summer season, which lasted
from July until December. This fishery occurred approximately between Bergen and Tromso, which in fact incorporates sixty-five per
cent of the entire coastline of the country. Like the spring herring, its
capture was by gill-net or seine-net, the latter in use to the south
while the northerners preferred the drift-net. Friele reported that the
reason the southerners used the seine was the herring there were full
of undigested food after their gluttonous feeding frenzy and could not
be salted down until this was removed. Thus the fish were left in the
seine for up to three days to allow the digestion of the stomach content before being laid in salt.

The same year, 1857, saw a thriving winter fishery around the
south-west part of the coast. Here 3,000 small, open boats, manned by
three or four men, caught between fifteen and thirty barrels each per
day over an eight-day period during the height of the season. The
total output was in excess of 200,000 barrels.

Moreover, the summer herring differed quite considerably in size,
much more so than their spring counterparts. There were traditionally
four categories: large merchantable herring of up to 10ins long, small
or medium merchantable herring (9.4ins), large Christiana herring
(8ins) and small Christiana herring (7.2ins). These were denoted in the
branding by the letters KK, K, M and C respectively. Again the main
markets were Sweden, Hamburg (Germany), Russia, and Denmark.

The third distinct herring fishery of Norway was the Nordland
Great Herring. This short-lived fishery occurred on any great scale
between the years 1851 and 1875 and again in the 1880s. It was
renowned for its largeness and excellent taste in the kitchens of
Nordland and southern Finnmark. Most was taken by seine-net in the
period between September and November to be cured and exported
to the German Baltic ports, Russia and Sweden.

The Norwegian fishing industry changed rapidly in the 1870s after
the herring deserted their familiar grounds. Inspired by the British

and Swedish fishermen, they built larger sailing boats and followed the cod off the north-western coast. When the herring returned in the next decade, these fishermen were still using their sail boats – especially those of the Hardanger and Lista types which had adopted the fore and aft rig instead of the old squaresails. However, with the advent of the internal combustion engine in the early 1900s, the fishermen were again quick to adapt. It has been said that the entire fleet of 15,000 open and decked fishing boats were converted to motor power between 1900 and 1920. Large catches of herring continued to be caught off the west coast in the twentieth century, even though much of it was used to extract oil. The price consequently slumped. However, as we shall see later in this book, Norway was to have an immense impact upon the stocks of herring within the North Sea and North Atlantic, which was to lead to a total ban on fishing as the century progressed.

In contrast to Norway, Denmark's herring fishing was tiny, probably as a result of Sweden and Norway being under the Danish crown for centuries, especially where the fishing was rich. For the west coast of Denmark is inhospitable with shallow seas. Here fishermen fought for a subsistence living and, not being able to sail far offshore, they concentrated on catching cod, plaice and haddock. Later they pioneered the Danish seine, opening the North Sea Fishery after the port of Esbjerg was built in 1886. Only on the east and north coasts was herring caught in any quantity. Here the fishermen used drift-nets and anchored-nets, both of which had to be set at the correct depth where the temperature suited the herring. The Bornholm fishermen ascertained this depth by lowering down a *gradeflaske* – literally a temperature bottle or thermometer – and taking readings at different depths. For this late summer fishery they used their small, open, double-ended boats called *sætebåd* which were rigged with one spritsail until decked boats appeared in 1867.

The fishermen from the north of the country followed the herring in the Skagerrak, the piece of water between Denmark and Norway. Here they used *sildebåd* – literally 'herring boat' – the design of which remained unaltered for centuries until motorisation. They were basically of Norwegian design, lightly built, double-ended with an s-shaped midship section. The Sound fishermen worked out of Skovshoved, just outside Copenhagen, and their typical boat was 24ft long, open and narrow and ideal for the short seas. Like the *sildebåd*, they were sprit-rigged. Slightly further north, the Hornbaek fishermen worked into the waters of the Kattegat that separated northern Denmark from Sweden, using a gaff-rigged vessel that more resembled the Norwegian craft, even though Skovshoved and Hornbaek were only twenty-five miles apart. This illustrates the way in which all fishermen adapt their craft purely to suit the conditions of their locality – the beach they work from and the waters in which they fish. To the maritime ethnologist this becomes all too apparent in studies of fishing communities and their vessels everywhere.

The Norwegians also had a massive influence in the herring fishing of Iceland. This was in the late 1860s, but the reason why it was the Norwegians and not the Danes who ruled the island until independence in 1944, or the Icelanders themselves, also great fishers, is unclear. Whether Norway somehow regarded the fishery as its inherent right stemming from its control over the island in the fourteenth century, nobody knows. But reports emerged in northern Germany in 1879 that an 'extremely superior' salted herring from Iceland that fetched an equally superior price had been imported into Gothenburg. The following year a cargo of the same herring was imported directly into Germany through Elmshorn, which lies on a tributary of the river Elbe, a few miles north-west of Hamburg. Apparently the vessel that brought it in had sailed specifically to Iceland to join in the herring fishing and had subsequently returned with the salted herring which reached the Hamburg market.

It seems that the captain of a Norwegian trading boat had noticed the shoals of herring off the east coast of Iceland, and this he mentioned to his ship-owner. This merchant of Mandal, Albert Jacobsen, immediately bought up a piece of land close to the Sejdis fjord and sent a vessel to fish. However, the first year was unsuccessful, so Jacobsen formed the Iceland Fishing Company along with seven other local merchants. Success followed further investment and an expansion in their on-shore facilities. But that was short-lived indeed, with the herring disappearing almost as soon as they made a return on their investment. The outcome was that the company was dissolved and the land was sold to another company with Jacobsen as one of its shareholders. Again they met with failure until only two shareholders remained – Jacobsen and Carl Lund. Then, in 1877, the herring returned and two years of mediocre fishing followed. In the autumn of 1879 vast shoals appeared so that they did not have enough salt or barrels to cure the entire catch. Yet they still managed to send back over 8,000 barrels, which realised a healthy profit for the company, such were the high prices paid for this herring. However, disaster ended the season when the Dutch steamer *Anna*, taking the final 2,117 barrels back to Bergen along with the shore workers from the fishing station, hit a rock at Feiosen and sank, taking with it the lives of the first mate, the pilot, two coopers and the director of the station, Captain Abrahamsen. Most of the cargo was also lost.

The success of the fishery, though, encouraged others to fit out vessels and voyage to Iceland. Thirty vessels alone sailed from Mandal. However, to get permission to fish these grounds, the foreigner must be naturalised. This necessitated the taking out of Icelandic citizens' papers at a minimal cost, swearing allegiance to the Danish crown and having an address on the island. To do this, they imported timber-framed buildings that were quickly erected close to the shore. In the summer of that year some 28,000 tons of herring was landed, mostly to the west of the island, and 40,000 tons followed off the east side in just one week in October. Total landings for that year were estimated at 100,000 tons. However, as has been the case with much of the fishing in Icelandic waters until the second half of the twentieth century, there was only a limited benefit to the islanders themselves.

Although the Norwegians commanded much of the herring fishery of the eastern seaboard of the Atlantic, it is worth noting that Russian fishermen made substantial landings from the north coast. The Russians were lucky in that they had four distinct areas around the coast of their vast empire where herring were caught. In the Russian-controlled part of Finland, small herring called *stromming* were landed in the spring in the Gulf of Bothnia. During the winter, when the gulf is frozen, herring were caught under the ice through holes, using a sort of seine-net. On the Caspian Sea, a particular strain of herring was taken especially for its oil until the benefits of salting the catch were realised. Up to 100,000 tons were taken for this purpose. Herring was also caught on both sides of the Bering Strait, mostly by seine-net or sometimes by fish weir. This was, of course, the Pacific herring, large amounts of which were landed into North America, where the history of the herring continues.

Smoked Herring Dip from America

Ingredients:
5 smoked herring fillets
Soured cream

Method:
Cut the fillets up into chunks and soak in soured cream in refrigerator for 24 hours before serving with crackers, crisps or raw vegetables such as celery, cucumber and carrot.

CHAPTER SEVEN

Herring for Sardines

the New England herring fishery in the nineteenth century

It was Captain Jonathan Carleton of Isle Haut, Maine, who was allegedly the first to return to the United States with the very first cargo of herring from the Magdalen Islands. This group of islands – these days known as the Islas de la Madeleine – sit in the southern portion of the Gulf of St Lawrence where the water is relatively shallow. Carleton arrived there in 1822 after sailing to catch the early spring cod, but finding this scarce, he decided it would be worth experimenting with a load of herring. After a successful fishing, he landed 350 barrels that were then smoked for the Boston market.

But, as everyone probably knows, cod was the sought-after fish off the banks to the east of Newfoundland. European fishers, when they first came here, found cod as big as humans and in such abundance that they could fill baskets by simply leaning over the edge of the boat and scooping them up. Herring didn't interest them merely because they were plentiful at home, certainly in northern Europe.

The early settlers of New England – the north-east corner of the United States that encompasses the coastal states of Maine, New Hampshire, Massachusetts, Rhode Island and Connecticut as well as the landlocked state of Vermont – had certainly known about the herring shoals off their shores. Being British subjects, theirs was the freedom to fish these waters without hindrance. They sailed up to the coast of Labrador in search of cod and found huge shoals of herring. After the 1775-81 Wars of Independence, the American fishermen, by a treaty of 1783, were given the right to fish in any of the British North American waters and to 'dry and cure fish in any of the unsettled bays,

A pinky, a traditional American fishing boat, unloading at Eastport, 1885, drawn by G.B. Goode

harbours, and creeks of Nova Scotia, the Magdalen Islands, and Labrador so long as the same shall remain unsettled'. Much of the herring was being salted in hogsheads and either being used as bait or as food for slaves, although since 1808 herring had been smoked at Eastport in the Scotch way. Indeed, Daniel Ramsdell was one of the first to move from Canada to Lubec, Maine, in 1797, starting a smoking business after being taught in Nova Scotia by a Scot.

An 1818 convention removed the right of fishing to within three miles of the shore in some localities, but Labrador, the Magdalens and the southern shore of Newfoundland remained open. Thus the cod fishers, fishing these waters, opened up the herring fishery. The Newfoundland herring fishery began in the late 1830s.

After Carleton's successful trip, others decided to try their hand at the same. Vessels sailed from Deer Isle, Fox Island, Mount Desert, Lubec and Eastport within two years, and soon all the fishing towns of New Hampshire were bringing home herring. During the period 1858-65 some fifty vessels went to the fishery.

Further west, in the Gulf of St Lawrence, lies the Island of Anticosti, where abundant shoals of herring were to be found, especially off the East Cape in June. When the fishery off the Magdalens proved poor, the fishermen would move west and fill their boats up here, although it has been said that there were other more accessible areas, so that this area was a last resort.

The problem for these American fishers was the need to salt the fish in pretty exposed locations if they chose to work on shore, where temperatures were low. Thus the majority salted the fish down onboard ship. Salt was carried in pans in the centre of the hold and, once the fish had been taken aboard, this salt was thrown over them. They were then shovelled into the hold with more salt being added. In this way they were carried home. However, as we have seen in the European market, herring really needs barrelling as soon as it leaves the sea and thus the fish landed back into the New England ports was inferior. Some was taken ashore and cured in the normal way while the vast majority was taken for smoking. The vessels they used were the 40-80-ton fishing schooners primarily built for the cod fishery, but as the trade developed, larger schooners of up to 175 tons were engaged. Sometimes the whalers fished for herring outside of their normal season.

Yet this was an inhospitable coast with uncertain weather. In August 1872, a summer hurricane in the Magdalens lasted three days. Eighty-three vessels were anchored in Pleasant Bay and of these forty-eight were stranded after breaking their moorings. The seas were breaking 100ft high against the cliffs, as many of the boats fetched up there. Amazingly, only three men died, these being from the crew of the schooner *E.J. Smith* from Wellfleet which went ashore just outside Amherst Harbour and broke up in two hours. That more were not drowned was due, in some instances, to the bravery of those on shore. Thirty-one men were saved by two islanders and their Newfoundland dog, which leapt into the surf and physically pulled them all ashore. This storm was remembered for years afterwards, both for its intensity and its duration, and was reckoned to have been one of the worst on record at the time.

The American herring, like its European counterpart, is prone to sudden changes to its migration pattern that might seem, in retrospect, like a deliberate trick to outwit the fishermen. In the spring of 1870, according to the *Gloucester Telegraph*, the fishery off the Magdalens was a complete failure. It seems that the herring arrived a month early that year, so that by the time the boats arrived, they had all but disappeared. Two vessels from Newburyport arrived home, one with just fifty barrels and the other with none. All the effort of a month's work for nothing.

The town of Gloucester lies to the north-east of Boston, close to Cape Ann, and it became renowned for its cod fishery. However, the growth of the port was due partly to the herring fishery in the second half of the nineteenth century. Before 1854, only tiny catches of the fish were landed, both for bait and home consumption. That year, Captain Henry O. Smith, veteran skipper of the schooner *Flying Cloud*, set out from the port and sailed to Newfoundland to bring home a cargo of frozen halibut, as reports were reaching Gloucester that huge quantities of the fish were being caught. Leaving in December, he found that by the time he got there the halibut catches were poor and, as an alternative, he decided to fish for cod. However herring was in abundance at the time also, so it seemed, by way of an experiment, a good idea to take onboard the herring – he caught up to 80,000 fish. It seems that on an earlier trip he had caught too much herring to use as bait for the cod and this had frozen on deck and remained in perfect condition.

Smith returned to Gloucester in the February of the following year and immediately sold a quarter of his catch of herring to George W. Floyd, who sold it to the shore fishermen as bait. Three schooner skippers bought 500 fish each and, after eight or nine days at sea, returned with massive catches of cod. Thus the idea of buying frozen cod developed into a leading herring fishery, with much of the fish going to the New York and Boston markets for human consumption.

As well as the deep-sea herring fishery, small herring were taken close to the New England shore. Very small herring are often known as 'brit' or 'spurling', depending on the locality, and for many years it was believed that these were quite a different species of herring from the usual *Clupea harengus*. However, as in Europe where certain species of herring such as the Thames Blackwater herring do not reach as large a size as, say, the Norwegian herring, these smaller herring are now recognised as being part of the same family of herring. In some extreme cases 'brit' are only 3-4ins long. Yorkshire fishermen use similar sized hering to bait their lobster and crab pots.

One of the principal herring fishing grounds off the New England coast was off Eastport, inside of Grand Manan Island, where the shoals

A herring horse was used to carry herring to be hung up in a smokehouse like this one in Grand Manan in 1885, drawn by G.B. Goode

arrived in July and stayed until September. Other shoals then swam into these confined waters, so that they continued to be taken until the late spring. With the expansion in the frozen herring trade, many of the Gloucester boats engaged in this fishery.

West of Eastport lay the fishing grounds of Jonesport and Boisbubert, where herring has been caught since at least 1830. Here the herring arrived in April and remained until the middle of June, these being favoured spawning areas. Fish weirs were common for their capture and, when the fishery was at its height between 1858 and 1863, it is said that a dozen or so of these weirs were regularly fished, with 75,000 to 100,000 boxes of herring being taken for smoking before going on to Boston.

Moving west again, the waters off Mount Desert Island were abundant in herring between May and October when they fed there. All, except those in the vicinity of the Cranberry Islands where they were caught in gill-nets, were taken in weirs. Penobscot Bay was rich during the same period where a smaller, or 'sardine', herring could be taken in the late autumn.

The best-quality herring along the New England shore was said to have been caught off Matinus Island and Ebencook Harbour. Most of the fish was caught by the local fishermen who then sold it on to the cod fishers from all along the coast for use as bait. However, with the development of the Magdalene fishery, it declined hereabout due to a depressed market. Between Portland and Boston, some of the finest spawning grounds in the States lay just offshore. Wood Island, a protected anchorage near the mouth of the Saco River, is typical. Here the herring came in September to spawn, with both large and immature herring being captured. Once they had spawned they left almost immediately.

According to Mitchell, herring swam up the coast of Carolina in January to arrive off Virginia in February, and it was after this time that they swam up towards the Bay of Fundy, thereby visiting the areas mentioned before. From there the herring swam around Nova Scotia where a considerable fishery took place in the autumn in and around the region of Chedebucto Bay. It was suggested by Yarrell that there were in fact two species of herring visiting these coasts, one of which was 'new' and given the name of *Clupea leachii*. However this belief of his was subsequently proved to be wrong. Much of the Carolina and Virginia herring was in fact another species of herring altogether: the alewife (*Pomolobus pseudoharengus*), an anadromous variety that ran up the freshwater rivers to spawn. Like the shad (*Alosa sapidissima*), another anadromous herring species, it was prolific off the North American east coast.

As well as in the Bering Strait, herring was once caught in the Kotzebue Sound, which lies just inside the Arctic Circle on the Alaskan side. On the northern coast of Canada, it has been caught in nets in Bathurst Inlet and at Sandy Bay.

In North America there were, up to the nineteenth century, three principal methods by which herring were taken. Two of these were derived from methods used by the Wabanaki Indians, who inhabited these coasts long before any European ever arrived. The oldest of these was called 'torching' and stems from the Wabanaki instinct of observing the habit of the herring to move towards light. For this purpose, the fishermen lit a fire upon an iron framework – called a 'dragon' for obvious reasons – which projected from the bow of a rowboat. They fished just as the sun went down, with one or two oarsmen rowing, another steering and one stationed at the bow, armed with a dip-net, with which he scooped up the herring as they were attracted to the bonfire. It is said that fifteen to twenty barrels could be landed in just a few hours.

Fish weirs were often built to capture herring, among other fish. The Wabanaki had been digging holes on the beach to catch fish and later lined their holes with rocks to catch more fish. Then they added thin branches of brushwood. Thus the fish weir was developed and these varied greatly in size, shape and materials. They were built in a number of ways: sometimes using netting fixed to poles that were themselves fitted into flat stones where the foreshore is rocky. Sometimes the net was held in place with stones and ropes alone. In other instances lath and boards were used in their construction and in others brush and poles were favoured. It simply depended on the nature of the locality, but what they all did have in common was that the weirs or traps were cleverly designed with wings in the structure that led the fish into the pounds from where there was no escape. A weir was kidney shaped with the entrance at the narrowest part. A fence was often built perpendicular to this to force the fish in, although it was said that the Deer Island style had no such fence, as it used the natural topography of the shoreline. Once the herring were enclosed in the weir they swam around and were directed towards the centre by the inward-turned mouth. Then, when the weir was judged to contain sufficient herring, the fishermen simply closed the entrance.

A traditional way of checking to see how many fish were in the weir was to use a weighted wire – the feeler – much like the one the Scottish fishermen used to discern the presence of herring. The amount of fish could be estimated from the vibrations caused by them bumping into it. To remove the fish, a purse-seine net attached to the poles was utilised by tightening up the sole and top ropes, forcing the fish into an ever-decreasing area. Once the herring were tightly packed in the net it was transferred to a carrier boat using long-handled lap nets. In more modern times, a pump was used, having the added advantage of being able to collect the fish scales that fell off, which were then sold to be used in the manufacture of colouring in makeup and paint.

The brush weir was used off the Maine coast to catch small herring that were subsequently used in the preparation of sardines. This trade in small herring developed after George Burnham, of the firm Burnham & Morrill of Portland, one of the largest canning factories in the United States, visited western France in 1866, buying quantities of olive oil and studying the way the French canned their sardines, which are, in fact, immature pilchards (*Clupea pilchardus*). Burnham was keen to develop a new market after the canning of lobsters, for which the initial canneries were set up, declined in favour of the fresh markets. Lobsters have been prolific along the Maine coast since before the early settlers, and markets developed in the early 1800s as well – smacks were introduced to take them to market. Canneries proved a stopgap until the demand for the fresh shellfish outweighed that for the preserved lobster. The irony is that much of the herring was subsequently used to bait the lobster traps, as in Yorkshire!

However, the experiment was unsuccessful because the canners seemed unable to rid the product of the flavour of herring oil. The fault lay, it appeared, in the drying of the fish.

The next experiments were with menhaden (*Brevoortia tyrannus*) which also went under the unlikely name 'mossbunkers'. Once these fish were canned with success they were sold into the European market, with a medal of merit being awarded at Vienna in 1873 and a silver medal in Bremen the following year. Menhaden pickled in vinegar and spices was marketed under bizarre names such as 'Shadine', 'Ocean Trout' and 'American Club Fish'!

However, in 1872, tins of 'Russian sardines' were being imported into the United States from Germany and these 'sardines' were small herring from Norway. Thus experiments began again to find a suitable way to use the Eastport herring for the same purpose. What soon became obvious was that it was possible to use the New England herring by ensuring that, as soon as they were landed, the herring were decapitated and gutted and put into salt. It was said that a skilled person could prepare 1,000 fish in this way in an hour, which equates to one every three seconds! After a twelve-hour soaking they were thoroughly washed in brine, although some merchants preferred to soak the fish first before removing the head and entrails. They were then dried in the open or inside purpose-made drying rooms until sufficiently dried, after which they were immersed in olive oil heated to 250 degrees centigrade for three minutes and immediately packed into tins with cold olive oil topping up the tin. The lid was soldered on and the can placed into boiling water for up to two hours. This made the air expand the tin, which was then punctured while hot to expel this unwanted air and immediately re-sealed. Once cooled, they were checked and ready for market.

In 1879, a superior way of drying the fish reduced the preparation time. Previously, drying could take up to twenty hours, and by this new patented method, the herring were steamed and baked or broiled in an oven after salting. This process only took ten to fifteen minutes,

Preparing the herring prior to tinning as sardines, drawn by G.B. Goode

after which they were canned, sometimes in mustard and other spices, to produce a variety of tastes.

Returning to the brush weirs of the Maine coast, it appears that these were peculiarly adapted to catch the small herring. This kind of weir was in use in the eighteenth century in Nova Scotia, and knowledge of these was imported into Maine in about 1820. John MacGregor and his son Jacob were said to have been the first to construct a large weir of this type specifically to catch herring near Lubec. It has been estimated that by 1849 there were 120 of these weirs in the area.

Fish weirs, as we shall see, need a considerable amount of preparation in deciding exactly where they are to be located. Each weir uses the natural topography of the beach – either a rocky ledge as a bar to prevent the fish from escaping, or the shore as part of the structure, or natural channels that force the fish into its grip. All are situated where there is a fast current which fish prefer swimming in.

Brush weirs, as their name implies, are built from wooden posts driven into the mud about 6 or 7ft apart with smaller posts driven in between. Brushwood is then interwoven between the poles to form an impenetrable barrier for the fish at the same time as allowing the escape of the receding tide. They were at their most effective at night and especially at the new moon, a time the fishermen referred to as 'the darks'.

Once the tide had ebbed from the weir, five or six men would enter it and remove the herring by using a seine-net (the third way by which herring were taken on this coast). Rarely, it seems, did the American weirs entirely dry out to leave the fish stranded, as the fish would then quickly deteriorate. Once landed, the herring was loaded aboard their small sailing boat and taken to the nearby canning factory for processing.

This 'sardine' fishery grew rapidly from 60,000 tins in 1875 to over 7½ million being sold in 1880 with a value in excess of $780,000. However, in 1881, some of the 1880 product remained unsold and the fear was that supply was exceeding demand, for the same year saw over $1 million worth of imports of canned sardines from, primarily, France, as well as other countries. However, within ten years since the first tins were produced, a major industry had developed which had a massive impact upon the fisheries of the New England coast. Their fears were ungrounded, for by the turn of the century the fishery occupied sixty-eight factories, employing 6,000 people and producing $3½ million for the country.

PART TWO
Catchin' Herrin'

The Fishermen, their Boats and Gear

Tonight the fleets are on the water.
Every boat that ever sailed
out to the fields of herring
cuts a burning furrow
in the living phosphorescence
of the powering ridges.
The fields are greeny water;
their crops are keen and glancing.

From Tonight the Fleets in *The Larch Plantation*
by Angus Martin

Super Sgadan
(Supper Herring)

Ingredients:
4 medium herring
1 large apple
6 medium potatoes
1 large onion
1 heaped teaspoonful mustard
1 teaspoonful chopped sage
Good knob of butter
3 teaspoonfuls tarragon vinegar
Hot water or cider
Salt and freshly ground black pepper

Method:
Clean and fillet the fish by cutting off the head, opening along the belly,
carefully loosening the small bones on each side with your thumb and finally
prising the backbone out with thumb and forefinger to pull it out with small
bones. Spread the insides of the fish with mustard, season and roll up. Line
a greased fireproof dish with sliced potatoes, sliced onions and sliced apples.
Fit the rolled fillets on top, sprinkle with sage, vinegar and seasoning. Cover
with the remaining potatoes. Dot with butter, cover and bake in a moderate
oven for forty-five minutes. Remove lid to let brown for a further thirty
minutes.

CHAPTER EIGHT

The Fish Weirs

The American fish weirs differed from their British counterparts in that they seldom dried out, whereas those in Britain, and many in Europe, worked until the tide had receded almost in its entirety, leaving just a mere puddle of seawater from which the fish were removed. The New England structures simply entrapped shoals of fish within their boundaries so that the fishermen had to use their seine-nets to capture them. Given that the difference in height between high and low water is similar to that in Britain, this difference is somewhat puzzling.

It has been suggested that the European settlers imported the practice of using fish weirs into the States, yet this seems unlikely. Given the Indian ability for catching fish, and the fact that primitive weirs are still used by Eskimos to catch Arctic char and salmon, it appears more likely that they were in use well before Cabot and others arrived. Indeed, it was noted in the 1940s that weirs were in constant use throughout Africa, the South Sea Islands and the East Indies. Theirs was by no means a European speciality.

Fish weirs – often referred to as 'fixed engines' – are, as we've already seen, ancient. Archaeological excavations have produced evidence dating back 6,000 years in the case of the Lake Kongemose site at Agerod V in southern Sweden. Stationary structures have also been discovered in Denmark that date from the Mesolithic and Neolithic eras. Some of these were constructed of wooden stakes with a series of wattle screens in between while others were in the form of basket traps. One weir actually contained the remains of a codfish.

Evidence in Britain is scarce, although some fish traps of the river Severn estuary have been dated around 4,000–5,400 BC. Another at Loch Beg, in Northern Ireland, dates from 1,000 BC. These, however, would not have entrapped herring for obvious reasons.

The earliest illustration of a weir is of one on the river Colne which appears on a 1460–70 estate map in the archives of Westminster Abbey. The first documented one is said to come from an Anglo-Saxon charter for Tidenham on the river Severn and is described as a *haccwer* or hedge weir. Other weirs in Essex have been described as being from Anglo-Saxon origins, which seems to suggest they were then in daily use.

In 1299 there were at least five weirs at Minehead which, within eighty years, had increased to ten and were subject to dues of 5d. By 1425 this had increased to an annual rent of 2s 11d for one of them. Most fish weirs were the property of the monasteries and, for example, Bath Abbey, in the late eleventh and early twelfth centuries, had 104 weirs at its estate at Tidenham. Today it is said that the remains of some thirty weirs can still be seen along the shore between Minehead and Porlock Weir.

In Anglesey, a fish weir at Porthaethwy (Menai Bridge) was noted as being among the properties conveyed to Madog Gloddaith by Einion and Goronwy ap Llywelyn ap Bleddyn in 1316. Further references to weirs at Porthaethwy were made in 1378 and 1394. On the east side of the island, the Ynys Dulas weir was farmed in the fourteenth century, at which time Dafydd Don was fined sixpence for illegally fishing the river Alaw estuary, possibly at the weir on the opposite coast of Anglesey. A weir called the 'yme-kiln weir, at Llanfaes, stretched between the 'lyme-culne' and the 'feryman warth' and was leased to Thomas Norrey in 1438 for twenty years, while Thomas Sherwin later paid sixpence a year for another said to be 'lying between the lyme-kylne fishery and the house of the Friar Minor of Llanfaes'.

In Scotland, documented evidence of ancient weirs is less forth-coming. In his survey of the weirs of the Island of Bute, John Ferrier noted eleven structures of interest and he added that 'the practice of fish-trapping may have begun in Scotland in the Mesolithic times and it continued in the Highlands and Islands within living memory'. Edward Patterson has noted some thirty-seven possible traps on the Ayrshire coast between Ardrossan and Hunterston while Dr A.E.J. Went and Dr Estyn Evans have recorded many in Ireland.

France's west coast has many weirs, which have been said to be more highly developed than British types, with a higher tidal height and larger area of retained water. Given the abundance of weirs along this western fringe of Europe, it is possible that the Celts were respon-sible for their development well over 1,000 years ago.

Classification and Shape

In Britain fish weirs go by a number of names, depending on what part of the country they are situated in. In Wales they are *gored* or *goreddau* (singular *gorad* or *cored*) while in Scotland they are variably referred to as *yair, yare, cairidh, doach* or *cruive*, although the latter term in reality often only refers to the catchment pool at the extreme of the weir. A *cruive* can also be a wicker basket sunk into the current stream or a weir in the upper reaches of a river where salmon are caught. In English, a crew is a term used for the catchment pool, which suggests a linguistic connection. In the Irish form, weirs are *cora* and in Breton *coret*. However it is only by shape that fish weirs can be classified with any success, and not by their geographical position.

The earliest documented form seems to be the passive weir in the shape of a V. In Whitstable, Kent, the earliest known weirs are the Snowt Weirs that are U-shaped with five sails and five conical baskets made of withies that fit over the apex of each weir. A plan of 1608 clearly shows these weirs, as it does the V-shaped Whitstable weirs that were built from oak posts spaced at 6ft and enclosed with transverse timbers. In 1786, four fishermen were drowned after their boat fell foul of these weirs, adding to the total of sixteen deaths attributed to the weirs. Two V-shaped weirs were a feature of the Lynmouth foreshore well into the twentieth century, while thirteen were situated on the beach at Swansea in the 1930s.

If the assumption is that fish weirs developed from rock pools, then it follows that the very earliest form of weir was a semi-circle of stones around such pools, with the ends turned towards the shore. These have been described as 'boomerang-shaped' or in the form of a 'crescent with horns pointing up the beach'. V- and U-shaped weirs probably developed from these, although this has never been fully documented.

The remains of a semi-circular weir at Llanon on the coast of West Wales are some one hundred yards long and built along the line of the low-water mark, thus forming a pool on the landward side once the sea has ebbed. About halfway along there are the remains of a sluice gate where one stone was laid flat for water to flow over. Here a timber gate would have been fixed, which could be opened to aid the flow of water from the weir, without allowing the fish to escape.

A few miles southward of this point lies the tiny village of Aberarth, and between here and Aberaeron, a town that was specifically laid out in Regency style to promote the herring fishery in the early nine-teenth century, some twelve weirs were once working, belonging to Rhys ap Gruffydd in 1184 and presumably catching herring. The remains of many of these are still recognisable on the beach, some being obvious while others are mere hints of what once lay on the beach. For in many years, Cardigan Bay teemed with shoals of herring during the autumnal fishing season, with the towns and villages bene-fiting from the bonanza that the herring could bring. In other years, however, the shoals just did not appear and the reader is directed to the author's book *The Herring Fishers of Wales* (Llanrwst 1998) for the full story of the Welsh herring fishery.

This semi-circular shape, then, categorises one group of fish weirs. They can be said to be passive because they do not necessarily rely upon the action of the tidal stream to be effective. They simply work through the twice-daily process of the tide filling and emptying the weir, thus leaving the fish stranded. All they need is a substantial tidal height – the difference between high and low water – which in Cardigan Bay amounts to some 16ft (5m).

This type of weir has been described as the 'simplest and cheapest mode of fishing that can be devised', according to the Old Statistical Account for Scotland, and by others as 'lazy fishing'! From the same source comes a fine description of weirs at Cardross on the Clyde. The Revd Alexander McAulay described these thus:

The zair or yair fishings, so productive in this parish, seem to be almost peculiar to it. A yare is built of stones gathered from the tide watermark about 4ft in height, and of a considerable length, and stretches out into the river in the form of a crescent, or three sides of a square; but to give it a probability of succeeding, it must proceed from a point of land so as to enclose a Bay. The distance which it is extended from the shore is such, as to make it appear, or to crown, as the fishers term it, about two hours before low water. Were it placed farther into the sea, or built higher, the surf would be continually beating it down. In spring tides, with the water retiring quickly, great quantities of fish, particularly herring, are occasionally taken ... the rights of these yare fishings prove them to be of very high antiquity, being granted by crown charters above 500 years ago.

In Loch Snizort, on Skye, the weirs caught such an abundance of herring that the fish became a nuisance before they could be cured. Presumably they rotted on the ground or were attacked by the ravenous gulls that, too, were a nuisance.

In another instance, in Loch Broom, a fish weir belonging to the local church often trapped copious amounts of herring and on one occasion, when the Revd Dr Ross was minister, 1,000 baskets of herring were left in the weir after all the people in the vicinity had taken what they wanted. The fish was left there and it rotted so much that the entire upper end of the loch became polluted. On another occasion 2,000 barrels of herring were taken from it on one night. After the herring deserted the loch, the local fishermen, blaming the trap for this, tore down its outer wall, although parts of it still remain today.

Another weir on Loch Broom, opposite the one mentioned, was a rectangular weir, which was remembered for its herring in 1910. Rectangular weirs, thus form another group within the passive category.

Sometimes the weirs are built using the natural conditions of the foreshore, such as rocks and channels. In the Menai Strait, one such weir was created by building short lengths of weir between islands, thus trapping the fish. The weir in the estuary of the river Gwendraeth, close to Kidwelly was described as having a 'stone wall of large grounders sitting on a stone scar… turning… as far as the edge of the scar'. The gap between was supposedly completed in stone or timber. As there are historical references of mediaeval traps belonging to Whitland Abbey, it is possible that this weir is of great antiquity, and its remains are still visible. This type, then, represents a second category.

Active weirs, on the other hand, work on the principle that the tide coaxes the fish into the weir and then, on the ebb, prevents their escape against the current. These are the third category of fish weirs and have been built in all manner of shapes and sizes. The earliest of these were probably rectilinear types, such as the Minehead weirs, and have been described as 'primitive'. These are constructed of loose granite stone and extend for 380 yards, are 4½ to 9ft in width and 4½ft high. It is worth noting that two survived in operation until recently.

As well as utilising the tidal stream to operate effectively, it is believed that active weirs – and possibly passive ones to a much lesser degree – also make use of the pattern of swim of fish, in that they tend to swim towards the shore when moving downstream. This, we shall see, was the philosophy behind river estuarine active weirs.

Several good examples of active weirs have survived on the Menai Strait, some of which were worked up to the 1960s. The largest one is the Penrhyn weir at the mouth of the Ogwen river, Bangor. In 1577 tithes were exempted from this weir, belonging as it did to the manor house of Penrhyn. In 1810 it was noted that there were two weirs here that captured an abundance of fish, including herring and salmon. Richard Price remembers the remaining one being worked in the 1960s and described it as a wall of wooden stakes, 6ft high, with wattle in between and a salmon pool at its extreme end. A sluice gate was opened once the tide had receded. The children would take whitebait home from within it, but only after the fishermen had taken what they wanted.

Across the water on the Anglesey side of the Strait, the 'gorad bach' lies two miles north-east of Beaumaris. A bigger version of this weir was once worked further along the coast as the 'Trecastell gorad', but it has virtually gone. These weirs were triangular in shape, with a section of wall absent between the crew and the landward end. This ensured the fish could swim into the trap, yet be unable to escape against the tide. The gorad bach was in operation until the 1960s when its operators, brothers Wilf and John Girling, decided that the upkeep of the weir, the lack of fish, and the locals' habit of helping themselves, was too much.

It was John Girling, the brothers' grandfather, who had first come to Anglesey from Devon in the 1960s to cultivate oysters, which he did until he was offered the lease on the weir. Presumably it was in operation long before he took it over. In its outer wall it had a sluice gate, known as the bass trap, for when this was opened, the small fish in the trap could escape, straight into the clutches of the waiting bass that lurked around the gate. These bass were then captured in a dip-net. Among other fish, copious amounts of herring were caught in the weir.

This weir consisted, like many others, of 4ft-high stone walls, up to 8ft wide, into which stout oak posts were driven, close to the outer edge, allowing the fishermen a platform to walk atop the wall, right around the inside of the weir. Between the posts were wattle fences of willow which were 6ft high or more. Repairs were constant, according to Bridget and Graham Dempsey (Bridget is John Senior's great-granddaughter), who still live in the cottage at the head of the beach close by. Spruce posts were used latterly instead of oak because of the cost.

It is fair to say that many of these fish weirs were built in this way. One such weir is at Scallastle Bay on the Island of Mull, where a semi-circular wall still remains on the beach. Another of a similar construction lies across the Sound of Mull at Inninbeg. Several more, of different shapes, lie further along the Sound on the Morvern side. There are at least four on the shores of Loch Torridon, and one on Loch Kishorn. The Aird weir on Loch Treaslane, off Loch Snizort in Skye, consists of an erratic wall of stone meandering out to a rocky outcrop, with the rocky shore forming its other wall. Many of these are built across the estuary of a small river, which forms the fourth group as estuarine weirs. A fine example of this type lies at the entrance to the river Alaw, on the west coast of Anglesey. Here the weir, consisting of stone walls some 4ft wide and up to 5ft high, runs off the landward side of the foreshore out into the middle of the low-water line of the river before running parallel to the bank for some 400 yards. At the end there is a 30ft gap to the seaward bank, enough to allow fish in yet not let them out because of their tendency to swim towards the shore when running downstream.

The final grouping are the semi-permanent weirs and these come in all sorts of variations. The oldest of these consist of a series of wooden posts driven into the seabed with a wattle of willow set in between, which can be removed as necessary. On the Schei fjord in northern Germany, some sixty of these herring traps were once in use, yet today only one survives. The 10ft posts are driven into the seabed from a barge – the tidal range is negligible – forming a shallow 'V' with a gap at the apex where a hoop-net is fixed to catch the fish. The willow, locally sourced, is woven from above, using a pole with a 'V' on one end to push the willow downwards into the water. This structure can therefore be removed out of season.

F.M. Davis, in his 1936 *Account of the Fishing Gear of England and Wales*, mentions an old man in Aberdaron, North Wales, who used to build small temporary stone weirs. On the river Severn, the fishermen use wicker baskets, which can be fixed into wooden frameworks – or hedges, as they are known – in the season, and later removed. These baskets come in two sizes – putchers, which are 5-6ft long and stacked three or four high and in rows many yards long, and putts which consist of three sections (kype, putt and forewheel) and are 6ft in diameter at their mouth and up to 15ft long. The latter, being so large, tend to not be removed off-season, yet must be closed off to make them inactive.

Legislation in the nineteenth century curtailed the use of weirs, such was their effectiveness at catching fish of all sizes and species, especially immature fish, which upset the opponents of weirs. 'Saturday flaps' were fitted into weirs to prevent their use for thirty-six hours from 6 o'clock on a Saturday evening. Licences were issued, but only where the title of a weir could be proved. No new weirs were allowed, until slowly their usage completely died out in the twentieth century.

However there is one exemplary weir that hasn't, hitherto, been mentioned. In the middle of the Menai Strait, in the piece of water between the two bridges that cross over to Anglesey, known as the Swellies, lies Ynys Gorad Coch. Here the tide can run at up to 8 knots, and has been utilised in two weirs upon the island. On either side semi-circular weirs catch the main stream, the fish being driven in on the ebb and unable to escape. Today one weir is in working order, although gaps in the wall of the weir allow the fish to pass through, so it doesn't actually catch anything. Both weirs are said to date from the fourteenth century when herring, both smoked and fresh, was sent to the monasteries of Amlwch, Caergybi (Holyhead) and Penmon. The old smokehouse can still be seen on the island, albeit as accommodation and not as a smokery.

Around the end of the nineteenth century, the weirs were operated by Huw Madog Jones, who was the last of three generations of the family that lived there until his departure in 1920. William Jones first leased the island and its fisheries in about 1800 and Madog Jones (Huw's father) was born there in 1820 and retired in 1894. Herring were said to have been plentiful during this period, as well as whitebait and salmon, and, according to Old Madog – as Huw's father was known – the odd 'nice pig' that would get into the weir when the swine were being swum across the Strait further upstream.

Visitors to the island had to ring a bell suspended on the Anglesey shore, whence Young Madog – as Huw was known – would row over. For a shilling, a 'Gorad Whitebait Tea' was provided on the island, with the basket of fried whitebait fresh from the weirs. It sounds idyllic to sit upon an island, gazing over the sea to the distant mountains, with the sun shining and a basket of fried fresh fish and cup of tea to hand. These are memories of a bygone age of a century ago that we still, in many ways, yearn for. But, like the structures we can find on many a beach, that is all in the past. Fishing is no longer about catching what you can using a skill; it is about selectivity and technology. And that is why much of it has disappeared.

Ramsholt Herring
(from Pearl Simper and some amount of discussion)

Ingredients:
8 herring, gutted, de-headed and tailed
Vinegar – we used distilled
Water
Onion slices
Celery slices
Thyme
2 bay leaves
Tarragon
Peppercorns
1 clove of finely chopped garlic

Method:
Place the herring in a dish, add all the ingredients and marinade overnight to soak up the delicate flavours. Cook in a moderate oven for about twenty-five minutes or until thoroughly cooked. Serve with toast or brown bread and butter. Pearl and I perfected this recipe after Robert and I had spent the day drifting for the herring on the river Deben. The marinating removes the overpowering oiliness of the fish and the resulting dish really brings out the true taste of the fish without smothering the flavour of the sea.

CHAPTER NINE

The Drift-Net

The drift-net is simply a train of gill-nets that are not fixed to the seabed but only to a vessel which, together, are free to move with the wind and tide. In general, especially when catching herring, they are set at or just below the surface of the sea, for herring, like pilchards, mackerel and sprats, are pelagic and swim close to the surface when they feed, mostly at night. Hence the fishermen's practice of setting their nets at dusk and waiting till dawn to haul them in.

What the Dutchmen from Hoorn actually developed in the late thirteenth and early fourteenth century is unclear. Whether he discovered that nets didn't have to be fixed to the seabed to be effective or whether he perfected a previous tendency to simply attach the net to a drifting boat is open for debate.

The story of the drift-net is one that encompasses much about the herring fishery and the romance for which it is often held in esteem these days. For, until the twentieth century, the drift-net accounted for most of the herring that was captured by man, although, as we shall see in subsequent chapters, not all. Such is the nostalgia of that era that today's writers and film producers make much of the reverence of the fishing. However there is one piece of prose of subtlety that really does make proper inroads into a superb description of the fishery.

Neil Gunn's *The Silver Darlings* is an epic piece of writing following the story of Finn as he wrestles with growing up on the north-east coast of Scotland in the early nineteenth century, where the herring was the only means of securing an income when it 'pushed poverty from the door and beyond the little fields'. For these fisher communities had little else to eke a living from except sailing their tiny open boats out each evening into the deeper water to set their drift-nets overnight, curling up in the bowels of the boat for a few hours of interrupted sleep before the process of hauling began at sunrise.

And Jim, who would one day be a fish curer, a cut above them all; and George, shouting his figures and spreading his salt − what were they when it came to the sea itself, the handling of the boat in a storm, the phosphorescent fires, the living dance of the silver darlings? They only saw the herring dead, and lived on them like gulls!

Certain words distinguish the fishermen, in their struggles, from those back on land into whose hands much of the profit from the herring found its way. Yet the determination of fishers like Finn wasn't confined to that part of Scotland. For around almost the entire British coastline those living on the periphery of the land looked to this seasonal bonanza to supplement meagre incomes, stepping out in their open boats to set drift-nets.

In a way, the buss fishery was no different. Each buss had up to four or five small boats and, in the same way as the larger whalers had smaller boats harpooning and finally killing their quarry, these open boats lay to their nets at night, hauling and landing their catch onto the buss each day, where it was barrelled. The same technique had been applied to cod fishing in the seventeenth century off the Newfoundland coast when small dories fished during the day.

In Yorkshire, large three-masted vessels called five-man boats drifted for herring during the season, although a few of them occasionally used a trawl for white fish. These were invariably built in the county at a cost of £600 for a 56-ton, 60ft vessel. The small creek of Staithes and the beach at Filey were the two main fishing stations in the eighteenth and nineteenth centuries. Then, in 1835, Scarborough boatbuilder Robert Skelton produced a two-masted version, which soon became popular with a lighter rig. These were flat-bottomed for beaching and were laid up outside of the herring season.

But the fishermen of the Yorkshire and Northumberland coasts are mostly remembered for their cobles, a particularly unique vessel within the British types. These, being constructed upon a shortened keel and what is termed a 'ram plank' in its place for two-thirds of the overall length, were built to work off the beaches exposed to the onslaught of the North Sea. They were adapted for all manner of fishing, from potting for lobsters and crabs to catching halibut, cod and ling. Larger cobles were specifically for herring drifting, these being called ploshers, and are said to have been an extension, albeit in miniature, of the older five-man boats. Their name supposedly came about from the tradition of thumping the bow of the boat with a length of rope to drive the herring into the net, although it has been said that it is also the term for barrelling herring, and that another possibility is that it comes from the sound the sea makes against the hull when underway!

It has been said that one of the differences between drift-netting, which is in essence a passive form of fishing, and other more active ways of catching herring in a net, is that the fishermen simply go out to sea and shoot their train of nets anywhere. However this is an injustice to the skill of these fishermen, for they determine with great skill the best location to set and drift with their nets. And to help them find this spot they use natural phenomena − called the appearances − which nature has provided as signposts. It is perhaps fair to say that the ring-net fishermen developed these appearances with a distinct eagerness, but unfair to dismiss the care with which the drift-net fishermen took in shooting their nets. The need to recognise signs before shooting was one reason the boats preferred to do so before dark, using the last of the day's light to search the horizon.

Seabirds were the principle tool of the drift-netters. The sight of a gannet − the Solan Goose − diving from high and plummeting into the dark sea was a sure sign of herring shoals lurking below. Seagulls feeding on the surface or flying in numbers also suggested herring. Likewise, the presence of other predators such as porpoises and whales searching for food indicated the presence of shoals. Off the coast of Norway, whales have been known to throw herring up into the air while rising to the surface and blowing. Basking sharks, who feed on the same plankton as herring, also act as pointers. Below the surface, a shoal was likely to be nibbled at its outer edges by dogfish and conger eels, and some fishermen were able to recognise signs of this happening, albeit deep down and out of sight.

As well as signs from the animal kingdom, variations in the colour of the sea, such as dark patches of water, signified the existence of herring in a particular place. At night, patterns in the phosphorescence, aggravated by thumping the hull of the boat, could show their presence. Herring, being an oily fish, sometimes gives off spots of oil which float on the surface, to which the fishermen were attracted. Some fishermen could even detect this oil by smell alone. In bright weather, the silvery reflection of the fish swimming below the surface could also alert the fishermen.

In many parts of the country, weather patterns were a deciding factor. Dark, moonless nights were best, for bright full moons allowed the herring to see the nets into which they were meant to swim and become enmeshed, trapped by their gills – hence gill-nets. Cloudy seawater was also beneficial. Wind direction could have its own effect, for calm weather often alluded to poor catches, as did thunderstorms, which were said to frighten the fish into deeper water. In the North Sea, some say that northerly winds brought no catches at all while south-south-easterly winds heralded an abundance.

In an absence of any natural signs of herring, fishermen resorted to setting their nets in spots that had previously been prolific in catches. Once the nets had been shot, after an intervening period of a couple of hours or so, and especially after it had gone dark, the first net was hauled to see if any fish were in it. If there were and the signs were good, the net was fed out again; otherwise, it was hauled in and shot in another spot.

Hauling was the hardest work and before steam capstans this was all done by hand with men standing in a row pulling. As the nets came over the side of the boat they were shaken to remove as many fish as possible. Some had to be removed by hand. The net was sent below into the net room for stowage while the increasing pile of herring had to be shovelled into the fish room. Flocks of seagulls were probably trying to grab a few fish, their cries adding to the shouts of the men. Although, in fishing, there is always an initial sense of winning over nature as the fish comes aboard in the nets – this is the skill of the hunter-gatherer – the whole task becomes mundane over a period of hours. Six hours on a pitching deck covered in fish slime, in cold and wet conditions, hands being torn by netting and stung by jellyfish, arms being pulled from their shoulder sockets and muscles aching, is not fun by any standards. It was simply a necessity and thus the work was completed.

From the small boat's point of view, the fisher has less chance of noting these appearances, for the lower down he is in the water, the less he can see. The chances are also that he is closer inshore, in shallower water. But at some point in the season, the chances are that herring get into any net thrown into the sea, even during the day. I once sailed down the river Deben in the late autumn with Robert Simper and his son Jonathan in their Suffolk beach boat *Three Sisters*, IH81. Reaching the open sea off Bawdsey Ferry, we threw over the side a train of about five nets and, after tying the end to the bow of the boat, settled down to drink coffee, eat sandwiches and spend a few hours chatting. After the tide had taken us several miles north around Orford Ness, almost to Aldeburgh, we hauled in, bringing up half a bucket of herring in the process. Although the sun had broken through what had earlier been a mist, and the wind was light, we had brought in enough of the silver darlings for a good feed for a couple of nights.

Boats like *Three Sisters* have been fishing these East Anglian waters for generations. Aldeburgh, like Southwold and Thorpeness, where *Three Sisters* had been built in 1896, were home to groups of longshore fishermen who would follow the herring during the season in the same way as the Yorkshiremen did. Then during the rest of the year they would trawl or work trains of pots. This, I find, has been the general tendency for many decades, centuries even, all around the English coasts. In Kent, the fishermen sailed out in their herring punts from harbours such as Broadstairs, Margate and Dover to shoot their nets. However, as in the case of Deal, sometimes other, more lucrative, work attracted the fishermen out of (and in) the herring season. In Deal, it was casting an eye to the Goodwin Sands and the vessels that got into trouble, often being stranded or sinking, that provided a better living for them until the 1890s, when an exceptionally good year for herring and sprats in 1892 was said to have enabled the local curing houses to flourish.

With herring being largely an autumnal or winter fishing in England and Wales, the fishermen often had the summer season to supplement their annual incomes. Sometimes, instead of fishing, they used their boats to take the thousands of Victorian holidaymakers on sea excursions, working directly off beaches that were crammed with trippers. In Kent, as in Essex, these were more often than not day-trippers from the city, while in parts of Wales and the West Country, the crowds came to the coast for several days. Tenby, already mentioned as being home to a vibrant herring fishery, was a popular watering hole, and the fishermen used their Tenby luggers to take the visitors out to nearby Caldey Island. Tenby luggers were the local craft that evolved out of the herring fishery; small half-decked boats of about 30ft in length, rigged with one dipping lugsail and a small mizzen sprit, and a foresail on a long bowsprit, a rig similar in many ways to that of the *Three Sisters*.

Across the other side of the Bristol Channel, on the north Devon coast, lies the delightful village of Clovelly, a haunt of many a tourist. According to Charles Harper in 1908, the 'Clovelly fishermen are famed for their endurance and Clovelly herring for their flavour', although this was written eighty years after the peak of the trade. The little harbour there, first built in the fourteenth century, was, in the time of Henry VIII, regarded as the seventh most important fishing station in Devon and, in the nineteenth century, one of the chief stations in England. According to the *Welsh Port Books*, herring was exported from here and nearby Bideford to Carmarthen, on the Welsh side. Further along the coast, Lynmouth was 'notable for the marvellous plenty of herring there taken' by Thomas Westcote in 1630, who also noted the Clovelly herring. The Revd John Robbins, vicar of Clovelly from 1730-77, reporting the ups and downs of the herring, wrote that

in this year 1740, God was pleased to send his blessings of a great Fishery among us after a failure of many years. This thro' His mercy continued in 1741. In this year 1742 the fish was small and poor and in less quantities. In this year 1743 but an indifferent fishing. In this year 1744 worse than in the preceding. In this year 1745 still worse. In the year 1746 much worse.

Could it get even worse?

Yet there must have been an improvement for, by 1800, there were sixty boats working from the harbour. Sixty boats would not have remained if the fishery had become 'even worse'. They would go else-where. The fishery lasted from September until December, and the fishermen used their Clovelly herring boats, which were heavily-built luggers, until these were superseded by the picarooner in about 1880. The picarooners were smaller and could be launched at any state of tide, unlike the bigger boats, so that they tended to get to the fishing grounds that lay a couple of miles offshore first. Because of this, they were given their name, which is Spanish for 'sea robber' or 'pirate', such was the vehemence from the older fishermen for the new type.

The catch would have been landed soon after the nets were hauled, and it was auctioned on the beach and pulled up the village on sledges behind donkeys. In 1832 the *Exeter Gazette* reported that the first catches arrived in Clovelly in September and were immediately dispatched to Bideford by horse and cart, where they sold for 2d each. The very next day the market at Exeter 'was well supplied with them at ten for 6d' which represented quite a price reduction!

Clovelly mirrored fishing villages along the entire coastline of Britain. They were tiny communities perched on the boundary of land and sea, largely inaccessible and detached from their surroundings, separate identities yet with their own real sense of spirit. Communities all facing the same danger, the ultimate danger some say, of a livelihood being spent in the job with the highest death rate.

The Isle of Man was once renowned for its fine herring, and still is for its Manx kipper. The capital, Douglas, and other harbours such as Peel, Ramsey, Port St Mary, Laxey, Port Erin and Castletown all had fleets of boats that were Scandinavian-influenced. These, the herring scowtes, were almost direct descendants from the Icelandic *skuta*, which were fast vessels with sails and oars. The scowtes, with their squaresails, drifted for herring at night. Legislation was introduced to regulate the fishery and, in 1610, one particular law enforcing a closed season from 1 January to 5 July within nine miles of the shore also prohibited the shooting of nets before sunset. Another 1738 law required all Manx fishermen who had located a herring shoal to inform his nearest neighbour.

After a particularly ferocious gale on the night of 20 September 1787, some fifty to sixty scowtes were wrecked when they tried to return to Douglas harbour. The lighthouse at the end of the pier had been devastated in a gale of the previous year and never replaced, so the returning fishermen were almost working blind in the pitch black. Estimates of the loss of life that terrible night range from six to twenty-one fishermen.

The result of the disaster was a sudden change to the decked, smack-rigged boat and it is said that over 600 of these worked from the island at the beginning of the nineteenth century, only thirteen years later. Many were undoubtedly wherry-type vessels that were popular within the smuggling business. Then, in 1823, the Scottish fishermen, and later the Cornish, arrived with their two-masted luggers. The Manx soon discovered the benefits of shortening the main boom and adding a mizzenmast with lugsail to increase manoeuvrability while, at the same time, allowing the main mast to be lowered, thus riding their nets under mizzen alone. Forty years later the nickey was introduced, on the lines of the Cornish lugger, and this vessel, with upright stems and sterns, also resembled boats of the east coast of Scotland. However these were relatively short-lived, for the Manxmen, in 1884, adopted a vessel similar to those of Loch Fyne. Manx nobbies, as these were known, were found to suit the waters around the island.

The east coast of Scotland a proportion of fishing villages. These grew out of the tiniest of beaches, landing places just capable of holding a few small boats, but close enough to the rich herring fields. The communities that evolved became their own self-sufficient settlements, quite apart from the rest of society who often treated them with distaste. In towns where the fishing community had to share space with society, all too often the fisher town became an area of that town in itself, a separate quarter, usually at one end, where the councils found they were able to push the fishers, boats, gear and all. And so the fishing communities grew from their own blood, marriages between fisher families being the norm, although sometimes they mixed with other fishers from along the coast. They became apart from the rest of us, their lives wholly dependent on the sea and the shoals they sought in earnest, working by night, sleeping by day.

However, as the scale of the herring fishery increased rapidly throughout the nineteenth century, these villages themselves flourished. This, in turn, led to bigger boats being built, as we shall see in subsequent chapters. For these the fishermen needed deeper harbours to enable the vessels to remain afloat around the clock. The fishing, then, became centralised into specific ports, although the fishermen retained their homes in the villages. Fraserburgh, for example, overshadowed the smaller ports of Sandhaven, Pittulie and Rosehearty, whereas a hundred years earlier the latter rivalled Fraserburgh as the chief herring port along this part of the coast. But, standing out among all the ports of the east coast, was Wick.

In 1767, three Wick-based merchants fitted out two sloops for the herring fishing and were successful. Fired up by this, the local MP Sir John Sinclair initiated the arrival of a party of Dutchmen to come over and teach the local inhabitants the art of fishing and curing herring. By the end of the eighteenth century there were over 200 boats. Sixty years later this north-eastern port, built, remember, by the British Fisheries Society as an extension of Pultneytown, became the herring capital of Europe. During the season there were as many as 1,000 boats filling the harbour to capacity. As Wick thrived, so did the herring industry, as it had become, distinct from a mere fishery. Technology increased production, markets developed, and with these improvements came new methods of fishing that were, ultimately, to lead to its collapse a century later.

Herring in Oatmeal

Ingredients:
4 herring fillets
Flour for dusting
Salt and pepper
½ teaspoonful dry mustard
4oz porridge oats
1 egg, beaten with a little milk
Vegetable oil for frying

Method:
Trim fillets and dust in seasoned flour. Mix mustard into porridge oats. Dip fillets in beaten egg and coat in porridge oats. Shallow fry, two at a time, for three to four minutes each side.

CHAPTER TEN

West-Coast Toilers

She's a solan's hert, a solan's look;
She canna thole a lee.
I'll coil her ropes and redd her nets,
And ease her through a sea.
She's a seeker, she's a hawk, boys.
Thon's the boat for me.

So wrote George Campbell Hay in the last few lines of his epic poem *Seeker Reaper* while toiling aboard Calum Johnson's Lochfyne skiff, *Liberator*, during the herring fishing in the 1930s. He'd noticed the skiff *Sireadh* as they worked in the Kilbrannan Sound and penned what has perhaps become one of his best-known works. A decade later Naomi Mitchison and Denis Macintosh were writing their joint documentary entitled *Men and Herring*, in which they followed the ring-net fishermen of Loch Fyne for a week's work. However, both were published well after the golden age of the sailing skiff, the boat that helped to lay down the roots to a thriving fishery.

Yet these works represent the two extremes of the fishery – the first somewhat romanticises in elegant poetic terms the sights and sounds of the task and the haunts of the fishermen, while the latter is much more down to earth in terms of the way of life of those engaged in their daily routines. Mitchison and Macintosh give us the yarns, the wiling away of time telling stories such as the drunken antics of 'the Tailor' and the cold, damp working conditions and the repetition: '"The damned net's no' worth barking, it isna fit to catch spiders, never mind herring." But they were just not wanting to be bothered, that was all it was.' That was the reality of the job on a wet and windy Monday morning after a weekend at home! Not even was Finn, in Gunn's *Silver Darlings*, given to such a non-committal lack of inspiration when he was about to embark on a voyage to the fishing grounds. The call of the sea, the hunter's sense, was always foremost in his mind, the pitting of his skills against nature his prime objective in his constant quest. All these writers, though, have given us, decades later, superb insights into an era now long gone, just in the same way as renowned artists have left their imprints of the herring upon our minds.

Nobody quite knows when herring fishing first began on Loch Fyne. It is probable that early settlers found fish lying in pools at the end of the loch, and progressed to fishing from small boats. We have already seen in Chapter Five how sixteenth- and seventeenth-century writers, and a host of travellers over the next hundred years, reported a healthy herring fishery in the loch. Their inference seems clear: Loch Fyne herring were plentiful and of the best quality. Indeed, Inveraray, close to the head of the loch, was once called 'Slochk Ichopper' which literally means 'the gullets where vessels bought or bartered fish'. The importance attached to the fishing is reflected in the town shield that depicts a net with a herring and the motto '*Semper tibi pendeat halec*' – 'May there always be herring in your net'. Three miles south of the town is Frenchman's Point, where traditionally French boats came to barter for fish. A further two miles south is the village of Kenmore, laid out and built by the Duke of Argyll in the early 1800s to clear the fishermen out of Inveraray while at the same time building himself a new castle.

In terms of the fisheries of the west coast of Scotland, which, in the eighteenth century, were largely a chaotic disordered affair worked by individuals in open boats, it was John Knox whose accounts had the biggest impact on the development of an organised coherent fishery.

However, anyone researching Scottish history today is fortunate that there were three statistical accounts undertaken. The first was in the 1790s when each parish priest was asked to submit accounts of everyday life. This, now referred to as the Old Statistical Account (OSA), included aspects of the fishery. The second account – the New Statistical Account (NSA) – gives us today another picture of the parishes in the 1840s. A further account was concluded in the mid-twentieth century.

From the available evidence of the relevant accounts and the various travellers – especially Knox – it is possible to piece together a picture of the vessels in use before the ring-net was introduced in the 1830s.

Scandinavian boat design influenced this coast, an influence that stretched back to the days of the Vikings settling in these lands. Thus the small open boats used by the fishers were something in the region of 16ft long in the mid-eighteenth century. These were double-ended boats – in other words they were pointed at both ends when looking down upon the boat. The stems and sternposts raked sharply, there was a considerable sheer along the line of the deck when viewing from the side, and they were of a relatively shallow draught under the water. When rigged with a sail, this was usually of the squaresail type. Boats as such were commonplace from the north coast, through the Isles of the Outer Hebrides and Skye, down as far as Mull, as well as over on the north Irish coast. South of Mull, and more particularly in the Clyde, there was an altogether different shape of boat working the herring fishing.

From a long association with the smuggling boats of the Irish Sea, the southern Scots adopted the wherry, a two-masted, lightly-built, boat with a fore and aft rig. Because of their speed, wherries were often used in the smuggling of goods from the Isle of Man – the central storehouse for illicit goods until 1765 – into south-western Scotland, eastern Ireland and Wales. These came mainly in two sizes – larger decked vessels and smaller open ones. In 1740 the Collector of Customs at Liverpool noted that there was seen 'a wherry at anchor and a great many horses and casks upon the shore ... the casks carried back to the wherry in yoals ... the wherry weighed anchor and went to sea'. The 'yoals' were presumably small rowing boats and the wherry of the larger type. From documented evidence, the smaller wherries seem to be 20ft long. Of the condemned boats at Ayr after being arrested for smuggling in 1778, there were 'small boats that none were decked ... boat number eleven measuring 19ft 12ins and 8ft 2ins in breadth is computed in the said certificate at seven and one fourth tons, though by his computation it should only be seven tons'.

According to yachtsman Robert Buchanan, in 1883, there was a wherry specific to the Isle of Arran that he described as nearly extinct and as being 'a wretched-looking thing without a bowsprit, but with two strong masts'. He was impressed with the vessel's sea capabilities: 'Across the foremast is a bulkhead, and there is a small locker room for blankets and bread. In the open space between bulkhead and the locker birch-tops are thickly strewn for a bed, and for covering there is a huge woollen waterproof blanket ready to be stretched out. Close to the mast lies a huge stone and thereon a stove... rude and ill-found as these boats are, they face weather before which any ordinary yachtsman would quail.'

Loch Fyne was home to numerous of these wherries. For example, in about 1790, Ardrishaig had thirty boats each crewed by four men and there were three, later five, boatbuilders. The village grew into a thriving place with 'regularly laid out streets, in which one house seems to march forward, while its neighbour makes a retrograde courtesy – its cheerful harbour, filled with the wealth of fishermen, the herring boats – the stillness prevails, alone broken by the plash of oars, or the harsh guttural Gaelic of the rowers...' according to Christina Brooks Stewart in *The Loiterer in Argyllshire* in 1845. Paul Fraser noted that Inveraray had up to 500 boats fishing for the season that came from all along the loch. There were only eight fishermen actually living there in 1790. Thomas Garnett came to Loch Fyne in 1799 and described it as being one part water and two parts fish. In Inveraray, he found a similar number of boats as Paul Fraser had counted, each boat being 'covered with a kind of sail-cloth, to form a covering for the four men who compose the crew'. During the day the fishermen gutted herring, slept and sang 'Celtic tales to the sound of the bag-pipe', which Thomas Pennant, twenty-five years earlier, had described as sounding cheerful.

Whether it was common practice to sleep aboard their boats is unclear, for the fishermen of the loch certainly did sleep in huts ashore. However, according to Angus Martin in *The Ring-Net Fishermen*, most of the scant evidence points to the fact that camping ashore did not exist to any great extent, although oral tradition might perhaps contradict this. However, as drift-netting was the mode of herring fishing throughout the loch until the 1830s, and thereafter predominant among the fishers of the head of the loch until the 1860s, necessitating working at night, it seems less likely that the fishermen did sleep ashore during the day. Only with the adoption of the ring-net, which at times was used in daylight, might night-time sleeping ashore be contemplated.

At some point in time between the Old and New Statistical Accounts being published, the fishermen of Loch Fyne adapted their wherries to the lugsail, which, according to the minister of Glassary Parish in the NSA, was introduced into Loch Fyne by fishermen from

Ayrshire, who moved into the area from Newton-upon-Ayr, primarily to collect bait, and subsequently for the rich fishing to be had. One report, however, described these men as not being 'so attentive as could be wished to cleanliness in their habits', and being fond of beer, which was taken to sea in preference to whisky. Whether this description applied to fishermen in general, or merely these from Ayr, is yet to be ascertained, but it is a well-known fact that east-coast fishers were given alcohol by the fish curers in lieu of wages. These men had, after all, formerly come from Pitsligo, near Fraserburgh, on the east coast. Whether they, in an alcoholic haze or not, had discovered the lug-rig there, or indeed if the French had introduced it to the Clyde, is unknown as yet. Nevertheless it has to be added that the Breton fishers were among the first to adopt the lug rig so it is reasonable to suggest that the latter might be a more obvious choice. At the same time they made a transition from transom-sterned boats to ones with a Scandinavian-type pointed stern, a change probably coinciding with the evolution of the ring-net.

The ring-net evolved from experiments using a drift-net as a seine-net from the beach. Ninian Ballantyne seems to be acclaimed for buying the first great catch of herring taken after drift-nets were used to enclose herring in a bay near Tarbert. This was probably in 1833, although a report in the *Edinburgh Observer* puts it as 1835. What seems to be clear to Angus Martin is that within a few years nets were being specifically designed for circling the herring shoals using boats. And double-ended craft are also much more effective at close-quarter work where vessels have to be able to turn about quickly, such as is essential when working a ring-net close to the shore.

A typical ring-net was some 150 yards long and several yards deep and consisted of separate sections of netting attached together. It was held afloat with floats attached to the back rope (the rope at the top of the net) and weighted into the water by lead being wrapped around the sole – or bottom – rope. As with a drift-net, the minimum mesh size was eventually government controlled, as it is today in all sea fishing nets.

When fishing, a ring-net boat always operated with a partner, referred to locally as the neighbour boat. Each carried a complete net with ropes attached, but only one was shot at each ring. When a shoal of herring was spotted – and here the fishermen gained a keen sense of the natural appearances – one boat shot their net with a buoy, or 'winky', at the loose end. Once the net was in the water, around the shoal, the neighbour boat sailed up to the winky to take it aboard and thus either end of the net was attached to the stern of each boat. The boats moved forward, towing the net, before hauling commenced and they came together, stern to bow, with the net between them. Thus the circle was made and the sole rope tightened to create a sort of bag with the herring inside. With a good catch the corks on the back rope would be bobbing up and down, increasing the excitement of the fishers as they hauled on ropes, backs breaking under the strain and hands ripped apart by the coarse rope and the sliminess of jellyfish – called scouders – stinging bare skin. And here was the skill, for not only did they have to tend sails and watch wind and tide, but grapple with a net in sometimes heaving seas, rain-drenched and wind-bitten. A thankless task at the best of times: four men and a boy from each boat wrestling with a seething, writhing net.

Yet once the net was closed and the herring unable to escape, the job was not over. The fish had to be taken aboard as quickly as possible, as dying fish weighted the net down further, squashing those below and possibly damaging them. Poor herring realised a lower price. So a brail-net was used to dip into the mass of fish before being swung aboard into the middle of the small boat. One advantage was that the boats did not have to lie all night to their nets, therefore being able to get the catch back to shore more quickly, for the early fisher-man always gets the highest price for his catch. However there was a drawback. Trawled herring fetched a lower price at market than drift-netted herring because the latter was usually in a better condition. Some also say that because trawled herring dies by drowning – in the other case the fish bleeds to death – the flesh is not as tasty. According to Denis Macintosh it was a matter of habit. He recalls the time he caught a heavy ring of herring during the war and gave some to a nearby drifter. Once they both reached Rothesay pier, the buyer declared the drifter's herring as being of better quality and paid 10s a basket more than the trawled herring – and it was exactly the same herring, although he didn't know it.

In the nineteenth century the arguments raged between the Tarbert fishermen to the south of Loch Fyne and those drift-netters in the north, the latter believing 'trawling' was about to decimate their fish-ery. Men against men, community against community, even one branch of a family against another. The fish curers, and even the landowners, entered the fray until legislation was passed under their influence to outlaw any form of trawling. Yet still some persisted, having invested in new smaller boats and nets. The navy arrived to patrol the loch with a gunboat, tracking down offenders, whose gear was confiscated. On one encounter in 1853, a gunner from HMS *Porcupine* shot and wounded twenty-eight-year-old Colin McKeich. Successive government bills passed through Parliament over the next eight years until a young Ardrishaig fisherman, Peter McDougall, was shot and killed while out aboard a trawl skiff (as they had become known) at night, an act of barbarity that saw the perpetrators being found not guilty in court. The fishermen of Tarbert effectively gave up and endured starvation and debt. Yet two years later a Royal Commission report condemned the repressive legislation and their hopes rose and fishing began within a year, albeit still illegally. Yet the report was enough for the government to reconsider, and in 1867 all the Acts were repealed and ring-netting's violent birth was at an end. The fishermen from the top end of the loch realised for themselves the advantages of taking up ring-netting.

In the openness, which had previously been lacking, the fishermen were free to advance the method. The trawl-skiffs became larger and, in the 1880s, half-decked skiffs were introduced. These Lochfyne skiffs, as they were called, had a forecastle for the four crew and the boy (the apprentice doing the menial tasks and sleeping on the cabin floor) to live in for extended days at sea. For the first time there was no sleeping under sailcloths, or in the open, or ashore, or indeed upon one of the converted smacks that were previously used as houseboats, following the fleet in their quests for the shoals. The boats became single entities, aboard which the fishermen could survive for weeks, and thus they were able to fish a much longer season, from the Outer Hebrides down to the Isle of Man, and even through the Caledonian Canal to the east coast. However their presence was not always welcomed, as in the Moray Firth and Lewis, where ring-netting was never accepted. Many a Clyde fisherman avoided Stornoway because of the reception he was likely to receive.

The Lochfyne skiff has been described as one of the prettiest of British working boats, and they were well tended by their owners. With their varnished hulls, scraped and scrubbed once or twice a year, and their single standing lug-sail and jib, they sailed like a dream, graceful and bird-like, yet deadly at their work in the fields of herring. Just like all the other regional sailing craft of the British coast, they plied their grounds, supplying the markets with herring, giving families a roof and full stomachs, and etching out their place in history. Certainly, sometimes the fishing was good and at others disastrous, but that has never changed with fishing. It is still like that, and every fisher knows, when times are good, that hard times might be round the corner. This is the nature of the profession, more so than others. For instance, 1929 was a bad year on Loch Fyne and many fishermen went off to work in the Glasgow shipyards or to work in the woods above Minard for £1 a week. They were living with extremes, just like the job itself, working in dangerous seas from open decks. It is not surprising that fishing has the worst death rate among all occupations, higher even than mining.

Then came the internal combustion engine that was to change the face of fishing forever. Boats were quickly converted to take motor units: in Loch Fyne, in the main, Kelvin engines came from the Glasgow factory. The *Sireadh* was built with a 13.15 Kelvin engine from new. She worked out of Minard, south of Inveraray, and was registered as TT150. The *Perseverance*, CN152, was built in Campbeltown by renowned skiff-builder Robert Wylie for Archie Mathieson, and had a similar engine from new. Such was the pedigree of these boats that both survived into the 1990s, and *Sireadh* was still very much afloat in 2003, making her an octogenarian. The *Perseverance* was eighty-three years old when she sank off the coast of Portugal in 1995.

With the internal combustion engine came a complete change in design of boats. Campbeltown fisherman Robert Robertson, who previously had been the first fisherman on the Clyde to install an engine into his skiff *The Brothers*, introduced an entirely different type of boat in 1922. Although not totally apart in shape from the sailing skiffs, these had a longer hull, a canoe-stern, a small wheelhouse, better accommodation and a shortened sail. Robertson had been influenced by Norwegian craft after a visit there. While other fishermen were dismissive of his innovation – as indeed they were when he had been the first to add an engine to *The Brothers* fifteen years earlier – Robertson increased his landings after a couple of years of experimentation. Wheelhouses were quickly added to sailing skiffs in the desire to duplicate his successes. Others copied the design, and, as engines became more reliable, the rig decreased proportionally. Thus evolved what was termed the motor 'ringer'. The herring fishing of the Clyde had never looked so good.

When *Men and Herring* was written, just after the war, fishing had resumed in earnest after a brief respite. Hauls of 800 baskets and up to 1,000 and more were being taken at one shot and they were fetching almost £1 a basket. Winches had taken the backbreaking element out of the job and derricks eased the brailing process and off-loading onto the shore. The feeling wire was more successful in locating shoals, another innovation from Scandinavia. Echo-sounders were developed in the 1930s and modifications to the ring-net had made it an even more effective tool. Fishermen were all over-adapting to innovation that was, after several decades of boom, to lead to the eventual downfall and disappearance of a way of life that stretched back over many centuries of man's achievements. The herring, that most fickle of fishes, was soon to desert Loch Fyne.

Cider Baked Herring

Ingredients:
6 herring
½ pint cider
2 small onions, sliced into rings
2 teaspoonfuls mixed pickling spice
8 cloves
Salt & pepper

Method:
Clean, split and fillet the herring. Season well with salt and pepper. Roll them up, skin inwards, beginning at the tail. Place them neatly and fairly close together in an ovenproof dish. Cover with the cider and sprinkle with mixed pickling spice and cloves. Garnish with the onion rings and bake in a cool oven – 275 degrees Fahrenheit, gas mark 1 – for one to one and a half hours.

Variation: Herring in Ale – instead of cider use ale and use bay leaves in place of the cloves.

CHAPTER ELEVEN

The Scottish East-Coast
Fishers and the Zulu Wars

As the eighteenth century progressed, so did the fishing fortunes of the herring men on the east coast of Scotland. In the dawning years of the new century, according to the various reports from the Commissioners set up to investigate the herring fisheries, the fishermen were using open boats, as they were on the west coast. Mr G. Stuart, when asked about the state of the fish themselves when landed, reported that he regarded them poor because 'the fish lay in open boats exposed to the weather'. Presumably these small craft were rigged with sails, for the first documented fishing boat, dating from the seventeenth century, was the 30ft-long, two-masted, square-sailed 'great boat'. These open craft seem to have acted as trading boats to and from the Orkneys, and were descended from Scandinavian-type craft in that they were pointed at both ends and had heavily raked bows and sterns.

The Scandinavian tradition, stretching back almost 1,000 years at that time, was the principal influence responsible for the shape of the vernacular craft in use around the whole coast of Scotland, and indeed much of the English, Irish and Welsh coasts. The open boat, described above, was generically referred to as the scaith or scaff, which by the middle of the century had become the scaffie. The first real evidence supporting this boat as an individual type comes from Captain John Washington's report of 1849. An unseasonal autumnal gale wrecked over 100 boats one August evening in 1848, when the fleets were just settling down to their nets and were unable to seek shelter in the harbours as they were tidal (the tide had fallen since their departure). Washington was instructed to consider all the elements contributing to this disaster that led to 100 fishermen losing their lives and 124 fishing boats being destroyed. Obviously this was sufficient for the government to take some serious evasive action.

In his subsequent and somewhat lengthy report, Washington highlighted several factors that he believed to have ultimately led to this disaster occurring. He was critical of the design of the boats and the fact that they were undecked. He criticised the lack of sufficient shelter for the fleets to seek. Furthermore, he found the system of inexperienced crews being taken from the landsmen – that is the farming community, if 'farming' describes the tilling of the hillside – unacceptable and he severely reprimanded the fish curers because of their practice of supplying whisky in part-payment to the fishers. Not for the first time do we hear of the fishermen being judged for their excessive drinking habits. But then, considering the nature of the job, is it perhaps not surprising that a little Dutch courage is needed to venture out into the North Sea night after night in their eternal quest for the silver darlings.

The report also supplies us with a fascinating insight into the boats in general use. He noted six different types on the east coast of Scotland, from Wick in the north right down to Newhaven on the Firth of Forth. The one with the strongest Norse ties seems to be the Moray Firth boat that resembles the scaith. He also documented various designs from other parts of the English coast, as far away as Penzance and St Ives, and even the Galway hooker, useful when comparing the vessels around the entire coastline.

However, from the plans he reproduced in the report, we can also see another distinct type of craft in general use in the area in question: the Newhaven boat is upright in profile. This design was the preferred option in the Firth of Forth and the coast southwards, and north along the Fife coast. Fife is an ancient kingdom, according to tradition, lying between the two great firths of the Forth and the Tay.

The men from Fife had been herring fishing for as long as anyone on the east coast, and probably longer. Theirs was a tradition handed down from the times before the Danes arrived in the eighth century, and one that continued when the Dutch dominated the North Sea. It is said that they managed to export herring into Holland at the time, and later, many of the families emigrated there when the Scotch government began to use the herring as a means of raising tax revenue. Thus it is said that this Dutch connection led to the Fifers adopting their upright vessels, although it has been suggested that they do in fact resemble Viking longships!

Of course, this isn't to say that the men of Fife fished endlessly, for there were the bad years. Peter Smith, in his *The Lammas Drave and the Winter Herrin'*, tells us that the years 1550–1655 were good, while there was no fishing between 1657 and 1693. From then to 1780 landings were good again. The title of his book describes the two annual fisheries: the Lammas Drave occurred in August and September and peaked in 1860, while the winter herring took place at the start of the year up to March. Both were centred off the coast of east Fife, the coast between St Andrews and Buckhaven.

Returning to the boats themselves, we have two distinct forms of hull shape – the scaffie, and what soon became known as the fifie. Washington identified others that were perhaps a variation of either one. The fifies were the larger of the two types and in the 1830s these vessels were costing between £75 and £100 each. Compare this to a trawl skiff on Loch Fyne at the time. which cost about £10. Yet, even with such a high investment, a string of harbours in Fife sent boats to the fishing. In the summer the first-class boats sailed up to Wick, Helmsdale and Fraserburgh. In Buckhaven, for example, out of a total of 144 fishing boats, sixty were first-class (over 15 tons), forty-four were second-class boats and the remaining forty were third-class. Second-class vessels were deemed, according to the 1868 Sea Fisheries Act, to be less than 15 tons but with a keel length in excess of 18ft. Small craft under 18ft of keel were classed as third-class. Although these regulations didn't come into force until 1868, the terms were in general usage (although many assumed 'first-class' to imply that a vessel's length was in excess of 31ft). Also in 1868, fishermen were required by law to paint on port registration letters and their individual fishing number. The port letters came after the number – i.e. 345KY – until 1883 when the letters and numbers were reversed – i.e. KY345 – and this system has survived right up to today.

Buckhaven vessels are worthy of note, for Lubbock, writing in *The Log of the Cutty Sark*, argues that Linton, the naval architect responsible for designing the *Cutty Sark*, was influenced in this by these Buckhaven boats, so impressive was their performance.

However, what seems clear is that the early great boats had a tiny forecastle that allowed some shelter from the elements, yet, when

Washington was collecting his information – and he travelled widely along the east coast – he found that almost all of the fishing boats were undecked. Presumably, working in the main directly off the shore, the fishermen required the lightest of boats. This appears to have been the case with both scaffies and fifies.

The two types were wildly different in design and shape. The scaffie had a steeply raking sternpost at the after end and an upright stem with a curved forefoot – the forefoot being the part of the boat between stem and keel. In contrast, the fifie was upright at both ends with hardly any forefoot or heel (the junction between keel and sternpost) at all. Both were double-ended vessels and were originally built with clinker – or overlapping – planks until improvements in the supply of timber allowed the planks to be fitted alongside each other or butted up, as in the carvel construction.

In the same year that Washington was critical about the habit of fishing from undecked craft, the boatbuilders Alexander Hall & Co. of Aberdeen prepared a design for a 45ft-long boat with watertight bulkheads and buoyancy compartments. The failure of this vessel seems to have been the inflated cost of the vessel, which the fishermen could not warrant spending. Washington asked naval architect James Peake to submit two designs that were incorporated into his report yet were ignored.

Two decades later and the National Lifeboat Institution sponsored the building of several decked boats that were handed over to certain fishermen from the bigger harbours for one year. The idea was to encourage other fishermen to adopt safer boats. At the same time the Duke of Sutherland entered the debate and ordered a similar vessel built at Helmsdale. And thus the fishermen, slow to change as we've already seen, eventually adapted to innovation. Decked boats were built, probably egged on by the building of deeper harbours that were accessible at all states of the tide. To the beach-based communities, after all, a large boat was of little use as the manhandling of it upon the beach was impossible.

And so by the 1870s a pattern had emerged. Large fifie vessels, entirely decked over and up to 70ft in length, rigged with two hugely powerful dipping lug sails, were the favoured option in the ports from somewhere in the region of Fraserburgh southwards to the English border. In 1872 Berwick had forty decked boats of about 45ft overall, that cost £200 new. Leith boats were bigger and cost up to £300. Newhaven had thirteen such boats delivered in eighteen months.

In contrast, in most of the Moray Firth and northwards to Wick, the fishermen retained their scaffies, some having decks or half-decks added while new boats were decked over in their entirety.

Taking for example the year 1872 once again, there were 4,530 registered fishing boats on the east coast employed in the herring fishery, with Shetland and Orkney having another 470. In comparison, there were 3,252 on the west coast between Stornoway and the Clyde. The total number of fishing boats for Scotland, at the same time, was 15,232 vessels with a total tonnage of 106,464 tons, employing 46,178 men and boys. So we can see that not every boat was engaged in the herring fisheries. Smaller yawls – the word comes from the Norse *yol* meaning small boat – fished for white and shell-fish. In the south, where they were prevalent in contrast to the bigger fifies, these yawls, or yoles as they called them in Fraserburgh, were distinct in their different mode of fishing. Thus they became known as 'bauldies', a term adopted from the Italian patriot Garibaldi, who was fighting a civil war in Italy. Why exactly the Scots adopted his name for a type of fishing vessel is unclear, but the suggestion is that they were very conscious of the English influence being wrought upon Scotland, so understood well the aspirations of anyone fighting to cast off external supremacy. This attitude to what was seen as English interference in their (and others') affairs was to manifest itself several years later.

There is a wonderful photograph of Wick taken in 1865 by Alexander Johnston. It depicts the 'Herring Capital of Europe' jam-packed tight with fishing craft of which it is said there were over 1,000 at the height of the season in early summer. Judging by the numbers of fishing boats on the east coast, there may well be many more, although counting them from the photograph is impossible. However, most of them appear to be open or half-decked scaffies. These single lug-sailed craft were suited to the local conditions, were cheap to build and easy to maintain. Yet their disadvantage was their size. Once the fishermen ventured further afield they found them unsuitable to build to the same scale as the fifies. Thus alternatives were experimented with, and so was born what, justifiably, has been described the greatest, most efficient sailing fishing boat ever to grace the European shores.

The Scottish Zulu herring drifter combined the principal aspects of scaffie and fifie in one vessel. The keel was long with a slight slope to its heel. The stem copied the uprightness of the fifie while, at the after end, a long raking sternpost echoed that of the scaffie. There are various stories as to how this design came about; most of them tongue-in-cheek. One says that a Lossiemouth lass was betrothed to a fisherman from the north who sailed in a scaffie and that a hybrid boat was built as part of her dowry. Another tale tells us that one fishing family from Lossiemouth had different opinions as to what was best, with the husband preferring the scaffie with its sloping stern while his wife opted for the straight stems of the fifie. Others recount that the husband came from Lossiemouth and the wife from either Fife or Fraserburgh. Another, yet further, account states that two local boat-builders, each preferring one of the designs, sealed the marriage between their son and daughter by building a vessel combining the best features of both. However plausible these all sound, the fact of the matter is that the first vessel built on these lines seems quite categori-cally to have been the *Nonesuch*, INS2118. Not surprisingly, given its mention in most of the above accounts, the boat's owner, William 'Dad' Campbell, was from Lossiemouth. The story accompanying the fact is that he was originally from Brandenburgh and his wife from the Taylor family, from Cairnbulg, so they choose the shape to please each other. Another yarn is that the *Nonesuch* was a copy of a smaller skiff they had seen in Portessie.

Nonesuch was 59ft in length on a 39ft keel. She was first registered on 5 July 1878 as a first-class clinker-built sailing drifter. Yet she was not referred to as a 'Zulu' fishing vessel in the Fishing Registry of 1878. The first reference to the word 'Zulu' in describing one of these boats appeared in the *East Aberdeenshire Observer* dated 30 August 1881 in a report of a severe storm off the north-east coast: 'The first to arrive was the Zulu, of Inverness, no. 3179'. This vessel was in fact called the *Renown*, INS3179, therefore it seems apparent the newspaper was referring to a class of vessels. In the next year a vessel named *Zulu*, BF662, was registered and thus described as a 'Zulu clinker-built boat; decked; lugger rig; jib, foresail and mizzen'. The same year saw the launch of the *Cetawayo*, INS358, and *Transvaal*, BF310. Other references to these boats described them as 'Buckie scaffies', the 'modern herring boat' or the 'new style of herring boat', although the term 'Zulu' was the one that stuck.

The choice of the name seems to have stemmed from the great amount of sympathy felt for, and admiration of, the Zulu warriors.

Their defeat in 1879 caused a considerable loss of life among the three Scottish regiments on duty on that continent, and a certain amount of resentment was felt as this was seen to be largely due to the ineptness of the British military commanders. Local opinion erred in the Zulu people's favour and, combined with an increasing distrust of the English by the Scots and the feeling that the Zulus were simply fighting to preserve their rights, the newspapers portrayed the Zulus as noble people, worthy of respect, defying British imperialism. Thus the new breed of fishing boat, with equal nobility and strength, deserved a fitting name, and the Zulu came into common usage.

Nobility and strength they certainly had. The largest of the Zulus was over 84ft long, with a huge overhang at the stern and an extremely raked sternpost, the angle of which measured forty degrees or less. They were built wholly from timber, especially when carvel boats were commonplace. The rig was two equally massive dipping lug sails of over 3,500sq ft that needed the full complement of nine crew to handle. Going about took up to ten minutes, as the sails were lowered and 'dipped' around the masts, which themselves weighed over 2 tons and were over 2ft in diameter where they passed through the deck. Even with steam capstans, which were later fitted to both fifies and Zulus before the end of that century, the work was arduous. The number of drift-nets they set also grew in size – up to over seventy nets – with the introduction of the capstans to aid the hauling in, and with the advent of cotton nets as against the older hemp nets. When fully loaded with fish they could carry 80 tons, with 30 tons of ballast to counteract the sails.

At the beginning of the twentieth century there were 480 Zulus registered at Banff alone. A string of yards all along the coast turned them out, sometimes in eight weeks, which is fast boat building by any standards. It is said that they were easier to build than the fifies because the straight stem allowed this to be cut from a single piece of oak while the long overhang had less tuck-in to bend the planks. By now they had become the principal boat in the Moray Firth and northwards, while the southerners continued to build their fifies. The design found favour outside Scotland and many were built on the western coast of Ireland with grant funding from the Irish Congested Districts Board.

But with the introduction of motorisation in the late first and second decades of the twentieth century, it was found that the sloping sternpost was not suited to receiving a propeller aperture, whereas the upright fifie was perfect. Thus began a decline in their numbers so that, like the Lochfyne skiffs for the same reason, their actual lifespan was short. Thus many ended their days abandoned on beaches, or sold on to be replaced by the new breed of motorised fifie and, later, the cruiser-sterned herring drifter. Some were chopped up, such as the *Muirneag*, SY436, the last Zulu to work under sail, which was sawn up into fencing posts in 1945.

One Zulu remained at the fishing until 1968, albeit not under sail. The *Heather Bell*, BF1206, was built by W&G Stephens of Banff in 1903 and owned by Alexander Paterson. He sold her to William Ritchie of Rosehearty in 1912 and she was re-registered as FR498. She worked all along the coast during the herring season and, during the winter, fished for white fish with great-lines.

In 1935 she was sold to George Anderson of Whalsay, Shetland, replacing his earlier fifie that was broken up into fencing posts and fire-wood. At this point her name was changed to *Research* and she was again re-registered as LK62. Except for a brief period being requisitioned during the war, she remained fishing from Shetland until her owner retired in 1968. Luckily she escaped the fate of her predecessor and was bought by local fish merchant John Philips of Lerwick, and later the Shetland Maritime Trust was formed to oversee her retirement. The project was unsuccessful and the *Research* was eventually, in 1979, pur-chased by the Scottish Fisheries Museum of Anstruther, Fife, and placed in their collection. After several years of languishing in Anstruther har-bour and several stints of repair work, the vessel sank at her berth. She was subsequently lifted from the water and now sits in a purpose-made exhibition hall inside the museum. Only now, by standing on the plat-form alongside, can the massive size of this vessel be appreciated. The only sadness is the realisation that this vessel, after so many of its like were built in its era, is the last remaining full-size first-class example.

Of course the bauldies and Zulus weren't the only fishing craft to be named after current world events influenced fishermen. The seine-net boats of the 1960s were given the name 'sputnik class' after the Russians launched their satellites. But as often as not these boats were sub-classes of a particular type. The Zulu was different in that it heralded a com-pletely new design capturing the best of the two boats that were, hith-erto, in constant use. Some would say a hybrid; I say an innovation.

In conclusion, the spectacle of these fleets of Zulus is best left to those who experienced it. Thus Herbert Warrington Smyth, in his book *Mast and Sail in Europe and Asia*, published in 1906, can have the last say:

> *It is truly one of the finest sea sights of modern times to see this great brown pyramid come marching up out of the horizon and go leaning by you at a 10 knot speed, the peak stabbing the sky as it lurches past some 70ft above the water.*

Tollesbury Christmas Pickled Herring

Ingredients:
16 Blackwater herring
1 ½ pints white vinegar
4 onions, thinly sliced
1 ½ pints water
1 ½ oz pickling spice mixture
3 oz brown sugar

Method:
Remove bones, head and fins from fish. Soak the herring overnight in cold water and then drains; if required, remove any black membranes. Cut the fillets into bite-sized pieces. Place a layer of herring into a large dish (earthenware preferred) and cover with a layer of onions and a generous sprinkling of pickling spices. Continue layering and seasoning until the dish is three-quarters full. In a non-metallic bowl combine the marinade ingredients, mix thoroughly and add to the dish. Cover dish tightly and marinade herring in a cool place or refrigerator for three days. Gently stir herring with non-metallic spoon, then re-cover and marinade for at least another day. Note: Herring greatly improve with prolonged marinating. For best results at Christmas commence this recipe at the end of November.

CHAPTER TWELVE

The Fishermen and their Pipe Stalkies

Big, powerful luggers were not, of course, confined to the east coast of Scotland. The East Anglian herring ports of Lowestoft and Great Yarmouth had their own fleets, as did the mackerel and pilchard fishers of Cornwall. On the west coast, it was the Manx fishermen aboard their nickeys, and later the smaller nobbies, who competed in the herring markets. And, coupled to the fact that the herring fleets travelled all over following the shoals, it was not unusual to see a harbour crammed with luggers from all over Britain.

Lowestoft luggers differed from their Scottish counterparts in many ways. They were counter-sterned, less upright at the bow, had shorter masts, and often a mizzen topsail. Many changed over to the 'dandy' rig of main gaff and topsail and mizzen lugsail in the late nineteenth century, primarily for trawling purposes for which the fishermen preferred this rig. The surviving smack, *Excelsior* LT472, is one such example of a trawler, albeit gaff-rigged, while the smaller *Integrity* LT457, is a dandy-rigged herring drifter built in 1895. However, although both are beautiful boats in their own right, neither is as spectacular, in my opinion, as a Zulu or a fifie, the *Reaper* FR958 being a good example of the latter.

What the Lowestoft lugger can be said to have given us, though, is the steam drifter, for it was here that the first successful wooden drifter was launched with a steam unit inside. This was the *Consolation* LT718, which emerged from the yard of Chambers & Colby in 1897. She appeared much as a sailing drifter except for the addition of a tall funnel.

Yet this was not the beginning of the story of steam within the fishing fleets. In general, steam-driven vessels had been around for over 100 years. Luggers and smacks had been towed out of their harbours by steam-powered paddle tugs since the 1850s and doubt surrounds the date at which the first steam fishing boat was built in Scotland. Iain Sutherland gives us a Wick vessel in 1869 and Peter Anson one from Aberdeen in 1871. Neither was, it would seem, very successful. In England it was 1867 when the *Thistle* was launched at Dartmouth. In 1877, William Purdy, a tug owner from North Shields, used his tug *Messenger* to trawl for fish. Astonished fishermen looked on at this 'absurdly new-fangled and impractical' idea. With relatively successful results, four years later the first purpose-built steam trawler, the *Zodiac*, was built for the Great Grimsby Steam Trawling Co., and immediately its catches grew four-fold. The following year saw the first successful steam trawler working from a Scottish port. The *Rob Roy* LH92 was soon succeeded by the 87ft *Hawk*. In 1878 the steam trawler *Integrity*, from Northumberland, was in collision with a ferry in the Firth of Forth and sank.

The first trials of steam drifters occurred in Scotland in 1875. This was at Fraserburgh where the experiments lasted for three years, and was followed up by the building of ten vessels in Leith between 1880–84. Another drifter, built in Thurso in 1879, worked the herring season that year, beam-trawling afterwards. Yet success was not theirs for the nets always ran foul of the propeller which resulted in many of them being destroyed; these boats were adapted for line-fishing. Until the drift-net was modified by the addition of the 'tarry leader', allowing better control of the net, the steam drifter was but a dream.

Not for the first time, arguments between the trawling and drifting communities rattled on. Steam trawlers were accused of ripping drift-nets by steaming straight through regardless. In some ports violence erupted as the traditional driftermen believed trawling both destroyed herring spawn and their nets. In Wick, fishermen were stoned while mending their trawl nets in 1884. The following year, again at Wick, a cargo of white fish was attacked and dumped into the sea by furious drift-netters. Some of these local fishermen received a thirty-day gaol sentence for also assaulting the crew and the fish salesman.

The conflicts between fishermen and trawlermen continued in various parts of the country until the government was pressed into setting up a Commission that reported in 1885, giving the Fishery Board for Scotland the right to regulate the trawl fishery. Thus trawling was banned in certain areas, much to the delight of the herring fishers.

1 *The Herring Basin at Lowestoft Harbour in about 1880.*

2 *A typical snipa from Bohusland.* (Fisheri og sofartsmuseum, Esberg)

3 Above: *The Dutch logger fleet was centred on Vlaardingen.*

4 Right: *Seals of the town of Hamburg in 1743 showing the importance of fishing and the sea to the town. Note the spelling of 'heering' as against today's 'hering' in German, suggesting that the word does originate from 'heer'.*

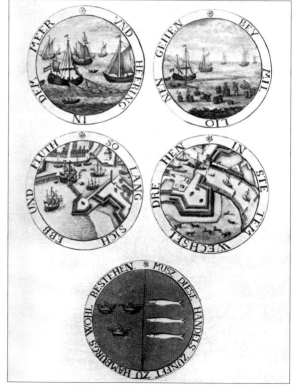

5 *John Girling using a dip-net to collect whitebait from his fish weir, Gorad Bach.* (Bridget Dempsey)

6 *The Gorad Bach weir in the 1960s.* (Bridget Dempsey)

7 *Unloading the catch on the beach at Clovelly in the 1890s. The boats are picarooners.*

8 *Unloading the catch onto the pier at Ramsey, Isle of Man. The woman on the right with the white apron is Mrs Killin, a well-known herring saleswoman.* (Joe Pennington)

9 Above: *A considerable catch aboard the ringnetters* Alliance *CN187 and* Maryeared, *c. 1984.* (Angus Martin)

10 Right: *A dual-purpose ring-netter, the* Fair Morn *BA295, built 1966.* (Nigel Munro)

11 *Wick in 1865, with the harbour full of, mostly, scaffies.*

12 *The steam trawlers were almost identical in shape, but spent much longer periods at sea. This Dutch trawler is the* Bergen IJM16.

13 Opposite: *The first-class fifie* Reaper *remains in the ownership of the Scottish Fisheries Museum, Anstruther.*

14 Above: *The typical scene in a herring curing yard with troughs (farlanes or farlins) full of herring and barrels awaiting filling.*

15 Opposite: *Fish wife at St Andrews, Fife. The women took as active a part in the fishing as did the men.*

16 Right: *Yarmouth has long been renowned for its fine bloaters, as this 1930s postcard suggests.*

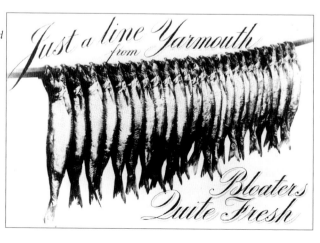

17 Above: *Jennie, a Scots herring lass.*

18 Opposite above: *Inside the kipper house where herrings are prepared.*

19 Opposite below: *Yarmouth had its own unique basket for carrying herring known as a 'swill'.*

KIPPERERS AT WORK

20 Above: *A motorised fifie being unloaded of herring at Castle Bay, Barra in the 1930s.*

21 Left: *The sign of the three herrings hangs over a house in Nefyn.*

22 Opposite: *"Aren't Herrings delicious?"*

THE NEW
HERRING BOOK

Scores of Simple Recipes

"*Aren't Herrings delicious?*"
SAYS MERLE OBERON
FAMOUS "LONDON FILMS" STAR

HERRING COOKERY

NOTE

THE REPRINTING OF THIS PRE-WAR
BOOKLET IN UP-TO-DATE FORM HAS BEEN
POSTPONED UNTIL THE PAPER SITUATION
ALLOWS THIS TO BE DONE. THE TEXT
AND RECIPES ARE, THEREFORE, IN A FEW
INSTANCES, INAPPROPRIATE TO PRESENT-
DAY CONDITIONS IN THE UNITED KINGDOM.

Issued by

THE HERRING INDUSTRY BOARD, I GLENFINLAS STREET, EDINBURGH, 3

Issued by

THE HERRING INDUSTRY BOARD, 184 STRAND, LONDON, W.C.2

24 *Landing herring at Stornoway.* (Campbell McCutcheon)

25 *Keiss harbour.* (Campbell McCutcheon)

23 Opposite: *The continued printing of the* Herring Cookery *book, despite warime paper restrictions, is testament to the popularity of herring.*

26 *Herring drifters leave an East Coast Scottish port.* (Campbell McCutcheon)

27 *Fisher folk at Buchanhaven, Peterhead.* (Campbell McCutcheon)

With the launch of the *Consolation* at Lowestoft, the herring fishermen realised the benefits which these vessels could supply. For sure, the investment was far greater. A steam drifter cost in the region of three to four times the price of a sailboat. For example, in 1900 a Zulu cost £700 and a steam drifter £2,400. But with the added investment came the increased earnings, and Britain's fishers – and those of Europe certainly – passed into the steam age extremely abruptly from then on. The sailboats were sold, or often abandoned, through the lack of a second-hand market, and drifters bought through joint ownerships.

At Peterhead, the steam fleet increased seventeen-fold between 1900 and 1909, with most of the vessels being owned by individuals, shared persons or companies. The cost of the gear was also shared.

Many of the earliest steam drifters were in actuality simply the older luggers with compound steam engines added with a modification to the sternpost to allow a propeller aperture. The rig was retained until the reliability of the engines could be guaranteed. In appearance it was the tall funnel that gave rise to the term 'pipe stalkie', or in England the 'Woodbine funnel' after the cigarette that many fishermen smoked. Some remained steered by a tiller until wheelhouses were added abaft of the funnel. In time this was moved forward of the funnel to a more obvious siting. At the same time the lines of the boats were adjusted, with the resultant classic drifter shape – low freeboard to work the nets, higher bow and engine casing and galley behind the funnel – evolving. The early engines were in the region of 15hp on a 75-85ft hull, and these increased in size with the introduction of triple-expansion steam engines. A whole range of engines became available from manufacturers such as Elliott & Garrod of Beccles. Coal consumption was around the 15-20 ton mark for an average trip while some of the more clumsy vessels needed 25 tons. Several authors have recounted the tales of these fishermen at sea, the best perhaps being David Butcher's *The Driftermen,* in which he gives a fine insight into the daily toil and the customs and ways of life of these fishermen.

There is a certain nostalgia surrounding the steam drifter much as there is for the sailing fishing boat. One reference was that life aboard was much improved for the impoverished crew. Generally the engineer, fireman and cook were paid a wage whilst the rest of the crew took a share. The standard of accommodation was comfortable in comparison, with the sleeping quarters aft, beneath the galley with its big stove that kept them warm. There was no hot and cold running water though, and no toilet except a barrel on the after end which was emptied over the side. The deckies worked for hours on a rolling deck, and the corrosive seawater and chafing oilskins often caused large boils on their wrists that became more and more painful without treatment. The big difference, it seems, was that there was no rig to tend.

However, the cook's job was probably the hardest, as was the case on the sailboats. For the sum of £1 a week in the 1930s (in some parts of the country the boy was expected to work for his instruction only) he was expected to buy and produce food as well as keeping the galley clean. During the shooting operation his job was to pay out the 2½in thick tarry leader rope. Once the 81 to 101 nets – always an odd number – had been shot and the crew retired to the cabin, it was he who would cook up a number of herring, brew gallons of tea and provide loaves of bread for the hungry men. However he did normally get one of the ten or so bunks to sleep upon. Once the hauling process started in the first light, his job was to return down into the forecastle and coil in the tarry leader. As on the sailing boats, he was the apprentice learning the ropes and he would soon join the crew on a full share.

During this hauling operation, the engineer would often appear on deck to lend a hand while the fireman remained below stoking the fire for the donkey engine powering the capstan and winding in the net. These two were the 'black squad', whose job it was to keep the vessel working. Two crew shook the net as it came aboard to clear the fish, although some often remained enmeshed, to be thrown up by the three men below in the net room who neatly stowed the net. On average, the crew numbered nine or ten including the skipper.

Monotony characterised the herring fishermen at work. Even after the advent of steam. The nets were shot in the early evening, after which the crew snuggled down to eat and sleep, and they were hauled at first light. Once they were hauled they made for port at full steam, packing the herring in the fish room. In harbour they jostled with the other boats to get the bow onto the quay. Often a drifter would force its way between two other boats to gain a nose onto the quay and hulls were sometimes damaged in the process. With the introduction of iron, and later steel, steamers in the late 1890s, the chance of damage was slighter. Once on the quay, a sample basket was taken ashore and a deal done with the buyers before the main catch was unloaded. Then began the laborious task of making repairs to the net, cutting out tangles in the process. Dogfish and conger eels can wreck great lengths of netting in their zest to get a free feed.

In the East Anglian ports, the herring ground lay some forty miles offshore, so it was easy to offload the fish on a daily basis. In the remoter parts of the country, such as in the Western Isles of Scotland, if catches were poor, the boats often stayed away from port for two or three days. Castle Bay, on the island of Barra, became a major herring port, as did Stornoway on Lewis. The expansion of both was largely due to the curers from the east coast moving across country after the spring herring there. Mallaig grew up in early twentieth century as a major west coast landing port, due entirely to its proximity to the fishing grounds and the West Highland Railway that was opened in 1901.

By today's standards, coal is of course a filthy polluting fuel, yet a century ago it was regarded more as a godsend than a pollutant. Images of the high funnels belching forth clouds of black smoke serve to compound the belief that fishermen were a class of dirty people always smelling of fish and coal smoke. On the sailing boats the former was undoubtedly true, but the driftermen were relatively clean. Indeed it is said that once paraffin engines were introduced towards the end of the first decade of the twentieth century, the smell of oil was all-pervading aboard the boats and the fishermen stank accordingly.

1913 was the peak year for the herring fishery in Britain and the most successful year for the drifters. With the onset of war in the following year, the markets in Europe, specifically those of Germany and Russia, collapsed. That year there were 1,163 Scottish drifters fishing the autumnal fishery at East Anglia, 854 of which were steam driven. A third of these came from the Moray Firth port of Buckie. Only Lowestoft had a higher number and the combined British fleet numbered more than 1,800 steam drifters. 1,359,213 cran of herring were landed at Yarmouth in the fourteen-week season while the total in Britain reached its maximum figure. The official measure of a cran was about 1,000 fish, although in reality it was often closer to 1,300 fish. Each steam drifter was said to give work to 100 people, from the crews, the gutters, dock workers, tug crews, railwaymen, shipwrights, engineers, salesmen, curers, fishmongers, coal-miners, coopers, rope-makers, net-makers, sail-makers and others. Furthermore each steamer earned on average £795, while motor boats averaged £365 each, and sail boats £235.

When the hostilities began, the steam drifters and trawlers were put to further use – they were requisitioned by the Admiralty for minesweeping and patrol duties. 1,502 drifters and 1,467 trawlers were thus employed, while forty-nine per cent of fishermen joined the navy, crewing these boats. In Scotland this accounted for 17,000 men. Others joined the army. It is said that out of all the working communities in Britain, the fishermen contributed most to the war effort in terms of percentage. During the war, 394 fishing vessels were lost on naval service, of which 246 were trawlers, 108 drifters and eighteen Admiralty trawlers. Of the 2,058 men lost on active duty on these vessels, most were fishermen.

Another 439 fishermen were killed and 675 vessels lost while actively fishing during the war years. 270 of these vessels were drifters and the majority of crew were either elderly or too young for service. Likewise, the boats that were not commandeered by the Admiralty agents were the oldest and slowest. Although many of these were strengthened with iron plating, especially around the wheelhouse, many were attacked by German submarines and strafed by gunfire or simply sunk. In some cases, when vessels were working in convoys, the Germans made all the fishermen gather on one boat which was allowed to sail home while the others were sunk by gunfire. Aircraft bombed boats on occasions, while minefields accounted for other losses.

Some drifters gained recognition for outstanding service during the First World War. The *Gowanlea* FR105 was one such vessel. She operated in the Mediterranean and saw active service in the Adriatic, ferrying troops into Corfu, until she was hit by enemy fire in 1916. However, holed and without a funnel, the vessel reached port for repairs, even though several of her crew were killed. Credit was given to First Engineer William Noble, who kept the vessel steaming at full speed under the most arduous of conditions. The *Gowanlea* later gained repute the next year while standing up to the might of the Austrian navy by firing on a cruiser and escaping sinking, even though the crew had been instructed to abandon ship by the Austrians prior to them sinking the vessel. She returned to Britain after the war and recommenced fishing, although she was sold to Lossiemouth some years later.

Such was the performance of these vessels during the conflict that a building programme for a standardised boat was begun to replace those sunk. These vessels became known as the Admiralty 'standard' drifters.

Herring steam drifters were not solely confined to the North Sea as we've seen in the case of the west coast of Scotland. Milford Haven Docks, situated by the water of the same name that has often been described as Britain's finest natural harbour, was opened to craft in 1888. Those responsible for the investment were hoping to capture the transatlantic liners that plied a nearby track to and from America. This they spectacularly failed at, the first vessel arriving at the port being the steam trawler *Sybil* LT77. One can only imagine the shock on the faces of those whose money had built the harbour as a fishing boat arrived and not a liner. However, within a few years, they were not to regret this, for with some fifty-five steam trawlers based there around the turn of the century, four steam drifters arrived. These vessels, *Girl Daisy*, *Boy Fred*, *Cato* and *Favo*, were locally owned to work the herring along the west coast and, at times, into the North Sea. Two years later there were forty drifters and, in another two years, 200 of them. By 1925, Milford Haven had become the principal English herring port, landing 124,000 barrels (over 50 million fish) during the previous year. This was an amazing turnround of events, considering the amount of herring being landed before in East Anglia, and no doubt bettered the fortunes of those investors more than the occasional transatlantic liner.

Seasickness tended to be a problem aboard the drifters. Some say the awkward motion was due to the heavy engine situated abaft of amidships, while others put it down to the hull shape and the increased speed from the sailing smacks. John West of Gardenstown fished after the Second World War and was sick every day he was at sea, even when he was the cook at the age of fifteen, the normal age for boys to begin their apprenticeship after leaving school (although this had been raised from fourteen only a couple of years previously). Indeed, in the case of the steam trawler it was not uncommon, because the accommodation was in the forepeak of the vessel and caused a sleeping body to be thrust 10ft upwards as the boat ploughed into heavy seas, hovering in thin air for a split second before person and bunk plummeted the 10ft back down again. The sensation in the stomach and head is well known! The steam drifter, with its after accommodation, was not so uncomfortable. It is also worth mentioning that herring fishing, by its very nature, usually meant returning home each night. Trawling, on the other hand, involved long trips at sea – two weeks in the home fishing, longer at Iceland – with only a couple of days leave at home, especially in war time. With almost twenty out of twenty-four hours being worked shooting and hauling, gutting and stowing, it was a tiring job. Such a physical demand put strains upon men living in the cramped conditions of the steam trawler. The herring fishermen, by comparison, were lucky!

Steam propulsion had dramatic effects upon the herring fleets of other northern European countries. Steam drifters entered the Dutch fleet, primarily based at Vlaardingen, close to Rotterdam, in the very early years of the twentieth century. Most were steel built, yet their characteristics were similar to the British craft; they had the same tall, thin funnel and the 'telephone box' wheelhouse in front. The story was similar in the French channel ports and the Belgium coast. In Germany the advent of steam overwhelmed the fishing with 200 steam trawlers working out of Bremerhaven. Drifters were scarcer, although a number worked out of the main herring ports of Emden, Bremerhaven and Cuxhaven.

In the steam drifter we saw one of the most effective herring fishing boats for its size. Yet, like most things, events overtook the herring fleets. With the collapse of the main European markets after the First World War and a corresponding crash in the price of herring, the high costs of building these drifters prevented further building and the fishing industry underwent a period of depression. At the same time the petrol/paraffin units, and later diesel engines, were becoming a better choice for smaller boats. Only a handful of new steam drifters were built after 1920 so that, when 437 were commandeered in 1939 for active service, many of which never returned, and the majority of the remaining fleet broken up, only six drifters were left in Scotland by 1954. Unfortunately, at the dawning of the twenty-first century, when there is an awakening of the important part in history played by Britain's steam drifters, only three remain in the country that I know of. The *Lydia Eva* YH89, one of a few vessels built at Kings Lynn as a drifter/trawler between the wars, survives between Lowestoft and Great Yarmouth. She is regarded as not being typical because of her greater length and 'big bluff bow'.

Another of the three vessels, the *Feasible* LT1191, was built by John Duthie of Aberdeen in 1912 for herring drifting. Called up for service as a patrol boat in 1914, she assisted in the sinking of a U-boat three years later before returning to the herring fishing after the war, registered as LT122. In 1936, while sailing with the drifter *Shorebreeze* off the south-west coast of Wales, she was turned over in massive seas. She righted herself but her wheelhouse was swept away and crewmember Ben Halliday was drowned after being swept over the side twice that night. Towed eventually into Milford Haven by the trawlers *Gozo* and *Gordon Richards*, the remaining crew discovered that the *Shorebreeze* was lost with all eleven hands. *Gordon Richards* was lost herself ten days later.

The *Feasible* became a veteran of both wars when she was called up again at the outset of the Second World War as a minesweeper. In 1940 she joined in when Operation Dynamo evacuated troops from the Belgian and French beaches, herself embarking troops from La Panne. On the return voyage to Ramsgate she was bombed and disabled. After the war she was sold to Norway, renamed *Meloy* and fitted with a 1903 Brunvall 3-cylinder diesel engine. In 1990 she was sold and returned to Britain and in 1997 she changed hands once again. She was based in Penzance for several years before sailing to Bristol for restoration in the autumn of 2002, returning back to Penzance some months later. A decision is currently awaited on her future. Because of its rarity, the Brunvall engine has been replaced and sent back to the company museum at Molde, in Norway. According to the vessel's owner, Roy Mildon, on three occasions, after sailing around Lands End, the Brunvall engine stopped in approximately the same vicinity off Padstow for no apparent reason. Perhaps the boat had unhappy memories of the Bristol Channel and only a new engine managed to achieve what the Brunvall couldn't!

The third steamer is the 1908-built *Norfolk County*, which was taken to Norway where she was converted for general cargo use for many years before returning to Britain, where she is currently(2003) for sale. The price tag of £75,000 obviously reflects her good condition and the fact that she is described as a 'cruise/liveaboard' boat.

Three vessels, with possibly a few more scattered about the globe, out of over 2,000 in total built in Britain, seems surprising. But fishing steamers were a stopgap between sail and motor, a junction between fishing as a way of life and fishing for profit without consideration of the effects, and thus have been largely ignored. Coupled with the fact that, in their time, they were short-lived, and that they are today still costly to refit and run, this probably accounts for the fact that only three have survived. However, from the herring fishing point of view, their place in history dwarfs that of a very many other vessels. Let that be their silent epitaph.

Fried Herring Fillets with a Lime Pepper Crust

Ingredients:
2 herring fillets 6-7oz each
1 rounded teaspoonful whole mixed peppercorns
Grated zest and juice of 2 limes
1 rounded dessertspoonful plain flour
2 tablespoonfuls olive oil
Crushed salt flakes

Method:
Crush the peppercorns coarsely in a mortar and pestle. Grate zest of the limes and add half to flour. Mix thoroughly and spread mixture out on flat plate. Wipe the herring dry and coat the flesh side with mixture. Press fish well in to give a good coating and dust with any remaining flour. Heat oil in a large frying pan until very hot and fry herring flesh-side down for two to three minutes until golden underneath. Then turn the fish over and fry on the other side for two minutes. Drain on crumpled greaseproof or kitchen paper before serving. Serve sprinkled with crushed salt and the remaining lime zest and limes cut into quarters to squeeze over.

CHAPTER THIRTEEN

Herring Fishery after the Depression

In 1935 the *Maison Prunier* restaurant opened in St James's Street, London. Coming from France, Madame Simone Barnagaud-Prunier, the granddaughter of Alfred Prunier, the restaurant's founder, assumed that the English knew their fish, seeing that they ate more of it than most other European nations. What she soon discovered was that, although the British ate a lot of fish, they were ignorant of how to cook it. Thus encouraged to teach us what we could do with the plentiful supply of fish, Madame Prunier soon became a household name. One of her amazing feats was to induce the fashionable diners of London to ask for herring, and enjoy them once they had been served. This was remarkable in that, previously, this group had only tolerated herring as a breakfast kipper. Madame Prunier's restaurant specialised in the preparation of succulent dishes with rough fish as their base – herring, mackerel, John Dory, hake and skate. One of her goals was to popularise herring. The same year she visited both Great Yarmouth and Lowestoft for the first time and saw for herself the difficulties associated with catching, marketing and selling fresh herring.

With this in mind, she had the idea of giving a prize to the skipper of the boat that landed the largest catch during the East Anglian autumnal fishing. The first year of the Prunier Trophy was 1936, when it was won by the Scottish drifter *Boy Andrew* BF592, and the tradition continued until 1966 except for the years 1939–46, during the war and 1965, when the Herring Industry Board felt they were unable to donate the cup. In 1966 it was won, for the last time, by another Scottish boat, *Tea Rose* FR346. The highest catch was 323 crans in 1953. The full story of the trophy is told in Les Hawkins' *The Prunier Herring Trophy*.

Sir Robert Boothby, Member of Parliament for east Aberdeenshire, donated a cup with a similar idea in mind in Peterhead. The first winner of the Boothby Cup was the *Pilot Star* in 1937, which landed 198½ cran. Furthermore, the winning boat also received a set of binoculars and a weather glass (barometer). This set a precedent and continued for a number of years.

With incentives like this, and government intervention in the form of grants to build boats, the herring fishery was pulled out of the depression. However it was against this background of depression that the motorised herring drifter *Efficient* FR242 was launched from the stocks of J&G Forbes of Sandhaven, near Fraserburgh, in 1931. Owned by the Ritchie family of Rosehearty, she drift-netted for herring. She was powered by a Petter Atomic Diesel of 160hp, an innovative engine which the company photographed, using the picture of her owner standing alongside the unit in their publicity brochure.

We have already seen how internal combustion engines were fitted to fishing boats in the first decade of the twentieth century and how the impact of these was to have a dramatic and continual effect upon the fishing fleets. Although the Danes were the first in Europe to experiment with this, the first British motorised vessel was the aptly-named *Pioneer* LT368, launched in 1901 at Lowestoft. Another *Pioneer* appeared in Scotland in 1905 from Anstruther, and in 1907 the first engined boat appeared on the west coast of Scotland: the Lochfyne skiff *Brothers* CN97. Many boats were thus converted in the same way, while new builds were engined from the outset.

The sloping sternpost of the Zulu was found to be unsuited to a propeller aperture whereas it was suited to the upright fifie. Thus many boats continued to be built on the fifie lines, both aboard larger 70ft+ boats and those in the shorter range of 45-55ft. The true motor fifie was born. As many herring fishermen turned to seine-netting in the 1920s – seine-netting was developed on the west coast of Denmark and provided hard-up fishermen with another effi-cient means of catching white fish – fifies suited their purpose, the 50ft *Marigold* being the first purpose-built seiner from Woods of Lossiemouth.

In 1928 J&G Forbes launched the *Cutty Sark*, distinguished by its cruiser stern. Although Robertson's canoe-sterned boats had been fishing successfully on the Clyde for several years by this time, the

Cutty Sark appears to have been the first cruiser-sterned vessel in Scotland – the forerunner of hundreds that were to be built over the next forty years or so.

The *Efficient* was cruiser-sterned. At 76ft overall, she was a large boat by the standards of those days when boats tended to be built smaller due to the decline in fishing fortunes. However, after only six years at the herring, she was sold to new owners in Cornwall.

W. Stevenson & Sons are trawler owners based in Newlyn, and they fitted her out for trawling. The war intervened and the boat was one of those requisitioned in 1941. She spent the war sailing between Scotland and Norway ferrying refugees and acting in other secret operations, details of which remain lost in the realms of the Official Secrets Act. After the war she returned to Newlyn, was re-engined and renamed *Excellent,* PZ513, after the original lugger of William Stevenson, the founder of the family firm. Almost sixty years later she remains part of the Stevenson fleet, and is renowned for being the oldest first-class boat in the British fleet, and possibly within the European one also. Her accommodation aft was probably not much better than the steam drifters and the *Excellent* received her first toilet in 2001! Before that it was the bucket in the tiny on-deck 'cupboard' and the proverbial 'sling-it-over-the-side'.

Of course herring fishing resumed after the Second World War but lining and seining provided a more secure future for fishermen. Some 203 steam and 57 motor drifters sailed from Scotland to the East Anglian autumnal fishery in 1946. The government had set up the Herring Industry Board in 1935 to 're-organise, develop and regulate' the fishery but conditions were much worse in late 1945 than they had been in 1918. A building programme did get going with all new-built Scottish vessels having cruiser-sterns except for the canoe-sterned ring-netters that yards such as Nobles of Fraserburgh, Walter Reekie of St Monans and Weatherheads of Cockenzie were producing. When Alexander Noble began work in Girvan in the 1950s he produced a whole line of fine ring-netters, as did Dickie of Tarbert. Admiralty MFVs (Motor Fishing Boats) standardised the design much as the standard steam drifters had done after the First World War. The forerunner of these was said to have been the *Poppy,* built by Thomsons of Buckie in 1933 and said to have had a 'Thomson stern'. Admiralty-type vessels, up to 75ft in length, were built by a number of companies such as Jones

Buckie Slip & Shipyard of Buckie. Boats such as these fishing for herring and supported by air cover were called the 'kipper patrol'!

Throughout the 1950s herring continued to be landed, although by the beginning of the decade the British fleet had been reduced from over 40,000 boats over 40ft in the 1870s to just over 12,500. Landings were down to 176,000 tons of herring. In 1956, the last Scottish steam drifter, the *Cosmea* KY21, fished the East Anglian fishery. By the 1960s catches declined rapidly. In Peterhead, which inherited the title of 'herring capital' for a time, catches fell from almost 109,000 crans in 1952 to less than 7,000 twelve years later. By 1959 the English fishery was as good as over, with the annual landing for that year from both Lowestoft and Great Yarmouth equalling what would have previously have been landed in one night. Inshore landings were sporadic and generally only for local consumption. Only the ring-netters off northwest Scotland were landing significant amounts of up to 100 cran a day.

What this proved to many fishermen was that, to catch herring, an aggressive method of pursuit was more successful. They saw the success of the ring-netters as proof of this, which is ironic given that 100 years earlier the same drift-netters had been advocating a total ban on the trawl-nets. Then, from across the North Sea, came word of a method that was even more effective than ring-netting. The Norwegians were perfecting the purse-seine, a killer method of catching herring with catches of 1,000 tons in one haul. In 1965 it was reported that 259 Norwegian pursers caught 615,000 tons off Shetland when the entire British landings were only 10,000 tons. Ridiculously, much of this herring was being turned into fishmeal.

The purse-seine is basically a very large ring-net, although the Norwegians developed it for fishing inside fjords. They are said to have started using ring-nets in the 1760s, yet this net is up to 2,000m long with rings in the bottom of the net through which a rope passes. When tightened, the net forms into a bag – or purse – within which the fish are trapped, unable to escape. This pond of fish is progressively made smaller by hauling the net aboard until the fish remain in a tight mass in the bag at one end of the gear. The position of the bag is the main difference between this and the ring-net, where the bag is in the middle of the net. Once the fish is so placed, it can then be loaded onto the vessel. Ironically, an Aberdeen man called Bruce was said to have tried out such a design, again in the 1760s, as did various ring-netters much later, although their nets were deemed too shallow to be effective in this manner.

So, as the drift-net became obsolete after centuries of successful use, the fishermen began to turn to the more aggressive methods. With hindsight, common sense would have told anyone that the North Sea was just not able to sustain catches of 2,000 tons aboard one vessel. With start-up costs high – a net was over £10,000 while a boat needed a powerful winch and a power block costing another £5,000 – and unsuccessful landings to begin with, the fishermen persevered and the gear came right, leading to higher landings. Once the fish were in the bag-end of the net they were brailed aboard, a ton at a time. Then came pumps to quicken this process, and refrigerated sea-water (RSW) tanks to keep the fish fresh. Consequently the vessels had to be bigger. The killer method was about to wipe out the whole fishery in the North Sea.

The designs of vessels changed fundamentally about this time, as the old wooden Scottish fishing boat began to become obsolete. Transom sterns allowed more working space aft while steel boats became more universal. Shelter-decks became an integral part of the boat, providing cover for those fishermen working on deck. A shorter, stubby type of boat evolved for the white fishery while deepwater vessels became bigger.

At the same time some boat owners were developing the mid-water trawl towed by two boats. The Dutch and the Danes were the first to work these trawl nets after Robert Larsen had invented a trawl to catch pelagic species off Jutland just after the Second World War. So keen was the Herring Industry Board that it paid for fishermen to go over to Denmark to see exactly what was involved so that they, too, could develop such a method. Two Scottish boats from Fraserburgh were among the first to work the pair trawl and took good hauls. Others followed suit.

By 1966 the total herring catch from the North Sea was 1.2 million tons, a level nearly double of what it had been a decade before. The Icelanders were purse-seining and it is said that Norwegian and Icelandic fishermen took more than 200,000 crans of herring during one week's fishing off Shetland. The Scottish fleet of pursers and trawlers grew at the mere whiff of a bonanza. By 1969 there were fifteen purse-seiners, forty-three mid-water trawlers, fifty-three ring-

netters and fifteen drift-netters fishing in the Scottish fleet. Yet, unfortunately for them, landings fell dramatically over the next ten years
until it was estimated that over seventy per cent of the entire stock of
the North Sea was being taken out. By 1975 landings were down to
200,000 tons. Some of the fishermen were questioning the use of such
aggressive methods of fishing and refusing to participate, but there
were others who had no qualms about it. 'Fish for profit and damn the
consequences' was the phrase of the time.

Politicians are not renowned for acting with speed. In the case of
the North Sea herring the signs had been dire but largely ignored as
the Norwegians, Scots, Danes and Dutch emptied it of herring.
Britain was still reeling from losing the Cod Wars and access to
Icelandic waters. Entry into the European Economic Community had
just been negotiated and these politicians were well aware of the price
Britain had had to pay for entry. It had negotiated away the long-term
security of the country's fishing rights to its territorial waters that
contain sixty-five per cent of European fish stocks. They were therefore hesitant to act swiftly. Yet, in 1977, the full brunt of Brussels
descended upon the pelagic fisheries and the North Sea herring fishery was closed. The west coast was closed the following year. The
excesses of some of the fishermen had come back to haunt them.

Left free to spawn on their favoured sandy banks, the herring
recovered sufficiently for fishing to recommence in 1981. To begin
with effort was limited, but landings increased to 800,000 tons by the
end of the 1980s. By then the Common Fisheries Policy had come
into force. By setting quotas for specific areas, fishing capability could
be limited through legislation and, given that the principle of the CFP
is equal access regardless of nationality, Britain's share of the herring
quota displeased most. The final nail in Britain's fishing coffin was
about to be hammered home.

Today, the vast majority of herring is taken by mid-water trawling.
Most comes from the North Sea and west of Scotland, although a very
limited fishery was introduced back to the Isle of Man in 2001 after a
fifteen-year gap. The 2002 British quota was 265,000 tons for the
North Sea and 36,380 tons in the west coast of Scotland sector. The
Total Allowable Catch (TAC) for both areas was about 1.2 million
tons, shared throughout the EU and Norway. The current recommendations, as this is written, are for increases between fifty and seventy per

cent for 2003, although many regard this as a threat to sustainability and, perhaps, a return to the 1970s level of fishing. However, as politicians and environmentalists envisage a total ban on the cod and haddock fishing within the North Sea, there will be those that relish an increase in the pelagic TACs.

Two factors alone altered the face of fishing in the period after the 1980s. Firstly, engine power increased dramatically and secondly, electronic technology led to a much more effective means of finding the fish. Skippers simply gazing at screens have replaced the old ways of men leaning out of the wheelhouse and watching for the signs of bubbles on the surface or diving gannets. Seldom do they even look out of the window these days.

The modern pelagic trawler is a far cry from the early scaffie. *Daystar* BF250, at a mere 49.28m in length, is by no means the largest of these trawlers. The 71.1m *Serene* LK297 is the largest in the UK fleet, has an 8,280kw engine and can carry over 1,000 tons at any time. However *Daystar* can be said to be typical of these vessels. Her RSW tanks can carry 300 tons of herring – or other pelagic species, as these boats do not solely concentrate on herring – which is pumped aboard from the trawl-net through an 18-inch diameter hose and pump. The bridge is a mass of electronic wizardry through which Alex West, the skipper in 1999, searches for and controls the net to envelope the shoals in deeper water. For no longer do they have to wait for the herring to rise to the surface at night to feed – they sink their nets down instead. *Daystar*, built in southern Norway in 1987, was pair trawling at the time with another Fraserburgh-based boat, *Convallaria* BF58, an older vessel built in Holland in 1974.

To shoot the net it is first trailed out behind one boat before a line is thrown across to the other boat – this is the dangerous part, with the two 600-ton boats pitching in the sea some 15ft apart – and this line eventually feeds across the tow warp from one end of the trawl. Thus the net is released and trawling commences, the depth of the net set on the bridge from data from the instrumentation. Sonar 'eggs' attached to the net fire off signals to the bridge when the net is full and hauling can commence. Once winched in sufficiently, the line is thrown back across from the second to first boat, and the net gathered alongside the starboard of the vessel before pumping operations begin. Such is the technology of this fishing, and the high cost, that a trawl of 7 tons in the net would be deemed too small to operate the pumping gear, and would thus be let go. Unfortunately, most of the fish would be dead.

But *Daystar* has been replaced, as are other Fraserburgh trawlers. Three new ones have joined the Scottish fleet in 2003. At over 60m in length with an RSW tank capacity of 1,600cu.m, these vessels are monsters. With investments in such vessels the owners expect returns. Banks want their share. The only losers are the fish and the fishermen forced onto the dole.

I recently saw the new 70.7m long *Research* LK62 alongside Lerwick's Victoria Pier, the fourth *Research* belonging, in part, to the Williamson family. The first they owned was the Zulu *Research* that now languishes in the Scottish Fisheries Museum. Ignoring the fact that her generator kept everyone sleeping alongside the quay awake all night and the crew didn't care a fig when challenged about the noise, the boat is simply awesome. Three more of these gigantic mid-water trawlers are set to join the Whalsay fleet – the *Charisma, Adenia* and *Antartic* arriving soon. These boats can carry 1,000 tons of fish in RSW tanks with a 1,984-cubic-metre capacity, thus being even bigger than those above. Where does it end?

Fishing on this scale is obviously having a major impact on fish stocks. Unfortunately, mankind's ability to use the technological advances cannot be stalled, and the result is fewer but bigger vessels requiring less crew and an end product of unemployment. Deepwater fishing destroys the livelihoods of the coastal fishers as fish are removed before the artisanal fishermen can reach them. Even more boats and fishermen are made redundant in an ever-spiralling decrease in the numbers of fishing craft.

There is, however, one very great advantage that simply cannot be overlooked. On 14 October 1881, a storm engulfed the fishermen off the south-east coast of Scotland. With the herring season over, the fleets were fishing for haddock that evening. Within just a few hours almost 200 fishermen were dead, drowned or dashed against the rocks. Out of these, 129 came from Eyemouth alone: one third of the adult male population gone in an instant. This was Scotland's worst fishing disaster. There were others, of course, and we have already seen the results of the 1848 gale at the coast further north. Even in the twenty-first century, fishermen continue to perish while at their work and fishing remains the occupation with the highest percentage death rate. That today's new breed of fishing craft are inherently safer than the older wooden craft is obvious. And the degree of comfort is greater; instead of bunking down in the aft cabin, fishermen often have a cabin to themselves, with TV and video, hot showers and washing machines. Five-star accommodation in fact. Who can fault any of this? The balance, though, seems to be one of safety and comfort at one end of the scale against fish stocks, unemployment and the break-up of communities at the other. Like the fishermen wondering at the introduction of steam propulsion, or the trawl-net, or computerisation, the only question is where will it lead the fishing industry?

Salmagundy

This is an unusual recipe for a traditional British salad which was popular in the seventeenth and eighteenth centuries. It is built up as a small pyramid with brightly-coloured ingredients and garnishes. A very large round plate is needed and a shallow pudding basin or large saucer is used to build the pyramid. The butter 'statue' is very traditional to this dish but may be omitted.

Ingredients:
1 teaspoonful vegetable oil
½ medium curly endive (chicory), coarse outer leaves removed, washed, shaken dry and shredded
1lb cooked chicken meat, sliced
1lb lean cooked tongue, sliced
6 hard-boiled eggs, separated and finely chopped
8 rollmops or pickled herring, drained
2 large tomatoes, quartered
1 large lemon, quartered
1 large orange, quartered
1 small cooked beetroot – finely chopped
8 black olives, stoned
1 small gherkin, finely chopped
8 tablespoonfuls chopped fresh watercress
8oz butter frozen in 1 piece

Method:

Lightly grease the outside of the shallow pudding basin or large saucer using the oil and place it, inverted, on the large round serving plate. Sprinkle the endive over the saucer. Arrange chicken slices around edge of the serving plate and the tongue in another, slightly smaller, circle. Make a circle with the chopped egg yolks and then arrange the herring around on top of this egg yolk. Place a quartered tomato between each herring. Make a circle with the egg whites and place the lemon and orange quarters alternately around. Sprinkle the beetroot, olives and gherkin around the edge of the endive. Make a final circle around the outer edge with the watercress. Place the plate in the refrigerator and chill for at least thirty minutes. Place the butter on a wooden board and, using a sharp knife, carve into a decorative shape such as a flower, fruit or bird. Remove the plate from the fridge and place the butter 'statue' in the centre of the endive. Serve at once.

CHAPTER FOURTEEN

Fishing – a Deeply Bred Way of Life

'No herring, no wedding' is a familiar saying among many fishing communities even today. In the last century the evidence is clear. In the year 1871 Fraserburgh had an excellent herring fishery and there were eighty per cent more weddings by the end of it than there had been the previous year. But over on the west coast, in Tarbert, Loch Fyne for instance, the herring catches were miserable and consequently the marriage registers show no weddings that year. Likewise for Lochgilphead: not one single marriage in 1871. What this suggests is that, in almost every aspect of the fisherman's life, the success of the year's fishery governed his well-being and was reflected throughout the community. A bountiful fishery not only swelled the marriage registers, but also the pockets of all the local businesses. In the words of Dick Evans of Moelfre, Anglesey, when the fishing was good in the 1930s, everyone in the village saw an increase in trade, from the butcher to the baker. 'Even the local tailor benefited, when the fishermen didn't think twice about buying a new suit for £5 to go courting', he told me. Furthermore the local pub did more trade before breakfast than throughout the rest of the day!

Fishing communities have attracted a massive amount of attention from writers and artists, especially in the nineteenth and twentieth centuries. Before that it was travellers, as we've already seen, who wrote down their accounts of fishing communities. In the nineteenth century the beginnings of a melancholic approach to fishing communities are apparent, although some artists did portray something of the realistic side of the job that was fishing. With the introduction of photographic techniques in the mid-part of that century, the stark reality of that life began to be conveyed upon an ignorant populace. Then, in the twentieth century, writers began to approach the subject from a nostalgic angle, some writers almost elegising the everyday reality of the job as it was.

Fishing communities have remained separate from the rest of society throughout these times. Before, they were very often as much physically apart as they were mentally. Indeed, there are instances when local councils voted to remove fishermen and their beach-based activities right to the very perimeter of a town so that their previous quarters could be developed at a time when tourism was at its roots as an economic boost to that town's fortunes. The rich were keen to rush to the seaside to gain the health benefits of seawater, and the town fathers were as keen to receive them. In other parts of the country, particularly on the east coast of Scotland, it was only those whose livelihoods depended upon the sea that would contemplate living right along its edge. Thus fishing villages grew up with only fishermen in their midst.

Fishermen tended also to only marry girls born into fishing families. I say 'girls' because the chance was that they were young when marrying. From a very early age, all members of a family were regarded as part of the machine that was fishing. Thus the children were expected to collect mussels to bait the long lines outside the herring season, or to assist with the mending of nets, or even their setting up. The womenfolk often as not hawked the catch around the locality, carrying big heavy baskets of fish upon their backs as they did. Sometimes they even carried their menfolk out into their open boats to ensure that they at least set sail dry, although they seldom stayed in this state for long. And not only that, but it was those members of the family on shore that had to bear endless hours worrying for the safe return of their loved ones and, on occasion, watch helplessly as they were drowned before their very eyes. Fishing was an altogether family affair; thus it isn't surprising that a young fisherman looked to his own to gain a bride when he reached a suitable age.

Fishing was also a way of life in that son followed father into the job. It produced a certain sense of belonging, and a tradition not to be broken. The only on-land equivalent is coal mining, in which generations followed each other down into the pits. In most cases there was, after all, no alternative. In Scotland, where landlords were often the beneficiaries of the fishermen's toils, the threat of expulsion from the croft forced many an offspring into a life on the sea. This remained the case until the late 1800s, when the Napier Commission advised on the revision of the law.

However, the inheritance of a life at the fishing remains even today. Many a fisherman I've spoken to speaks of no alternative but to go to sea. It is in the blood, they all iterate; yet sometimes you get the impression that there's an intense love-hate relationship with the job. The same can be said for many fishermen who have retired. Their letters are full of lamentations for a heartfelt way of life, of passing traditions and time-honoured skills. It seems to be only the land-based academics and writers that bemoan fishing as an ugly and painful profession. That it was dangerous the fishermen didn't need reminding.

So were fishermen filthy and their villages stinking and iniquitous? Were fishermen drunkards who were both immoral and decadent? The answer is probably no more than any other section of the community, although there was perhaps a tendency among them to drink more than others. Indeed, most fishing communities were God-fearing. Drinking was encouraged in instances such as where they were paid by the fish curers in whisky. Also, given that the job is the one with the highest death rate, it is hardly a surprise to find that fishermen drink when they reach solid ground. This is further compounded by the rich pickings that can be made when the herring season was in full swing. In today's world, it is drugs that the fishermen often turn to to offset the reality of being on shore. They live a life of extremes and this does not instantly cease the moment they hit dry land. When wages are high, they are spent. In 1971, for example, an Irish fisherman could easily earn £500 a week, which was a massive amount at that time. Imagine arriving back from sea and having that sort of money to burn!

Fishing is by its very nature a smelly operation. Herring, especially, go off very quickly and can putrefy in hours in hot conditions. Given the state of many of their villages in pre-twentieth-century Britain, when sanitation was not available to the 'likes of them', their tiny houses were clustered very close to each other and doubled up as both living quarters and the storeroom for their fishing gear; that a fishy smell was omnipresent is far from astonishing. Not only that, but their diet was one of fish, mostly herring in season, which doubtlessly added to the general whiff of fishiness.

The Church played a heavy part in their doctrines and it always had. It was the Druids who had first regarded the sea, and all that was in it, as sacred and thus nothing from it could be eaten. In more recent times, in most parts of Britain Sunday fishing was regarded as taboo. In the instances that fishermen persisted in fishing on the Sabbath and landing in areas where the ruling was upheld, such unease was caused that, on occasion, it led to rioting. Scotland was particularly steadfast in its opposition to Sunday fishing. In Dunbar and Stonehaven there was a belief that the herring had deserted purely because men had sailed to sea on a Sunday. On the other hand, the fishermen of Prestopans regarded a start to the week's fishing on that day to be lucky. In the Clyde, weekend fishing activity was common in the latter part of the nineteenth century when ring-net boats fished contrary to legislation passed in 1889, prohibiting fishing between sunrise on Saturday and an hour before sunset on Monday, thus also preventing daylight fishing at the beginning of the week. However, according to Angus Martin, skippers were fined either 10s or £1 for this offence, which was hardly a deterrent.

Weddings, always an important part of community living, often took place on a Friday so that bride and groom had two days to honeymoon before fishing recommenced. However, Peter Aitchison notes that, in Eyemouth, very often the wedding would be early in the morning so that they could catch the train to Edinburgh to enjoy a day out in the city before returning that evening to enable the groom to fish the very next day. Indeed, on the day of the Black Friday disaster in 1881, the minister, Stephen Bell, had performed two early morning weddings that week.

As well as generally observing the Sabbath, the Church had additional influences upon fishing communities. Fishing tithes had been a tradition for centuries whereby fishermen were required to hand over one tenth of their catch to the parish. The practice was brought to a head in Eyemouth when the fishermen, led by Willie Spears, refused to pay. Troops were brought in and an unsuccessful attempt made to arrest Spears who later surrendered and was imprisoned and subsequently fined. The tithe was eventually 'extinguished' by the payment of £2,000. However this episode, and the Church's involvement, led partially to the circumstances that resulted in so many deaths during that Black Friday. It is said that the herring deserted one part of the coast when a new minister had declared his intention to tithe the fishery.

What sets fishing apart from other forms of livelihood is their many customs and habits. Very often fishermen in all sorts of different locations held belief to similar manners and superstitions. Their clothing was often very individualistic and was worn in great diversity. The importance of warm and waterproof clothing was obvious, yet fishermen could more often than not be identified from their dress. Gansey sweaters were common, knitted by the man's wife, so that it was sometimes possible to identify a drowned fisher by the pattern upon his sweater. Thick trousers were worn from serge, flannel or even moleskin, and flannel underwear, waistcoats and hats in different styles. High leather boots, so often the reason for a drowning when falling overboard as rarely could a fisherman swim even without the weight of his boots, kept his feet relatively dry while his torso was wrapped in oilskins coated in oil and barked with the nets. Rubber boots superseded the heavy leather ones in the early twentieth century, and a bit later the yellow oilskin smocks appeared, still worn by many fishermen today, albeit in modern lightweight materials. Even ashore, fishermen wore suits and waistcoats, and wide-brimmed hats, especially on a Sunday when the finest clothes came out of the cupboards.

The nature of the herring fishing is that it affected communities in different ways. In parts of the country the herring was followed for almost the entire duration of a year, with boats circumnavigating Britain in their quest. This necessitated long periods away from home. However, in other parts of the country the herring season was short, sometimes even more of a by-product of the seasonal fishery. In Beer, for instance, in southern Devon, herring fishing didn't figure much of an importance in the fishermen's calendar. However, in 1911, some 300,000 herring were caught in one single late-winter's night. All along the English Channel, herring was never bountiful, yet on occasion, it was profitable. At the same time, the Lowestoft steam drifters might be found landing into Milford Haven. In Kintyre, the ring-net fishermen were most likely beginning their preparations for the start of the spring fishing in the Clyde.

Superstition has always played a major part in the lives of those going to sea. In the words of David Butcher, 'the subject would make a story for a book in itself'. In the seventeenth and eighteenth centuries, when fishermen were ever intent in avoiding the roaming press-gangs to force them into a life in the navy, superstitions were blamed when they were detected. Superstitions were blamed for poor catches, for successful catches, for wind, for death, indeed for almost anything deemed out of the ordinary. That superstition affected their attitudes throughout life is generally assumed to be a result of the occupation being both dangerous and of mixed fortunes, especially when fishing for herring. However, these didn't just affect their life at sea, they were prevalent throughout their time spent at home as well.

Various factors affected their journey from home to boat prior to leaving. Catherine Czerkawska, in *Fisherfolk of Carrick*, suggests that this period is 'a time of preparation for the state of being at sea, and many taboos belong to this transitional period'. Thus a fisherman never washed his hands on a day of sailing for fear of washing his life away. He should never turn and wave when leaving home as this is deemed to be waving his life away. On an occasion when an item is left behind at home, his wife never runs after him with that item. To do so would be for him to return home without setting sail. And while away, it was deemed unlucky for a wife or mother to wash a fisherman's clothing, again for fear of washing his life away.

Encounters with certain people *en route* to the boat sometimes resulted in the fisherman returning home. Old women, people with deformities or a minister were usually deemed instances when setting out to sea was unlucky. Cats running across the path of a fisherman on his way to the boat often meant poor fishing, although in Shetland a cat running before the man was lucky. Asking a fisherman where he was going was considered ill-mannered and unlucky. Lowestoft fishermen would shout 'Iron! Iron! Iron!' on seeing a nun and run to touch iron.

Certain words were never used on board and these included 'pig', 'rabbit', 'salmon' and 'rat'. Pigs were 'grumphies', 'curly tails' or 'doorkies', depending in what part of the country you were. Peter Anson goes as far as to suggest that pigs were the most feared and that the mere mention in writing is risky! Some refused to have bacon brought aboard. Churches were sometimes used as landmarks yet were referred to as 'bell-hooses', while, in Lapland, fishing in sight of a church was unlucky. Fishing using stolen fishing gear was deemed lucky in Sweden. In the Clyde, white stones in the ballast were instantly thrown over the side. In some parts, red and white stones were included in the ballast on purpose, bringing magical properties with them. Ballast removed from one boat into a new boat brought bad luck upon the new boat.

Superstitions affected the way boats were built. John MacAulay always whets a new keel with whisky and buries a threepenny piece in the transom of the boat. Often a coin is placed under a newly stepped mast. Some boatbuilders could foretell the luck of a new boat by the way a chip of wood came away as they commenced work on the hull. When putting to sea, the boat was always turned with the sun rather than against it. To do the latter would entail turning back to shore. Hatch boards were always stacked with their painted sides upwards, and were never turned. Whistling at sea was considered to be 'whistling up the wind'. Nets would never be taken aboard on a Friday, and always an odd number of drift-nets would be shot. When hauling in the herring, one particular herring – King Herrin' – was picked out for its quality and thrown overboard to bring luck in the future. How the old men chose this one fish seems unclear, whether for the colour, the freshness, or shape of the tail, but they knew it right enough and picked it out.

Sundays were not days for setting sail (except in Prestopans). Boats with cats aboard were deemed unlucky. In northern Germany it was considered that herring eaten on New Year's Day would bring luck throughout the next twelve months. In parts of the Moray Firth fishermen would fill up a flagon with seawater and collect a bit of seaweed and take these home. The seawater was sprinkled over the house and the seaweed hung up over the door and fireplace. Spitting in the hearth was lucky while taking a light from another man was not. Even today, taking a light from a candle is considered to be 'killing a seaman'. Taking third light is considered unlucky, but this superstition is said to have come from the First World War trenches – first light, notice: second, take aim: third, fire. The burning of fish bones and shells was also unlucky.

Many superstitions differed from coast to coast, as some of the above examples illustrate. Many, such as whistling up the wind, exist today in many different sectors within the maritime field, so that the crew of a many a yacht will hold the same belief. By-names – that habit of fishermen of calling each other by a nickname – originated from the superstition of not referring directly to people. Thus the owner of the *Perseverance* was Archie 'Try' Mathieson, his by-name obviously originating from the name of the boat.

Other superstitions have become lost with time, as have many traditions from the sea. One thing is certain though, and that is that many of these superstitions stem from early religious beliefs in which the Church and the community played equal parts in the fisherman's life. Today, many of the fishers' superstitions would seem eccentric as everyday rituals in thinking and actions are less relative to our twenty-first century lives.

Of course it is important to remember that a fisherman's life was not just one of being at sea. There were many harbourside tasks for him to undertake before he could consider sailing out. Nets had to be set up, that is having their ropes attached, along with floats at the top and lead weights along the bottom edge. Buoys were often home-made from pig or bullock bladders, and I have seen one in a museum made from a whale's bladder, according to the museum's curator. There is also evidence of dogs being specially bred for buoys in parts of the country in the nineteenth century, and probably earlier. Sometimes the dog was killed by having its head bashed in on rocks, although, on more than more occasion, they were killed by having their heads attached to the rope that was used to pull the boat up the beach, thus killing them instantly. However it was done, the important factor was to ensure the skin was not damaged. The animal was skinned and its head and feet cut off (if the mode of death hadn't done this already) and inflated with a wooden bung in the neck. The hair was removed and the skin soaked in oil and Archangel tar before being dried. Sheepskins were often treated in the same manner. Heavy hemp nets being superseded by cotton ones in the nineteenth century, nets needed barking to infuse liquid to preserve them after use in seawater. Unpreserved nets would not last long under these conditions. Bark was taken from any tree rich in tannin such as oak, although cutch began to be imported from the East in the early nineteenth century. This came from the bark of the acacia tree, which was heated up and then poured into wooden boxes, in which it was imported into Britain. To bark the net, though, it was immersed in the boiling solution of cutch, hauled out, left to drip over the tub, and then hung out on the net poles to dry thoroughly. The fishermen usually undertook this task in groups, thus assisting each other in what was otherwise an arduous task. Sails were tanned in a similar manner to afford them protection in the harsh conditions under which they worked. Once man-made fibres were introduced in the twentieth century, these practices wholly disappeared.

Fishermen's houses were once lowly single-storey affairs with one room, such as the ruins which can still be seen in places. In the nineteenth century an awareness of their cramped living conditions produced some building of two-storey houses specifically for their use. On the east coast of Fife, these usually had external steps leading to the upper floor where sometimes they lived, the basement being used as a store. In parts of the country, the fishermen were loath to move upstairs as they considered an earth floor to be much healthier than a solid one, and so they used the upper floor as the store. However it wasn't unusual for ten people to live in one room. When the police decided that external steps constituted a nuisance in the street, obstructing the thoroughfare of traffic and accumulating rubbish, dormer windows were added to the upper floor, through which the fishermen could haul their gear. In time these dormers were moved to the rear of the property, and often were the third floor up in the roof, with two floors below being given over to living accommodation. Thus evolved fishermen's housing in the later nineteenth and early twentieth centuries. Today, in many towns across Britain, the layouts of these planned villages are just as apparent as the day they were erected. And by their position and architecture, it is easy to see exactly why 'fisher toons' were independent and set apart from the rest of society because of the nature of the work of the inhabitants.

PART THREE
Curin' Herrin'
Salt And Smoke

The herring is a lucky fish,
of good health he is ensured.
For whenever he gets ill,
immediately he's cured.

Anon.

Baked Herring Fillets with Fennel and Coriander

Ingredients:
1lb herring fillets
1 small fennel bulb, thinly sliced
½ small red onion, sliced
2 tablespoonfuls olive oil
Salt & pepper
1 tablespoonful balsamic vinegar
1 tablespoonful fresh chopped coriander
Pinch brown sugar

Method:
Lay each fillet onto a large square of baking foil. Add the fennel, onion, oil, seasoning, vinegar, coriander and sugar. Fold the baking foil to make a parcel and place onto a baking tray. Place in a preheated oven (190°C/375°F/gas mark 5) and cook for fifteen to twenty minutes and serve with potato salad.

CHAPTER FIFTEEN

'Guarented Fine
Westcoast Herrings'

From the Revd Herbert Marsh's statement given to the Commissioners of the House of Commons reporting on the British Fisheries (see Appendix Two), it is clear that Britain was struggling to maintain a constant supply of good cured herring to market and that politicians were aware of the need to act quickly to capture the German market while the Dutch fleets were out of action in the aftermath of the wars. However, twenty-five years before he gave evidence, the merchants of the north-west of Scotland were one step ahead of Parliament and striving to produce good-quality cured herring.

Roderick Morison of Stornoway – described as a sober man – and John Mackenzie of London formed a partnership in 1783 and founded a herring curing station on the island of Tanera Mor, the largest of the Summer Isles some miles to the north of Loch Broom. Here they built a series of terraced houses and five smokehouses within a courtyard, and a pier between the two settlements on the island. These were Ardnagoine and Garadheancal, the latter translating to 'cabbage patch'. This new settlement became known as Tigh-on-Quay, and was visited in about 1820 by William Daniell during his circumnavigation of Britain. He noted two ranges of buildings, 'furnished with conveniences for curing and smoking herring, and for salting grey fish'. Some 200 boats were seen in the bay during the height of the herring season, each boat – or buss – having two attendant boats that set nets in every cove of the island. The herring, it is said, was exported to the West Indies via merchants in London.

Mr Nicolson was the agent of the owner of the island at the time of Daniell's visit. This owner, Macdonald of Skye, had purchased the island from the original Morison/Mackenzie soon after Morison died in 1791.

Morison had been the manager and had overseen a lucrative fishing –
and profit for the company – with much of the herring going to Leith
and Greenock. Daniell noted that the lady of the manor was Mrs Hay
Mackenzie, who 'furnished the inhabitants with the means for carrying
on the fishery, awarded premiums to the most active, and thus conferred
on them a service which redounded to her own interests'. Whether
there is any connection between these two Mackenzies is unclear.

The idea of incentives to induce the locals to catch herring was
nothing new. Madame Prunier was certainly not the first to encourage the fishermen. In her case she was not motivated by the sense of
profit as the curers were in these out-of-the-way places. With bounties
being paid on the amount of herring landed at this time, there was an
obvious advantage to all, although the curers usually gained most
while the inhabitants merely covered their rent.

John McCulloch was renowned as one of Scotland's most observant
travellers in the early nineteenth century. He, too, called in at Tanera Mor
and noted the 'extensive establishment, provided with a range of smoking houses'. However, according to him, the herring had deserted and
the curing facilities were by then useless. Yet Daniell, a few years later,
appears to have found a fishery thriving. Evidence from Ullapool con-
firms that the herring catches declined substantially soon after the building of the settlement there in 1788, although presumably the herring
didn't desert in its entirety. Evidence in the 1840s supports the theory
that the fishing was intermittent but thriving at times. Thus Tanera Mor
was probably still active in its curing whereas the other nearby facilities
had ceased.

Isle Martin, lying at the entrance to Loch Broom, with a population
of some 100 people at the time, had curing facilities that had been
built by John Woodhouse, a merchant from Liverpool, in 1774, almost
ten years before Tanera Mor. Woodhouse had worked in the Isle of
Man, developing markets in the Mediterranean for Manx herring,
before turning his attention north. He built a huge smokehouse that
was said to have been able to smoke 1,000 barrels of herring at any
one time. They were salted for thirty hours, split through the mouth
and smoked for between two and three weeks. Spanish ships came
here to pick up herring to carry home, the Mediterranean being a
major market. Similarly, it has been said that Norwegian vessels came
to Tanera Mor, presumably prior to supplying the West Indian mar-

1 Dutch bomschuit off Scheveningen, *by Hendrik Willem Mesdag (1831–1915).*

2 *Fishermen's huts at Loch Hourn in 2002.*

3 Above: Fishing the
Weir, Swansea, *by*
Edward Duncan
(1803–1882).

4 Right: *Remains of a*
fish weir at Loch Torridon
in 2002.

5 Opposite: The Return
of the Fishing Fleet *by*
Hendrik Willem Mesdag
(1831–1915).

6 *Landing herring at Pointlaw, Aberdeen, 1902.* (Campbell McCutcheon)

7 *The* Excellent *as she is today.* (Billy Stevenson)

8 *The net surfaces during the hauling in of the pair-trawl operation.* (David Linkie)

9 *The* Convellaria *photographed from the* Daystar.

The Pier, Ullapool

10 *Ullapool's harbour, with fish being unloaded.* (Campbell McCutcheon)

11 *The herring curing station and pier at Tanera Mor in 2002.*

12 *Fishwives on the shore, Cockenzie, East Lothian, c.1900.* (Campbell McCutcheon)

13 *The author taking bloaters out of his smokehouse at the Portsoy Festival in 2001.* (Bodies of Banff)

14 Overleaf: *Dutch Herring Girl from a poster for Matjes herring.*

Hollandse *Nieuwe*

kets. However the enterprise at Isle Martin survived only until 1813, when it closed after successive years of falling catches.

To the north of Tanera Mor, Isle Ristol had herring curing facilities at one time, primarily to cure cod, but later herring. The nearby harbour of Old Dornie, perfectly sheltered, suited small vessels as, indeed, it still does today. These facilities, like the ones up and down the west coast, are invariably referred to as 'herring stations', a term that appears to give them an air of grandeur, yet, in the most, they consisted of nothing more than accommodation for the workers, a place to store salt and sometimes a smokehouse.

Today their remains are scant, although the Tanera Mor site is the most intact. Inside the courtyard, surrounded with a stone wall with entrances either end, is one row of housing, with the foreman's house – the largest – at the end closest to the pier. Sir Frank Fraser Darling had repaired this pier when he farmed the island between 1939 and 1944. His book, *Island Years*, tells the story of his experiences. Judging by his evidence, and the holes in the walls that once received joists, there was a similar row of buildings along the west side of the court-yard, although these have long gone. Fraser Darling tells us that these were the two-storey factories where, presumably, the herring was bar-relled. There were five arches in the inside wall so that its ground floor was open to the courtyard. This inner wall collapsed in the 1860s, the same evening that a child was born in one of the cottages opposite. These cottages were once three storeys high, the top storey having been dismantled by Fraser Darling when the roof was removed, it being in a dangerous state of repair. To the north of the buildings was a walled garden where Daniell noted an abundance of food. Apricots were supposedly grown against a south-facing wall, such is the effect of the Gulf Stream upon these western coasts.

The west coast of Scotland had numerous such curing stations around this time. Thomas Newte, in his *Prospects and Observations on a Tour in England and Scotland* (1791), describes one in Loch Torridon. In 1788, Mr Mackenzie of Firdon (a cousin to Mackenzie of Tanera Mor) erected 'a stage and wharf of 80ft long by 20ft broad, projecting about 18ft over a solid rock, which rises about 7ft above the high water mark' at Aird Mhor in 1788, on the south side of the loch. Any vessel drawing less than 14ft was able to come alongside and unload its catch, which was then cured, the salt being housed in a shed that had a slate roof.

Curer and cooper worked side by side, and white fish, such as cod and ling, were also gutted and salted on the site. Nearby was a granary where oatmeal, barley and peas were produced. The buildings were mostly of stone or timber and the facilities seem to have been extensively used, however, as Newte, in his own words, tells us that he relied upon the words of others and never actually went to the site, it is possible that he exaggerated the importance of the place. The remains of the stone wall perched on the rock above the south harbour, as he described it, are still very much apparent, although the distance from the top of the rock to the high water exceeded 7ft. However it was easy, visiting the site on a summer's day in 2002, to imagine small vessels coming alongside, discharging their catch, while bigger vessels presumably berthed to carry away the fish. Five vessels of the 20–40 ton range, according to John McQueen, were employed in the herring fishery in the closing decades of the eighteenth century, and Mackenzie himself, it seems, owned one of these vessels. Herring was fetching between 11s and 15s a barrel, although, when repacked for export, four barrels of herring went to make up only three. This, then, infers that the quality of herring for the home market was poorer than that for export and that there was an awareness that exported herring should be properly repacked.

Am Ploc, a spit of land at the eastern end of upper Loch Torridon, is said to have been the site for another herring curing station at about that time, upon which a house has now been built. The remains of three fish traps can be seen on the foreshore nearby, but these, according to local legend, were never effective at catching herring and any herring that did end up in the pool at low water were usually of a very poor quality. Another one was situated at Ardheslaig (Hazel Bay), on the southern end of the outer loch, again in the late eighteenth century, where herring cost 6d a barrel more to cure. Indeed, in the 1840s, some 200 tons of herring was landed in Loch Torridon in any one day during the season. Herring, it has been said, was sent from here to the Baltic, and the ships returned with barrels of vodka as ballast. Nearby is Sheildaig, a place name that supposedly translates from the Norse into 'Herring Bay', but there is no herring here, and another, contemporary suggestion is that the name literally means 'Bay with islands' which might seem more correct given that there's no history of herring being landed here. On the north side of the loch, Diabaig (Deep Bay) has had an association with fishing stretching back generations.

Nearby Alligin had some forty crofts when the herring fishery was at its height and one fish curer was kept busy. Here three generations of the Macdonald family built their boats up to the mid-twentieth century, their boatbuilding shed now selling fresh produce from the village. The last practising member of the family, Murdo, went out to Papua New Guinea to teach boatbuilding skills to the natives, before returning and retiring, such was the reputation for their craft. Several of their double-ended clinker-built skiffs still sail around the coasts in these parts and they were renowned builders of small slightly-built herring boats of about 15ft in the 1930s. One of their biggest boats, the *Queen Mary* UL138, can still be seen in her permanent concrete berth at the Gairloch Heritage Museum. This vessel, along with its sister boats the *Isabella* and *Lady Marjorie*, were built around 1910 for the cod fishing – Gairloch being renowned for its good quality of cod – although they did follow the herring at times. They were modelled on the Lochfyne skiff and the *Queen Mary* cost £62 to build. She was built for another Mackenzie – this time John – a fisherman from Badachro, Gairloch.

Badachro is a sheltered bay on the south side of the loch, once owned by Sir Hector Mackenzie in the late eighteenth century. Today there are the remains of three, possibly even four, herring curing stations in this small community. The earliest appears to have been the first building erected there. However, nearby are three others. One sits by the pier, close to the pub that, according to the locals, has been there for generations. This building housed a manager at its seaward end and, presumably, the rest of the stone building was a store for salt. Herring was undoubtedly cured outside and shipped out from the pier. On nearby Dry Island, an island that is connected to the mainland at low water, the herring curing station was established in 1884 and staffed by workers from Stornoway under the management of John Mackenzie, and today the small pier is home to a creel-fishing business. Between the island and Aird are the remains of a fish weir.

Across from here is Isle Horrisdale, the main populated area at the end of the eighteenth century. Indeed the schoolhouse, still remaining, was the original place of learning for all the inhabitants and closed when Badachro got its own school. Two settlements once existed on the island, the remaining one in the centre of the island and the only signs of the other being a few foundation stones among the grass at the southern end. The curing station is directly opposite Dry Island, and consisted

of a smokehouse and store alongside the natural harbour. The buildings have long since been turned into stores and workshops, but the
chimney of the smoker still exists. On one edge of the flat area where
the herring was packed into barrels sits a barking tub where the nets
were once dipped, although it is believed that was built originally to boil
cod livers to extract the oil. The cod fishery was the principal fishery of
Gairloch, and this curing station appears to have been originally built to
dry cod. One report suggests that the Dry Island curing facility was also
originally built for the cod fishery, hence the island's name. What is
known is that this fishery was encouraged by Sir Hector who, it is said,
gave the fishermen an annual bounty of 20 guineas and supplied them
with timber for their boats and in return received ¼d per cod landed.
He also ensured the fishermen were paid by the curer, and often made
up the difference and ended up being out of pocket. Thus some 20,000
cod were exported to Ireland, Liverpool, London and Spain at the
beginning of the nineteenth century, an amount which doubled to
40,000 over that century, with 1884 being a record one-off year with a
catch of 80,000 cod.

On a recent visit to view the remains on Isle Horrisdale, we were
kindly invited into the nearby house by Kate Wilson, whose family
has owned the house since the 1940s. In the kitchen I found, hanging
on the whitewashed wall, a branding stencil clearly denoting the
herring from these parts. 'GUARENTED FINE WESTCOAST
HERRINGS' was its label and thus any barrel so marked could be
instantly identified by the spelling mistake.

Having travelled to all these aforementioned herring stations –
except Isle Ristol – in the space of several days, one story soon became
familiar. This refers to black soil being 'discovered' alongside each site.
The story I heard, and indeed read, was one of Irish barrels being
brought to these places loaded with Irish black peaty soil for ballast in
the ships. This was then emptied prior to being filled with salted herring, or so I was told. However, this seems both illogical and contradic-
tory to the fact that much of the herring was exported to the West
Indies, Spain, Norway and, closer to home, sold to Leith and Greenock.
Herring, for sure, was exported to Ireland from Scotland, but the
majority of this seems to have been after the abolition of slavery in 1833
when new markets were being sought and in the 1840s during the
potato famine. Logic also suggests that the crew of a boat would not
heave a barrel full of earth along a pier and up to the curing area, but
would more likely throw the contents over the side of the vessel into
the sea. Furthermore, as most of the curing stations had their own
cooper, it seems unlikely that more than the odd ship would arrive
from Ireland with its own barrels. This would also necessitate the vessel
hanging around while its barrels were filled rather than loading up with
what is already there for export. But, nevertheless, what is certain is that
there are large quantities of this black soil around these curing places.

The answer, it would seem, lies in one of several avenues. Firstly the
curing process produces a lot of spilt brine which would naturally
flow around the site and be soaked up by the surrounding terrain.
Secondly, with a smokehouse operating, a great deal of ash from the
smoker would have to be removed and, presumably, be dumped upon
the earth. Separately, or perhaps together, these would nourish the soil
which, in time, blackened and became the rich fertile black soil so
prolific alongside these sites. I'm not a geologist, nor a horticulturist,
but the idea of tons upon tons of Irish peat being deposited outside
these curing stations, which in time would form mounds if brought in
any quantity, just somehow does not seem possible. Fraser Darling
suggests that some of the peat was brought in as ballast but not in
barrels. He also notes that the nets, heavy with sea slime, were hung to
dry alongside the buildings and the dried slime was rich in phosphates
and lime, and thus acted as a dressing for the soil. What is intriguing,
though, is how in Ullapool and Badachro, about Loch Torridon and at
Loch Hourn, I heard the same story. Maybe there is some truth in it.

The Shetland Isles are renowned for their herring fishery at Lerwick but both Shetland and Orkney developed herring ports in the outlying islands in the nineteenth century. Stronsay and Burray were bustling with activity at one time or other and in Unst, Britain's most northerly island, a huge industry grew up briefly around Baltasound, where there were fifty-two curing houses during the peak of the trade 1900-10. Some 600 boats landed here with markets in Germany and other continental European countries being supplied. In 1905 it is said that almost a quarter of a million cran of herring was landed. This is a massive amount comparable to that of East Anglia. However, as elsewhere, signs of it are all gone, except for the odd decrepit stone quay.

Loch Hourn was another inaccessible part of the west coast where the herring fishery once thrived. In the eighteenth century, fishermen's houses were built along the top of the foreshore at Arnisdale to establish a fishery. Loch Hourn herring was already renowned for its superb quality. In 1793 some 30,000 barrels were being caught every year and had been for several years. Yet, as elsewhere along the west coast, it was the Salt Laws that were preventing development of the fisheries. The fishermen were happy enough just to land a barrel or two to see their family through the long dark winter months. In 1803 there were between sixty and seventy boats working inside the loch, yet twenty years or so later there were over 1,000.

Thomas Telford's surveyors arrived at the latter end of the eighteenth century to view the possibility of building a harbour and on-shore facilities. John Knox was, at the time, advocating the building of forty such towns of sixteen big houses and twenty smaller ones, all around the coast from Campbeltown to Loch Dornoch (the Dornoch Firth). Several locations were suggested at the time, with Arnisdale the favoured site, but Mallaig, at the entrance to Loch Nevis which, too, was prolific in herring, was ultimately chosen, although not, it should be added, by the British Fisheries Society.

Daniell visited Loch Hourn and noted 300 vessels. A great shoal of herring swam up-loch and was stranded at the head. Seemingly, according to Daniell, the locals were unconcerned by this sudden bonanza and an amount equivalent to 6,000 barrels of herring was left to putrefy, the smell of which he found 'intolerably potent'.

Loch Hourn's herring fishery seems to have maintained a presence throughout the nineteenth century. In 1882 some 90,000 crans were harvested which, amazingly, accounted for about two per cent of the total British landings. The herring was smaller, fatter and sweeter in taste, in comparison with much of the west coast herring. Some, it is believed, spawned within the confines of the loch, which could account for its smallness if juvenile fish was being captured. Sgadan Beag Loch Hourn was well known outside the loch, with the Barra fishermen being one group of many who resorted to fishing there in the eighteenth century, and before. By the nineteenth century fishermen from all over Scotland were there. But, as John McCulloch wrote while visiting Tanera Mor, England and Scotland were 'herring mad, and avarice was more in mind than forethought, money more than wit'. The herring fishery was fast becoming unsustainable, although few recognised the fact.

When we consider all these areas where fishing was undertaken, the one thing that springs to mind is the inaccessibility of the curing stations. However, two centuries ago Scotland was a very different coast, in terms of access. Roads were, in most cases, paths weaving in and out of mountain passes while the sea was the best means of getting about. Today many wonder why herring stations were set up in places such as Tanera Mor, or Loch Torridon, or Loch Hourn, for instance, yet the answer is very simple. They were in the proximity of the herring shoals. The islands were populated then, unlike now when folk need access to the demands of modern living. They were flourishing communities in those days, and the herring gave work to these communities. The fish arrived by sea, was barrelled or smoked, and left by sea, so in reality it did not matter about being close to an internal network of roads. All that was needed was a suitable anchorage and pier, labour and a merchant to fund the project. Scotland's coastal communities everywhere have evolved in this manner. In the case of Tanera Mor, there was a superb anchorage capable of holding ships up to 2,000 tons, and twenty-one families residing on the island. Whether it be the tiny fishing settlements of the south-eastern shores of Harris, or the cliff-hanging villages of the Moray Firth, all have one thing in common: they were built with purpose in mind – they were ideal for the curing of the silver darlings.

Baked Buttered Bloaters

Ingredients:
4 bloaters
2oz butter
2 tablespoonfuls lemon juice
Salt & pepper
4 slices buttered toast

Method:
Cut off the heads, tails and fins and fillet the bloaters. Put in a greased ovenproof dish, dot with butter, pour over the lemon juice and season with salt & pepper. Cover and bake for ten minutes at 350°F, gas mark 4, and serve on the buttered toast.

CHAPTER SIXTEEN

The Fisher Lassies

an Unheard-of Phenomenon

In 1861 there were 42,571 fishermen and boys engaged in the herring fishery in Scotland and that part of England over which the Scottish Fishery Board had jurisdiction. Something like 900 million herring were caught that year and much of this fish was landed into Wick, on the north-eastern extremity of the country. The following year some 50 million herring were gutted by 3,500 herring lassies over a two-day period and more than 800,000 barrels of herring were cured in total that year. By far the majority of this was cured by the Scottish method – the Scotch Cure, as it was known.

We have already seen how the Dutch improved the curing in the fourteenth century and how the Scots had been curing herring possibly even earlier than that. However, as we have also seen, it was realised back in the eighteenth century that a constant and well-cured herring was what was needed to develop and maintain healthy overseas markets.

The Society of Arts offered a prize to anyone who was best able to duplicate, even improve upon, the Dutch method. In 1819 this was eventually won by J.F. Donovan from Leith, who had employed six Dutch curers on the west coast of Scotland. He was given 50 guineas for his troubles. Although employing Dutch curers might sound like cheating, his quality product was later adopted as the standard for the Scottish Exported Herring by the Fishery Board and Crown Brands were given to each barrel. Strict rules were laid down so that the herring had to be gutted as soon as possible after landing and certainly within twenty-four hours, and packed into barrels between layers of salt.

As the herring fisheries expanded in the last three decades of the nineteenth century, it became common for this gutting and packing to be undertaken by female employees who, as we've seen, were accustomed to working with fish. Thus commenced the tradition of women and girls from all over Scotland leaving their districts and following the menfolk around the coasts after the herring shoals as they swam southwards to their spawning grounds in the southern North Sea. It therefore was not unusual for them to begin the season in Shetland in June, work their way down the Scottish coast in the summer and arrive in Lowestoft or Great Yarmouth for the autumnal herring. Others worked in the Outer Hebrides and down the west coast of Scotland, thence over to the Isle of Man and later back over to East Anglia. Whatever route they chose, the East Anglian autumnal fishery was almost a must, such was the frenzied activity there and the rewards available to those keen to earn them. Once the fishing was over, the women returned to their Highland homes, spending the winter repairing nets and preparing for the following season. Some took a boat over to Ireland and worked in ports such as Ardglass for several weeks.

The annual migration of this female workforce lasted for almost a century and is unique in British history on such a scale. At its peak in 1913, some 6,000 women were on the move, mostly from the Highlands, although groups travelled over from the east coast of Ireland to join and a smattering came from England. In that year these women gutted 854 million herring in just fourteen weeks.

It is worth studying these impressively sounding statistics that sometimes all too easily get banded about. It has been said that a herring lass – as the women and girls were called – could gut a herring in one second, in other words sixty a minute. They worked in groups of three – two gutting from the trough of herring called the farlane (sometimes the farlin), and one packing the fish carefully into the barrels. They were generally paid by the hour, with bonuses for the number of barrels filled. Thus they seldom dawdled about. Ten hours a day of work was not unusual, and often they worked up to fifteen hours. It is not difficult to calculate, then, that one group could theoretically gut and barrel 72,000 herring a day, which would mean over seventy-five barrels. Each barrel held a cran of fish, being between 700 and 1,000 herring, depending on their size and fullness. However, seventy-five barrels per group is unmaintainable, although David Butcher reports that 288 barrels were gutted and packed in four days by one group working twelve hours a day. This works out at an incredible 3,000 an hour. However, Annie Watts, his informant, does note that the fishing was 'big' and she had a 'good crew'.

Take, on the other hand, the above statistics. Assuming they worked six days a week – Sundays were for church and singing – it follows on that 6,000 lassies – i.e. 4,000 actually gutting – gutted just over 10 million a day which works out at 254 herring an hour. Likewise, 3,500 women gutting 50 million in two days works out at a rate of nearly 1,100 an hour for a ten-hour day (750 for a fifteen-hour day), still a far cry from the theoretical 3,600 an hour. Thirty-seven barrels in one day, assuming a fifteen-hour day, calculates to between about 900 and 1,200 fish an hour, depending on the number it took to fill those barrels. What these statistics forget, though, is that some were gutted for kippering, which took longer, there was time spent awaiting fresh supplies and rest breaks had to be taken.

Far from belittling their work, I simply suggest that meaningless figures can be misleading. These women have been quite rightfully described as 'vivacious, hardworking and tough, and one of the finest type of women in the world'. They worked long hours, often outdoors in extreme conditions, and were never very well paid. Working from the long farlanes where the herring was tipped by labourers and mixed with copious amounts of salt, their hands suffered from cuts and salt wounds so that most, in an attempt to prevent these, wrapped their fingers in bandages of unbleached linen – called cloots – tied on with rags. Salt sores were common and would fester if left, so the Red Cross First Aid stations were visited. The lassies wore aprons that offered some protection from the blood, guts and fish scales that splattered them from head to foot. Headscarves, short boots and warm clothing were the normal mode of dress, although their sleeves would be rolled up when the sun was out.

As the girls gutted, the herring was thrown into one of five tubs according to their size. Once full, they were then packed into barrels with the herring laid dark side up at the bottom layer, and alternatively afterwards, each layer being roused in salt, until the top layer with the silver belly up. The barrel was sealed and left for several days before being opened and the brine poured off. By this time the herring would have shrunk as its moisture was removed, and the barrel was topped up with herring from another cured barrel, before being resealed and brine added through a bunghole. It was then branded under the eye of the Fishery Officer using a brass stencil, and Scottish Crown brands soon became recognised throughout Europe as a guarantee of quality. The stencil consisted of a crown, the word 'Scotland', the initials of the Fishery Officer, the year of packing and the type of herring in the barrel. These were:

La. Full: herring over 11 ¼ ins full with milt or roe
Full: over 10 ¼ ins and full with milt or roe
Filling: over 10 ¼ ins, maturing herring with long gut removed
Mat. Full: over 9 ¼ ins and full with milt or roe
Medium: over 9 ¼ ins, maturing with the long gut removed
Mattie: over 9ins, maturing with the long gut removed
La. Spent: spent fish over 10ins.

Maturing fish were those that were filling with milt or roe, while spent fish are those that have spawned, at which time their oil content reduces a mere three per cent. For the women, though, this ability to judge within which category a fish fits was second nature. With a deft movement of the knife, the herring's throat was pierced and the gills and intestines removed through the slit. These were thrown into another barrel. The fish was tossed without much conscious thought into the correct barrel. A later addition to the branding legislation was to add the letters G.B.K. for herring gutted by knife. When gutted by finger, G.B.F. was stencilled instead. U was ungutted.

It wasn't uncommon for a girl to start at the farlanes at the age of fifteen and many continued to the ripe old age of over sixty. The lifestyle was nomadic, to begin with at least, for often a herring lass found her match in a man connected with the trade – a fisherman, labourer, even a cooper – and settled down into married life, although the herring season was hardly ever shunned.

Grace Stewart was nineteen when she was photographed filling a herring barrel with brine at Lowestoft in 1904. She was born in Buckie and started gutting at an early age, and the photograph shows her as a strikingly beautiful girl, dark and mysterious, wearing an oilskin apron as she pours the thick liquid to top up a barrel. She married shortly after the picture was taken, and bore two sons and a daughter. A few years ago I met her granddaughter by chance at a maritime

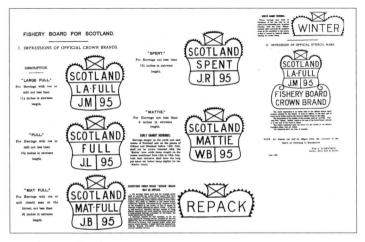

Scottish Crown brands

festival, where the image was on display in my 'Herring Exhibition'. This lady, in her sixties herself, was almost tearful as she noticed the picture and told me what she remembered about this lovely girl. In about 1920, she told me, Gracie earned ½d an hour and collected another 10s at the end of the season. Whether this is accurate is unclear, but contemporary evidence suggests a weekly wage of between 8s and 17s/6d and an extra sum for each barrel filled plus an hourly rate of 3d for topping up the barrels. Before 1914 the barrelage rate was about 18d, but fell to 10d afterwards. An average take-home pay was in the region of 10s before 1914, which had increased to 20s ten years later. In addition to this, they were paid an engagement fee by the curer they were working for, often called 'arles', at the beginning of the season. It fell to the lassie in the group responsible for packing the barrels to negotiate with the curer over wages and engagement terms.

To transport their female workforce about the country, the curers chartered trains. Each women or girl packed her clothing in her 'kist', or trunk, and these were loaded onto the trains as well. George Davidson, who in the early 1930s worked for A. Bruce & Co., fish curers of Fraserburgh, recalled that the kists went down to Yarmouth on the back of the company's Austin lorry at 40mph, while the gutting crews went by train.

So the railways assisted in the expansion of the herring trade not only through the ability to move fish quickly and cheaply around the country, but also in transporting the workers from port to port. On some occasions, the fishing boats themselves were loaded onto trains and carried about the country.

The herring lassie phenomenon has perhaps attracted more nostalgia than any other aspect of the herring fishing trade, more so than the boats and fishermen themselves. The idea of roving hordes of what were on one occasion described as 'buxom' women, coming from the coastal and highland regions of Scotland, was unheard of at the time, and the air of pride with which they undertook their arduous task has not failed to impress historians and writers alike. Often it is said how they would sing while at work, and when they were not working, they clustered in groups and the only sound heard was the rattle of knitting needles accompanied by the occasional laughter. That they were an unusual band of folk is accounted for by the fact that they invariably came from fishing communities which, as we've seen, were already set apart from the rest of society. Yet they were generally a lively bunch, dancing often while singing when not working. Annie Watts tells us how they would sing and dance while travelling down from Scotland by train.

The annual report of the Chief Inspector of Factories and Workshops of 1901 was severely critical of the working conditions of the herring lassies. Miss Adelaid Anderson reported that 3,000 women in Fraserburgh the previous year were housed in unfurnished sheds where barrels are stored during the winter. They would, according to her, 'bring everything – bedding, cooking utensils, and any furniture they need. In this room they eat, sleep, entertain their friends, and perform their domestic duties, with what I can only consider marvellous harmony.' In Yarmouth they worked on unpaved, undrained, uncovered plots of ground where the soil was awash with decaying fish.

Not surprisingly, then, strikes were common. When the rates of pay shrank after the First World War, the women downed their knives until the curers re-established reasonable rates. Rest rooms, canteens and first aid stations, as well as maximum working hours, were negotiated between the curers and the factory inspectorate after the war. Rest rooms were for use when work was slack and canteens ensured meals could be taken within the time allowed. First aid points about the curing yard provided cures for splinters from barrels and salt sores. In 1931 they went on strike again to insist on a minimum weekly wage and, in Yarmouth, agreed to 15s. Five years later 4,000 lassies, led by Maria Gott of Rosehearty, went on strike to regain a shilling for each barrel packed after the rate had been reduced to 10d two years before. They timed the strike to coincide with the busiest time of the season, stopping work for three days before their demands were met.

Saturday nights were for dancing or going to the pictures, and work was finished early to prepare. Sundays were reserved for religious observance and Sunday schools, and a visit to the Fishermen's Mission at four o'clock to listen to the weekly fishermen's singing. Their best dresses, carefully kept for the occasion in the kist, were brought out while their working clothes were hung out to dry after a morning's washing. Most girls after about 1910 lived in lodgings for which they paid up to 3s 6d a week before the First World War. Their landladies cooked their food in addition to this, although the girls had to supply the ingredients. It was not uncommon for three girls to share one bed. Tradition has it that they were often woken up at five o'clock in the morning with a bang on their door and the cry 'Get up and tie your fingers'. Such was the constant smell of fish about the girls that most landladies removed the carpets before the start of the season, replacing these with straw mats which could be thrown out at the season's finish, complete with the fish scales that were ever present. Things must have improved over the first decades of the twentieth century, albeit slowly, and not to perfection by any means.

For almost 100 years this tradition was handed down from mother to daughter to 'go to the herring', much in the same way as son followed father to sea. Possibly six generations of any one family survived the custom. Ever since the Scottish fishermen began the annual migration to East Anglia in the 1860s, the women also followed the fleets. In the 1950s the lassies worked for several seasons in Holyhead, which temporarily became a popular landing harbour for Irish Sea herring. Pickled herring – *pinog picl* in Welsh – became a household name in the principality while *penwaig Nefyn* (Nefyn herring) and *sgadan Aberporth* (Aberporth herring) were regional forms also well remembered about the Welsh towns and villages. Again, although the bulk of the catch was often hawked about the countryside fresh, small bands of gutting girls worked these rural areas. Mallaig, connected to the rail network in 1901, was said to have had thirteen smokehouses and accommodation for 1,000 girls in Chinatown, an area around the harbour. The season here was at its height around Christmas time, according to Fishery Board reports, so that many Highland lassies were able to prolong their working season not, relatively speaking, far from home.

By the 1960s, though, the phenomenon was almost at its end. In the 1930s there were some 2,000 migrants still at work, but, with a decline in the fortunes of the herring fishing after the Second World War, these numbers fell dramatically. By 1962 there were, according to one report, only a handful of girls – less than a dozen – still at it and by the mid-sixties it was all but over. By 1968 there were none.

The coopers had a fair amount of influence over the work of the herring lassies. It was they who sealed the barrels and, later, drilled the bunghole and re-opened them ten days later for re-packing. A leaky barrel might have to be re-packed, which would result in time-wasting for that team of lassies. The head cooper was also responsible for the quality of fish and checking that the sizing in each barrel was correct. In essence, the reputation of the whole company was his responsibility. Poor cured herring reaching its destination could be returned, and curers were known to go out of business in mid-season. In that case the herring lassies would have had to return north with no wages. Their fortunes were indeed as fickle as those of the fishermen: that was the nature of the herring fishery. As an example, Scottish coopers made 2,094,014 barrels and 422,080 half barrels in 1906.

Barrels consisted of 262-3 Imperial gallons, a measure set by legislation going back to George III. Legislation also governed the wood it was manufactured from (normally spruce), the maximum width of the staves and the number of hoops holding them together. Fishery Officers would pick at random barrels they wished to inspect by marking them with chalk, and these were opened by the coopers and the herring removed. The Fishery Board laid down that four out of 100 barrels should be thus inspected. This insistence, though, led in time to Scottish herring, and the Crown brand, being renowned throughout the world in time, although the majority of exports of cured herring, as against smoked, were to European customers. Britain had at last been successful 100 years after Herbert Marsh was advocating such an approach. However the Russian and German markets were destroyed by international politics, and the market for barrelled herring was in a decisive and permanent decline. So too were the livelihoods of the hardworking herring lassies, a phenomenon never to be experienced again in British society.

Kipper Fish Cakes

Ingredients:
1lb kippers
1lb potatoes, scrubbed
1 hard-boiled egg, chopped
2 teaspoonfuls English mustard
2 teaspoonfuls grated onion
2 tablespoonfuls chopped parsley
1-2 tablespoonfuls cream
A little nutmeg and cayenne pepper
Some butter and oil for frying
Watercress and lemon quarters for the garnish

Method:
Peel the potatoes and boil until tender, then drain off the liquid. Place in a bowl with the egg, mustard, onion, parsley and cream. Jug the kippers, flake off the flesh and add to the bowl. Beat to mix the ingredients thoroughly and season with the nutmeg and cayenne pepper. Form cakes by pressing the mixture by hand. Heat some butter and oil in a thick frying pan and cook the cakes for about five minutes each side until they are a golden colour. Garnish with the watercress and lemon quarters and a touch of cayenne pepper.

CHAPTER SEVENTEEN

Smoking the Herring

(and fresh, canned and iced herring)

There is a saying 'Herring and bread, go the bells of Minehead'. The people of this town also tell us that the prominent church of St Michael always had a light on in the tower to guide the fishing boats home.

Minehead, on the Somerset coast, is today a popular holidaying centre with its Butlin's camp close to the shore. Out on the beach, below the high-water mark, lie the remains of several fish weirs that were once abundant in herring. Today, though, the drying harbour is a shadow of its former self, when trading vessels crammed its quays. In the seventeenth and eighteenth centuries this quay was crowded with smoking houses producing red herring and kippers for the local trade. At the height of the fishing season, in late autumn, some 4,000 barrels of herring were cured and exported from this, one of the smallest of British fishing ports and one never associated with herring fishing. Compare this with the 20,000 barrels being cured on Loch Fyne at that time, and we see it was a fishery of substance. The smoking of herring was here, as in dozens of other small ports around the coast, a normal occurrence. Nearby Barnstaple had its herring salting and smoking houses on the Strand, where herring sold at sixty for a shilling at the end of the nineteenth century. Across the Bristol Channel, Carmarthen was said to have had a good trade in herring where pickled herring could be bought directly from a ship in any quantity from a couple to a barrel. And Bideford Bay – as we have already discovered in Clovelly – was particularly noted for its tasty herring.

It is impossible to say when man first learnt the benefits of smoking fish and meat to act as a preservative. Archaeological evidence suggests it has been done for thousands of years, often by simply hanging food up over a fire. The actual building of special structures – smokehouses – to preserve edible goods probably only dates back a few hundred years.

As for herring, John Woodger is credited with inventing the kipper in 1843 while he was conducting trials in the yard of what is now The Olde Ship Inn in Seahouses, Northumbria. He was experimenting with salmon, the word 'kipper' coming from the Old English *cypera*, meaning 'male salmon' (Samuel suggests it comes from the Dutch 'kippen' – to hatch – referring to spent salmon). By chance, it is said, Woodger tried splitting, gutting and salting a herring before hanging it in his smokehouse and discovering he'd arrived at the perfect recipe for a smoked herring. His innovation was surely the splitting of a herring down its back instead of along the belly.

For Woodger was by no means the first person to smoke kippers. Red herring, as we've seen, have been exported since the seventeenth century at least, and probably much before. Some say the east coast fishing communities were eating them 700 years ago. One report suggests that Scottish kings were ordering 'thousands of red herring from Yarmouth for their armies even in the thirteenth century'. Thomas Nash wrote *Lenten Stuffe, or the Praise of the Red Herring* in 1567. He was born in Lowestoft and described the red herring as a bloater more strongly cured. Nash regarded himself as the first person to write about fish and fishermen. Of the red herring he said, among other things:

is wholesome in a frosty morning: it is most precious fish-merchandise, because it can be carried through all Europe. No where are they so well cured as at Yarmouth. The poorer sort make it three parts of their sustenance. It is every man's money, from the king to the peasant. The round or cob, dried and beaten to powder, is a cure for the stone. A red herring drawn on the ground will lead hounds a false scent. A broiled herring is good for rheumatism. The fishery is a great nursery for seamen, and brings more ships to Yarmouth than assembled at Troy to fetch back Helen.

By stones he was talking about gallstones.

Many references note the massive numbers of red herring exported to the West Indies, where they were deemed suitable food for the enslaved population. Presumably those merchants from cities such as Bristol or Lancaster who dealt in this human misery deemed red herring nutritious and cheap for their enforced workers. Furthermore, red herring lasted months – at least six months if not longer – and therefore avoided the need to bring in fresh supplies more than twice a year. Much in the same way, armies were supplied with both smoked and salted herring.

Red herring are the longest smoked variations and the strongest tasting. For good reasons, then, did Nash say they put a hound off its scent. It is from this that the expression 'red herring' comes. Roused in brine for up to three weeks in some parts of the country – less in others – they were then hung high up in the smokehouse for anything up to three weeks, hence they were also called 'high-dries'. Other names prevailed: in East Anglia 'militiamen' from the vulgar term for a soldier in his red tunic as being a 'red herring'; in Scotland a 'Glasgow magistrate'; or simply a ham herring.

Nash notes that a red herring should be hung in a current of fresh air for between twenty-four and forty-eight hours before being smoked. Sometimes the smokehouse fire would be extinguished to remove fish from the lower areas so that the red herring can sweat, expelling some moisture. Then the smokehouse would be re-lit with fresh supplies at the bottom and the process continued. For the perfect red herring, an optimum fat content of between twelve and fourteen per cent is best. For it is this fat content that gives the fish its delicate flavour and its curing properties. Somewhere in the region of twenty-two per cent fat is the maximum they can attain, and this, when salted, tends to go mushy. On the other hand, once the herring has spawned, the fat content plummets to approximately three per cent. Thus, for the perfect smoked herring, it is important to get the fish just at the time when they are full with milt or roe, but still feeding – what is termed at red feed time. These full herring are sometimes referred to as 'maizy herring'.

Red herring come in two types. Golden herring, exported to Greece, Egypt and Africa, were the smokiest while the silver herring were only reasonably brined and smoked for between twenty-four and forty-eight hours and were preferred by the Italians. A good kipper, on the other hand, took about twelve to eighteen hours. A bloater is a lightly cured and smoked herring. *Blota* in Swedish means to soak, indicating a curing in brine. In Wales, though, a bloater is steeped in salt upon the ground for a day at least, before being washed and lightly smoked. In Yarmouth, the brine should be just strong enough to allow the herring to float, and they are held under with wooden battens. More salt is added before the herring are removed, dried and then affixed to the 'loves' by their heads in the smokehouse, and smoked over oak for twelve to eighteen hours. 'Buckling' were ungutted herring, which were hot-smoked in kilns and were preferred in Scandinavian countries.

Similarly, in Holland, herring were de-headed and gutted before being hot-smoked on spits over a mixture of beech and pine in metal drums.

It is perhaps misleading to speak in the past tense, although the great days of the herring are over. Kippers are a household name, even in Britain, where they were once regarded as breakfast food. Samuel Johnson ate a kipper for breakfast while stopping over in Loch Fyne. In his book *Journey to the Western Isles of Scotland*, Johnson notes that on Skye, the return of the laird to Dunvegan, after a long absence, heralded a plentiful supply of herring. On the other hand, if a woman 'crosses the water to the opposite land', the herring would disappear.

The poet Robert Southey regarded himself 'as a true lover and faithful eater of this incomparable fish' and ate herring at breakfast, dinner and supper. Those from Cullen, on Scotland's east coast were, he reckoned, the finest, although most were being exported to the West Indies and Mediterranean at the time. That was in 1819 when presumably he was referring to fresh herring being eaten and salted herring exported.

Hugh Miller, while cruising western Scotland aboard the *Betsey*, describes the time he first met his friend John Stewart in Tobermory. 'A door opened which communicated with the forecastle: and John Stewart, stooping very much to accommodate himself to the low-roofed passage, thrust in a plate of fresh herring, splendidly toasted, to give substantiality and relish to our tea.' Carlyle recommended herring to be eaten with vinegar, onions and prunes.

The vast proportion of today's smoked herring sold in Britain comes from the supermarkets – those multinational companies that have almost done as much to destroy the British diet and health as have fast food outlets. Their kippers, in my opinion, normally appear insipid and colourless, unless a dye has been used. Whether fresh or 'boil-in-the-bag', their taste is verging on the unpleasant!

It is pretty obvious that the natural golden brown colour of a kipper comes from the oak smoke it is infused with. Thus the practice of adding colouring to a herring prior to smoking started during the last years of the First World War. Herring were dipped in the vegetable dye *annatto* to save on the smoking time. However, all that happened was that inferior herring were made to look like kippers, which were in fact, tasteless. At a time of war, though, this was perhaps excusable, but once the war was over the practice didn't stop. With smoking times reduced, and the amount of moisture taken from the kipper reduced so that the fish were actually heavier than a true kipper, profits increased for the curers. Or, on the other hand, those that dyed their kippers could sell them at a cheaper rate than the traditional smokers, capturing a large share of the market. In Lowestoft, one famous brand of traditional kipper was the 'Kingkip', and the company responsible for these, and others, attempted to persuade the Herring Industry Board to establish a 'national mark' for kippers. The Board failed to accept this mark, and so the traditional smokers found that the only way they could compete was by adding the dye to theirs. Thus, by 1930, there were no large suppliers of traditional kippers and the 'Painted Lady', the dyed kipper, was invariably the only kipper available in Britain.

Some say a bit of dye added to a properly smoked kipper had no effect upon the taste. The Herring Industry Board advocated dyeing by saying that it was necessary to produce a consistent kipper from varying supplies of herring. Their excuse was that smoking was in fact a dying process in itself, and that the consumer only wanted a kipper that looked the right colour. That excuse would fail to convince consumers in these days!

The revival of the 'proper' kipper happened, quite unexpectedly, in 1955 with an article in *The Sunday Times* about smoked salmon. One Lowestoft reader sent in a box of freshly smoked, undyed kippers to the paper, and the following week another article appeared praising the quality of this box. Readers were instantly motivated to write in for the address and the family firm responsible received thousands of orders. The true kipper fought back for its position of top of the Smoke Parade!

Small smokeries do still produce a fine product, although the boffins at the European Commission endlessly seem to put barriers in their way in their ceaseless attempt to put them out of business. Seahouses, Craster, Whitby, Orfordness and Lowestoft join with Manx and Loch Fyne kippers as being household names. Theirs is a superior product, although much of the herring itself comes from Norway and Iceland. Vacuum-packed, postal-ordered kippers have become synonymous with the recent rise in status of the kipper. Manx smokeries have consistently refused to add dye to their product.

One of the biggest complaints I hear about kippers while I'm out and about with my Herring Exhibition are the bones. 'Ugh, it's got bones in it' is a cry from many a wrinkled-up face with contempt for the King of the Sea written all over it! Yet kippers, when smoked properly, are quite simple to deal with so that the bones remain on the plate and not on your palate. Proof is in the pudding, so I show them the smokehouse, take a kipper out, fillet the bone away and let them taste. I hope that I've managed to convince a few of you out there that eating kippers need not be such an ordeal. And the flavour is absolutely fabulous! The secret, it is said, is in the brine, for salt, according to the Michigan State University, 'removes water from the flesh and ties up the remaining water so that spoilage organisms cannot use it for growth'. Too much water and the smoking process falters.

Kippers straight out of the smokehouse are indeed a delicacy. I call it simply 'smoked herring' and often serve it with a piece of bread. For some shows I have even sold smoked herring rolls and watched as people immediately eat their fare. Rarely do I get a complaint. During one particular show in France, I supplied French bread, and the queue for the smoked herring extended along the quay. Demand severely out-stripped supply as my tiny backyard smoker is only capable of smoking 160 herring at one go, a process that takes some eighteen hours. The structure, a small wooden shed that some suggest looks like a toilet or sentry box, is a replica of a smoker that would once have been found in the backyard of hundreds of fishermen's homes, although many would have been built in brick. Mine is mobile, so it has to be easily assembled and dismantled for moving from one maritime festival to another. It is some 30ins square and about 7ft high, with a door, racks to place the tenterhooks on, a chimney and vents below. It works extremely well.

However, many prefer to cook their kippers. The best way according to, among many, the 'Two Fat Ladies', is to jug them by placing them, de-headed and rolled up, in a jug of boiling water for a few minutes and serve with a knob of butter. Grilling, frying, poaching and microwaving are alternatives. Some say they should be served with mustard, as mustard is excellent with all forms of cooked herring.

Americans have very different recipes for smoking their small herring. Gutted herring are pickled in Kosher salt, water, brown sugar, spices, hot Tabasco and soya sauce which is boiled up and cooled before the herring are soaked. Smoking follows a drying period of an hour or more. They are first smoked for several hours at a low temperature (120 degrees Fahrenheit) and then up to 190 degrees Fahrenheit for several more hours. Herring cured thus will last several weeks under refrigeration.

Although smoked and salted herring accounted for by far the majority of herring caught and landed, the onset of mechanisation had far-reaching consequences on the industry. In the same way as net-making machines improved the quality and speed of producing drift and other forms of netting, splitting machines quickened the pace of the smoking process. Likewise the development of freezing techniques enabled herring to be almost instantly frozen. Washed herring were placed on trays and drawn through an insulated tunnel, inside which they were blasted with very cold air at -20 degrees Fahrenheit. They emerged as solid blocks to be stored. Another method was to pack them into waxed paper in small quantities and to freeze them in a cabinet. The only downside of freezing was that the subsequent storage in refrigerators was relatively expensive.

Marinating herring is particularly popular in continental Europe, especially in the north. Although of Spanish origins, marinating is a form of preserving in a pickle of vinegar or wine, with added spices and sugar. Scandinavian herring comes in a vast array of marinades such as tomato, mustard, dill, yoghurt, cream, curry sauce and peppers. Sherry is sometimes used as the preservative. Swedish 'stromming' herring – small Baltic herring – are said to be pickled in a marinade of at least twenty ingredients, the taste of which the consumer never forgets. Rollmop herring and Bismarck herring are well-known forms of pickled herring.

In Britain, small herring were also regarded as delicacies. Kessock herring from the Moray Firth, Blackwater herring from the Thames estuary and those from parts of the Firth of Forth were generally noted for their flavour and small size. Cleddau herring from West Wales were, like the American Blueback herring and alewives, anadromous like salmon, in that they swam into rivers to spawn. Most herring spawned, and still do, on sandy banks, returning each year to spawn at their place of birth. Thomas Pennant's early migration theory, that herring swam each year southwards from the Arctic in one massive group, splitting into two groups at Shetland to swim east and west of Britain, was discounted over 100 years ago. Several different groups, identified in cases by a differing number of backbones, spawn in very different conditions.

Marinated herring is packed in cans in the same way the Americans canned their 'sardines'. The Herring Industry Board experimented with the process of sterilising the vacuumed contents of cans by heating at their research station at Port Glasgow in the 1940s. Mirroring the industry in northern Europe, they invigorated the British market by expanding the range available. Kippers, too, were canned, as were the herring roe that, even today, are generally overlooked. Some say sautéed herring roe is unbeatable. However, the majority of canned herring comes to Britain from Germany, in direct contrast to the days when Germany had, by treaty, to import an agreed amount of herring. That was until the advent of the Second World War!

Klondyke herring first appeared a few years after the Klondyke gold rush of 1897 when Benjamin Bradbeer noted a gap in the market with the decline of Norwegian herring supplying Germany. Herring was sprinkled with salt, packed in wooden boxes with ice and loaded aboard special ships. To begin with, it was almost exclusively a Lowestoft process and the boxes went, in the main, to the Hamburg port of Altona. Herring from western Scotland, Shetland, Wick and Fraserburgh, however, were exported in this way after the Second World War, although, as a total percentage of the herring industry, the trade in Klondyke herring was never very high. It was a cheap, easy way of disposing of herring during a glut. Previously, when herring was so abundant that the market almost collapsed, herring was used to fertilise the fields in many cases.

Nowadays, in what is widely regarded as a waste of resources, industrial fishing consumes some fifty per cent of herring landed. In this instance, good nutritious herring (and other species) is turned into fishmeal to feed to farmed fish and animals, the oil being used to produce foods such as margarine. However, with industrial fishing also targeting sand eels, a species lower in the food chain, the whole habitat of the North Sea has become under threat. Suggestions that krill and copepods can be fished commercially send shivers down conservationists' backs. Whereas the arrow-worm and comb jelly are capable of snatching copepods from the mouths of herring and sometimes even swallowing small herring, the idea of mankind stealing planktonic creatures from the food chain could possibly wipe out the whole of the North Sea fisheries.

The Bloater

Unlike a kipper, which is prepared in a uniform way throughout Britain, the bloater is a regional speciality and is cured in a variety of ways. It is said to have been devised in Great Yarmouth in 1830 from an accidental discovery when a curer named Bishop roused and smoked some leftover herring. This claim seems tenuous considering whole herring must have been salted and cured prior to this, not to mention the fact that the word originates from the Swedish *blota*, which literally means 'to soak'. This soaking relates to the steeping in salt. The general belief is that a light smoking follows this soaking, which is often, but not always, the case.

At Aberporth, on the shores of Cardigan Bay, there were two salt-houses where fresh herring was laid out on the stone-flagged floor before being sprinkled with salt. Once they had become supple enough, according to J. Geraint Jenkins, so that the head could be bent to touch the tail, they were removed and the salt-house cleaned. Once again the herring were laid on the floor with clean salt in between and left for three weeks. Again the salt-house was cleaned and the herring washed in clean water before being sprinkled in dry salt and left for a few more days. Sometimes they were then steeped in fresh water for three days and nights, the water being replenished on a daily basis. Only then were the fish left to dry in the open. These were never smoked.

At Nefyn the herring were usually salted in barrels for about ten days. Subsequently they were dried in the sun, laid out on ferns on the ground. Once packed with salt in willow hampers, they were shipped out as *penwaig sychion* – bloaters, again unsmoked.

Throughout rural Wales it was quite common for a household to have its own barrel of salted herring lying in a dark corner through late winter and into spring. A quantity would be removed when needed and rinsed out in fresh water overnight. Often these were then hung up inside the chimney to smoke for several hours before being consumed.

In contrast to the Welsh herring, a Lowestoft bloater was always smoked. Reggie Reynolds never salted his for less than four hours before smoking them overnight. Others were only smoked for two or three hours after a longer salting. In Yarmouth they smoked them for anything between twelve and eighteen hours. The common factor was that they were never gutted. Sprats were salted and smoked in the same way. I once did the same to pilchards and the resultant fish was delicious. Sometimes the Lowestoft people dried their salted herring in the wind in their backyard, before giving them a light smoke. Buckling, sometimes confused with bloaters, were ungutted herring that were hot smoked and thus not as tasty. They were common in Sweden and Germany and were in direct contrast to the Dutch method of smoking in which the herring was both gutted and filleted.

Creamed Herring Roes

Ingredients:
1lb soft herring roe
½ pint milk
Salt & pepper
1 ½ oz butter
1oz flour
Chopped parsley
Buttered toast

Method:
Simmer the roes in the milk for five to ten minutes and drain, keeping the liquid. Mash the roes and season with the salt and pepper. Make a roux sauce from the butter, flour and liquid and add the roes and parsley when the sauce has thickened. Serve on the buttered toast.

CHAPTER EIGHTEEN

Herring and its Legislators
and Administrators

We have already seen how the Church was taking tithes from fishermen and how royalty often demanded part of the catch. Edward I made the fishermen of Llanfaes, in Anglesey, pay one penny per mease of herring landed to help fund his building of Beaumaris Castle in the late thirteenth century. In 1576 Liverpool magistrates set fines for fishermen. For fishing on holy days £5 was levied, 40s for fishing from a ferry, 20s for each 'bloude wype' arising from a fishermen's quarrel and 12d for fishing with a net less than twelve roods from the next one.

In 1738 a law was passed in the Isle of Man requiring any Manx fisherman who had found a shoal of herring to inform his nearest boat. Just imagine that today, when fishermen spend hours on their radios talking to each other about the lack of fish when, in reality, their holds are full! The days of the North Sea drift-netters notifying their neighbour and passing on the surplus herring in their net because they could not take on board any more are over. Then the only requirement they would ask was that the neighbour boat brought their net back to harbour undamaged. Nowadays some fishermen prefer to dump eight tons of herring back into the sea rather than waste time turning their pumps on for such a paltry catch. Yet the fishing industry is subject to more control than ever due to the increasing consumer demand to ensure sustainability of stocks.

Bounties were introduced for the white herring fishery in the Act 23, Geo.II. Cap.24;1750, whereby 30s was paid for vessels of 20 to 80 tons, after petitioning from London merchants, increasing the bounty to 50s in 1757. Various acts between then and 1786 tinkered with the legislation until the bounty was reduced first to 30s and then to 20s.

Robert Fall, a fish curer from Dunbar, wrote in a pamphlet that year that the rate of 50s should be reintroduced, and that 10s of that should be paid to the captain and crew of the vessel, instead of the owners. However, to get bounties was a pretty tedious affair, as licences had to be obtained, oaths sworn and vessels had to rendezvous at particular places and times. Furthermore, the injudicious salt laws were preventing a serious expansion of the trade. The levy on salt was first introduced in 1643 and, according to Lord Dundonald, netted the Treasury £700,000 in 1784 at a rate of 3s 4d per bushel. The use of salt was restricted and heavily taxed for the fisheries so that many fishermen believed it was easier to throw herring into the sea than pay the tax. Even when the tax was reduced, the restrictions upon the fishers and curers alike was such that they might have to sail tens of miles to land at one particular customs house. The legislators, sitting in their London offices, were about as much good as they are now! Throughout the last quarter of the eighteenth century a whole string of 'learned gentlemen' visited the coasts of Scotland, writing their reports. Boswell, Anderson, Newte, Garnett, Knox and Pennant all commented on the salt laws and their effects upon the fishing.

In 1785 the First Report from the Committee appointed to enquire into the State of the British Fisheries echoed Fall's comments. In 1787 bounties of 1s a ton landed were thence paid to encourage small open boats to participate. In total three reports were submitted by the Committee in 1785 and four in 1786. One boat applied for the open boat bounty in 1785 when £27 was paid out, whereas £17,904 10s 6d was paid out over the next nine years. However, Scottish boats were denied this because they were unable to conform to the requirements of the Act until alterations were made.

Further reports were made to the House of Commons in 1798, 1799 and 1800, and part of the 1799 report has been discussed in Appendix Two. In 1801 the Committee recommended the abolishing of the salt tax, but instead Parliament raised it. Not until 1825 was it totally repealed.

In 1808 commissioners were appointed to promote, regulate and administer the fishery whereas previously they had reported on the 'Manufactures and Fisheries' as a whole. The ambition was to develop the herring fishery into a major resource. Their annual reports covered all aspects of the herring fishery including recommendations and

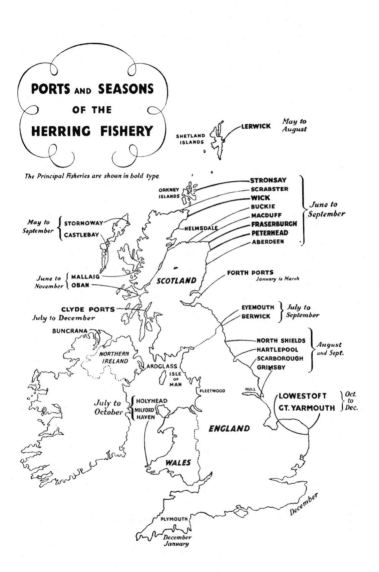

PORTS AND SEASONS OF THE HERRING FISHERY

The Principal Fisheries are shown in bold type.

LERWICK — *May to August*

SHETLAND ISLANDS

STRONSAY
SCRABSTER
WICK
BUCKIE
MACDUFF
FRASERBURGH
PETERHEAD
ABERDEEN

ORKNEY ISLANDS

June to September

May to September — STORNOWAY / CASTLEBAY

HELMSDALE

June to November — MALLAIG / OBAN

SCOTLAND

FORTH PORTS *January to March*

CLYDE PORTS *July to December*

EYEMOUTH / BERWICK — *July to September*

BUNCRANA

NORTHERN IRELAND

NORTH SHIELDS
HARTLEPOOL
SCARBOROUGH
GRIMSBY — *August and Sept.*

ARDGLASS

ISLE OF MAN

FLEETWOOD

HULL

July to October — HOLYHEAD / MILFORD HAVEN

LOWESTOFT
GT. YARMOUTH — *Oct. to Dec.*

ENGLAND

WALES

December

PLYMOUTH
December January

appendices with financial accounts, various declarations and the number of boats and amount of fish landed. From 1820 they were given responsibility over the white and other fisheries.

The Act 48, Geo.III. c. 110 of 25 June 1808 was one of the most substantive laws relating to the herring fisheries passed and covered many aspects from the bounties paid (which were increased to £3 a ton) to giving powers to Fishery Officers to go aboard busses to count the crew and inspect the fishing journals. A fine of £100 could be handed down to anyone found guilty of obstructing an Officer or his assistants. It placed certain onuses on the masters of vessels to keep accounts of salt, which was to be verified on oath in front of an Officer or Justice of the Peace. Barrels had to be branded. However, the Act did legislate for the crew of a buss to be paid a bounty of 2s per barrel of herring, divided among them in a set way.

The 1815 Act (55, Geo.III. c.94) introduced the cran measurement which was set as 32 gallons English wine measure. Not until the Cran Measures Act of 1908 was this altered to the present 37½ Imperial gallons. The thickness of barrels was also set at half an inch throughout. Bounties were extended and powers were given to Officers to seize nets. Bounties were reduced in 1821 and again by the Act 5, Geo.IV. c.64 of 27 June 1824. However it wasn't until another five years later that they were abolished altogether. A period with no government encouragement followed.

Over the next forty years or so successive Acts amended differing aspects of the fishery, the most fundamental being the Act 14 and 15 Vict. c.26 of 24 July 1851 banning the use of all forms of herring fishing except by 'the usual drift-net' and thus allowing nets for trawling or otherwise to be confiscated. This particularly affected the ring-net men of Loch Fyne. The same Act repealed certain aspects of the curing of the fish, such as no longer requiring herring to lie in barrels for fifteen days. Legislation against the ring-netters was strengthened in 1858, which allowed one half of the profit from the sale of 'all boats, nets, buoys, floats, or other fishing implements or apparatus which shall be forfeited under the provisions of the recited Acts' to 'be paid to the captor or informer'. In 1861 this was widened to include the forfeiture of any illegally caught herring. Herring closing times were amended in 1865 before the Act 30 and 31 Vict. c.52 of 15 July 1867 repealed aspects of the 1851 Act, making it 'lawful to fish for and take herring and herring fry at all places on the coasts of Scotland, in any manner of way, and by means of any kind of net having meshes of a size not less than that now permitted or required by law, or to have in possession herring or herring fry so fished for and taken'. The Act stressed that this only applied to Scotland.

Captain John Washington submitted his report into the disaster upon the east coast of Scotland to the House of Commons and this was published in 1849. Many of his recommendations concerning the safety of vessels were repudiated, not just by the fishermen, but by the Commissioners as well.

The Sea Fisheries Act of 1868, for the first time, placed requirements on fishermen to register, letter, number and name their vessels, as well as display lights. The same Act, among other items, carried into effect a convention between Britain and France regulating the fishery in the adjoining seas. However, back as far as 1833, the Commissioners for the British Fisheries were reporting that names were not being painted on the back of vessels, that no grants were payable to such craft and that they could be seized.

Ten years later, in 1878, the Report on the Herring Fisheries of Scotland appeared. This substantial report was prepared by Frank Buckland, Spencer Walpole and Archibald Young and was perhaps the first real attempt to thoroughly investigate the fisheries by means of public enquiries in fishing harbours all along the coast. For the purpose they were given the use of HMS *Jackal*, the gun boat that had previously been patrolling Loch Fyne during the prohibition years and whose officer and marine had shot and killed the Tarbert fisherman Peter McDougall while he was fishing illegally. Buckland and Spencer were Inspectors of the Salmon Fisheries for England and Wales, and Young was a Commissioner of the same. Buckland had been appointed an Inspector in 1867, at a time when legislation to regulate the salmon fisheries was introduced. One aspect of that legislation relevant to the herring fishery was their 'fixing' of fish weirs in use, thus ensuring a phasing out of the use of these structures over the next 100 years. Buckland had also already reported into the crab, lobster and other sea fisheries on the coast of Norfolk in 1875.

For this later report he and his associates held their enquiries during the months of September, October and November 1876 in England and subsequently throughout Scotland between August and November the following year (and returning to Ballantrae in February 1878 to report on the winter fishery). They made a number of recommendations, too numerous to mention in this short space, but they found an expanding industry little affected by government intervention. Surprisingly, they found no evidence that man's operations were having effects upon fish stocks. Buckland was indeed held in high esteem and widely respected and, from the lack of action on over-fishing, the establishment obviously chose to accept some of the advice. He did feel, however, that research into the fisheries and its problems were vital and that the public should be made aware of its importance in the national diet.

Some facts of his report make fascinating reading, especially some of his statistics. He reported that a million barrels were being landed annually, amounting to 800 million herring (about the same number landed into East Anglia in 1912!). The total of the Norwegian, Irish, Scottish, English and Dutch herring fishery he put at 2.4 billion fish. A cod, ling or hake, he estimated, consumed on average two herring a day although on occasions six were found inside a cod's stomach. Assuming they feed in these waters for 210 days a year, that 3.5 million cod, ling and hake were annually landed and that one in twenty were captured, then these fish devour some 29 billion herring a year. In other words these predators take twelve times more than mankind. Likewise he estimated the Scottish gannet population to consume 1.1 billion herring a year. Other figures he worked out were that Scottish herring nets would stretch some 12,000 miles if laid end to end, which is roughly equal to crossing the Atlantic three times. It was also said that if all the herring eggs laid hatched out, the sea would be so full as to flood part of England!

Buckland also wrote profusely and lectured widely. *The Log-Book of a Fisherman and Zoologist* was published in 1875 and he wrote the preface to his *Natural History of British Fishes* two days before his death in December 1880. A few days earlier he had bequeathed £5,000 after his wife's death to set up a trust under the name 'The Buckland Professorship'. In 1930 the first of many Buckland Lectures were given by individuals, a tradition to carry on to the present day except throughout the war years and a few odd interruptions. In 1933 the lectures were given by William C. Hodgson, D.Sc. under the title *The Natural History of the Herring in the Southern North Sea.*

By 1882 the Commissioners of the British Fishery had become the Fishery Board for Scotland, although their duties were much the same. Parts of England were under their jurisdiction. Meanwhile the government continued to issue legislation covering requirements such as registration, fishing times and close times and more. However, the emphasis gradually spread away from concentrating solely on the herring fishery, with regulation of the mussel, oyster and white fisheries.

Fishery Research laboratories were set up in St Andrews (1883) and Dunbar (1893). The latter was moved to Aberdeen in 1900. In 1883 the International Fisheries Exhibition would have been a dream fulfilled if Frank Buckland had still been alive. Within the next ten years the sea fisheries districts were established around England and Wales.

In 1903, the newly established Board of Agriculture took over responsibility for the fishing industry. Echoing Buckland's suggestions, the new Board of Agriculture and Fisheries was authorised to conduct scientific research, some directed by the International Council for the Exploration of the Sea. Stock control was top of the list of priorities. A separate Board of Agriculture was established in Scotland in 1911. By the time of conflict in 1914 confidence between fishermen and the Board had increased. After the war the Board declared that 'fishermen and fishing vessels constitute an invaluable auxiliary arm of the navy. If it is true that the navy has saved the country, it is equally true that the fishing fleet saved the navy.'

The first Scottish national fishermen's association was set up under the name of Scottish Herring Producers' Association Ltd (SHPA) in 1932. In England and Wales it was the 'English Herring Catchers Association', based in Lowestoft, that fulfilled the same service. 1933 saw the appointment of a Sea Fisheries Commission that eventually led to the establishing of the Herring Industry Board in 1935 whose annual reports gave statistics for the industry. One of its first tasks was to hand out loans to fishermen for the purpose of reconditioning vessels, building new boats and purchasing new gear. Some 130 steam drifters were scrapped. SHPA had, after the financial collapse of the late 1920s and the loss of the Eastern European markets, recognised that the industry was facing dire times and the fleet was ageing. Likewise the Fishery Board Reports had drawn government attention to the plight of the fishermen. Part of this was why the government had set up the Board in the first place. In the 1870s there had been over 40,000 fishing

boats, but this had been reduced to 17,000 by 1920. By 1950 it had further depleted to 12,500.

The Board's position was strengthened in the early 1950s in response
to the traumas of the war and the post-war period. Prices were controlled with minimum prices being created in 1957. More boats were
withdrawn from the fleet through scrapping and eventually the entire
fleet was motorised through loans and grants. Herring catches continued to decline until the Board authorised grants and loans for vessels to
adopt the purse-seine. Industrial fishing was encouraged, and export
contracts negotiated and canning and freezing processes advanced, as
we've seen. However, Britain joined the European Economic
Community, and the North Sea herring fishery was closed in 1977
after advice from the ICES. Total Allowable Catches (TACs) were
agreed just prior to this but were too late to prevent a total collapse.
With boats having to target mackerel in place of herring, the former
SHPA altered its name to the Scottish Pelagic Fishermen's Association.
With Britain's entry in the Common Market some of the Herring
Industry Board's functions were taken over by new bodies so that the
Board was wound up in 1981. The White Fish Authority and Herring
Industry Board's remaining work was combined into the Sea Fish
Industry Board, which today is known as Seafish.

The much-maligned Common Fisheries Policy eventually came
into force in 1983 after years of negotiation by the Council of
Ministers. Thus control of what had once been one of Britain's
strongest natural resources passed into the hands of Europe's bureau-
crats. From an initial control of over sixty-five per cent of European
fishing grounds, Britain suddenly found this had reduced over night
to about thirty-six per cent. British fishermen were to bear the blunt
of political negotiations for the country's entry into Europe's inner
clan who regarded this rich resource as a major prize for those other
fishing nations of the community.

Today most of the herring caught is by large pelagic trawlers. The
2002 season has been deemed fair, with prices for fresh herring aver-
aging £170 per ton, down £30 since the previous year, according to
Fishing News. Stocks of herring appear healthy and quotas for 2003 are
set to rise by up to fifty per cent. Meanwhile Britain's fleet has been
slimmed even further with over 120 boats decommissioned in 2002.
However, environmental and fishing groups have been lobbying the

government against this policy of scrapping perfectly seaworthy boats. Forefront in the campaign to highlight the 'enforced destruction of Britain's fishing heritage' is the 40+ Fishing Boat Association.

The newly formed DEFRA, which replaced the Ministry of Agriculture, Fisheries and Food (MAFF) in 2001 after the fiasco of the foot and mouth episode, simply enforces European policy, although interpretation among different nations can have a drastic effect on the fisheries. While Britain's herring fishery might have a secure future in the short term, and negotiations are on-going and another Common Fisheries Policy has recently been agreed, the long-term future of all of Britain's fishing is by no means guaranteed. Whatever lies ahead, there is one thing that is clear. Nostalgia and sentiment might play a part in history, but in reality the herring, once an employer of a quarter of the working population in some areas, will never again rise to the occasion. He might still be the King of the Sea, the silver darling, the prince among fishes, but never again will he alter the course of European history. Never again will a hundred boats sail out to catch what one boat alone now can. No, not only has the British government lost control of this resource, but so have the fishermen themselves. No longer do old fishermen want to come back as seagulls after their death, for they prefer to remain with Old Nick.

Harengs Frit with Sauce Moutarde

A Recipe from Buckingham Palace

Split open the herring and remove the roe. Then take out the bone and dry well after washing. Arrange roe on the herring down the centre. Pass through flour and dip in beaten egg and pass through breadcrumbs. Fry in hot fat till crisp and golden brown.

For the sauce, make a little béchamel. Flavour with a little mixed mustard that has been made with vinegar. Add salt and pepper to taste. Serve the sauce separately.

CHAPTER NINETEEN

The Legacy of Herring

Just a month before submitting this manuscript to the publisher, I travelled over to America, journeying up the Maine coast, finding, among
other things, cans of Scottish sardines in the local shops. Of course,
these were herring, for, as we all know by now, no sardines are caught
in Scotland. The Americans still insist, though, on calling them sardines
and much is caught by their own boats. The 'Beach Cliff' variety,
another I bought, originated from Prospect Harbor, Maine, canned by
Stinson Seafoods, only one of a few canneries still in existence.

The herring season was well underway. Bob Gardner works aboard
the *Starlight*, a Gloucester boat working out of Rockland. I met him in
a bar at Gloucester while he was home for the weekend. The *Starlight*
is one of around a dozen boats working pair-trawls for herring. The
season had been good, with 47,000 tons of fish being landed so far.
The annual quota had been set at 54,000 tons for Area 1A, which they
were fishing at that time and is a strip lying offshore along the Maine
coast. Inside of this there are three closure areas where the herring
were spawning, according to James Becker of the Department of
Marine Resources. I met him at Rockland when he was collecting a
sample of the catch from the purse-seiner *Western Seas*. She was landing 150 tons of herring caught off Boon Island, to the west, the bulk of
which was going to bait for the lobster industry. Lorries from the bait
suppliers lined the quay, awaiting their turn to load under the shoot
from the pump. Only one tanker waited, his load going to one of
those few canning factories left. Whereas the Maine coast once had
something like seventy factories canning herring, only a handful now
remain. In 1899 the New England herring fishery directly employed
1,796 people, according to the Commissioner of the Department of
Sea and Shore Fisheries: 100 years later I doubt it employs a fraction of
that number.

Glen Lawrence is the skipper of the *Double Eagle*, a 1929-built sardine carrier. I had met him on the previous day at Rockland. His boat had been built for the north Lubec Manufacturing and Canning Company by Charles Ingall of East Machias and had been named after one of their brands of canned sardines. After being subsequently lengthened and having several owners, Glen bought her in 1990 and rebuilt her. 'Want to see the most beautiful boat here?' he asked me by way of an introduction. I didn't need persuading!

His principal activity is now transporting bait herring out to the islands. Maine is renowned more for its lobsters than any other fish. Indeed, you can't really travel anywhere along this coast without coming across a 'lobster shack' where live and cooked lobsters are sold. It is a sort of ritual for tourists to buy a lobster and sit overlooking the sea, chomping their way through a whole crustacean. Indeed much of the tourism of the State – often referred to as 'Vacationland' – is centred on the lobster fishery. Even the vehicle number plates used to figure lobsters! But the lobster story is another for a later time.

Glen had no herring the day I met him, and he worried that his customers, the lobster fishermen, had no bait. No bait meant no lobsters, and no lobsters meant no money for the 500 families that relied upon his cargo. But the next day he was out, and I heard he had taken a full load of 35 tons of herring off of the *Western Seas* prior to her unloading at Rockport. What I also learnt from Glen was the distrust between the seiners and the pair-trawlers, both of whom constantly verbally attack each other. The purse-seiners accuse the trawlers of taking immature fish and destroying stocks (James Becker told me that there was no evidence that this was true) whereas the trawlers reckon the purse-seiners use the same arguments that the stop-seiners had when purse-seining was developed, and weir fishermen before them when stop-seining began. These are familiar arguments. The fact that only four boats were working seines perhaps suggests the direction the arguments were going.

Bob Gardner was out fishing when I was in Rockland. The 90ft *Starlight* was pairing with the *Retriever*, a 145ft trawler with six RSW tanks. A couple of months earlier they had been fishing off Matincus Island, thirty miles south-east of Rockland, finding plenty of herring. Now they, too, had gone off west to find herring. Pair-trawling, like purse-seining, always takes place at night when the herring come off the hard seabed. It is the way forward, Bob told me, for mid-water

trawling doesn't destroy the seabed and trawling in pairs is more efficient in terms of the pull of the trawl as no energy is used in keeping
the net open as in conventional otter-trawling. The boats do this
simply by being apart. The days of seining and trapping in weirs are
probably almost over, in the same way as the sustainable methods of
herring fishing have disappeared in Europe. Efficiency hardly ever
goes hand-in-hand with sustainability.

Stop-seining is in actuality an extension of weir-fishing using fixed
gear. A net, buoyed at the top and weighted on the sole, is set across
the mouth of a bay or cove so that the fish enters and becomes
trapped once the tide recedes. As with a weir, the fish is then removed
using a dip-net or, more likely these days, pumps.

Weirs are still in use along the extreme east of the coast and up into
Canada, but their numbers are in certain decline. At Bar Harbor, on
Mount Desert Island, I searched for the remains of the one at Bar
Island. I found the spot where I could identify its position from a photograph but the beach was quiet with only the odd seagull plodding
around searching for an uncertain meal. Somehow I expected to hear
the sound of the wind rustling through the brush. This weir had been
built around the mid-nineteenth century by David Rodick, the
owner of the island. In the late 1860s it was observed by Benjamin
DeCosta who wrote:

*[Weirs] are huge traps, built on shallows and bars, in which silly fish are
impounded. Selecting some spot on the shore where the tide recedes at low
water, a fence of wicker-work is made with strips of deal or spruce saplings,
enclosing an area varying from one-half to three or four acres. A good-sized
gateway is left for the fish to go in, and when once in they do not have wit
enough to attempt to go out, at least in season, but go circling around the sides,
shooting past the open gate. When the tide has gone nearly down, the fisherman enters the weir with a skiff, closes the entrance, and, taking a great scoop-
net, jumps into the water and soon loads the boat with handsome herring,
which are conveyed ashore to be put in pickle or hung up on sticks in the great
curing-houses whose smoke, in these parts, ascends forever.*

While watching the process of capturing the fish, DeCosta noted that
the herring:

... rushed about the weir exceedingly frightened. When dropped out of the net
into the boat, they set up a prodigious drumming. The herring in the water could
be distinctly seen, their sides flashing like silver. The rest of the fish did not seem
to mind our presence, and swam leisurely around the boat, or lay still while we
paddled among them. Besides herring there were menhaden, silvery hake, dog-
fish, rockcod, sculpin, flounders, pollock, skate, and goose fish or monkfish.

He also noted the amount of immature herring caught, which probably accounted for the dismantling of the weir in the early 1900s.
Nearby weirs were once to be found at Hull's Cove, Sunken Ledge
and Burnt Porcupine Island but all signs of these were gone, or so I
was assured in the harbourmaster's office.

  I mentioned the alewife in Chapter Seven. This anadromous herring is still in abundance and I found signs of it in many parts of the
coast. At Damariscotta Mills I visited the restored fish ladder that
allows the alewives to swim from the Great Salt Bay into Damariscotta
Lake to spawn. The alewife, also known as the sawbelly, wall-eyed
herring, big-eyed herring, spring herring, ellwife, buckie and cat-
thrasher, had, from about 1800, been harvested and subsequently pickled or smoked. Damariscotta in Native American, means 'the meeting
place of an abundance of alewives' which proves the authenticity of
the fishery, and legislation was passed in 1741 protecting its spawning
grounds in many of the rivers, some of which are still called 'Herring
River' (I also found a few 'Herring Coves'). The ladder was first built
in 1807 by John Perkins and Ephraim Rollins to aid the fish on their
42ft ascent from sea to lake. At the base of the ladder there is a
mechanical dipper that was built in the late 1940s to catch the fish, but
with a dramatic decrease in the fish population in the 1990s, a ban was
imposed on disturbing the fish on their migration to spawn each
spring. Thus the restoration of the ladder was begun in 1995, and now,
once completed, it is a popular tourist attraction to see the swimming
of the great shoals of alewives upstream. The remains of the smoking
shed can also be seen at the ladder's base.

  And so the legacy of the herring remains in America and Canada,
just as it does in Britain and the rest of Europe. The Viking incursions,
the Hanseatic league, the British navy, the British Empire, colonisation
in the East and West, slavery, war, famine, the Highland Clearances –
these too are the legacies of herring in terms of history. But these are

redeemed to some extent by, of course, the positive side of the industry: by the employment it provided for thousands of families and for the source of food it gave to millions in almost every corner of the globe.

But what of herring today? We have already discovered how today's herring comes in tins, in tubs, as kippers, marinated, rolled up with a wooden pin stuck through, and, indeed, fresh. Most supermarkets stock a few on their fresh fish counters. Yesterday I spotted some Norwegian herring selling for £2.59 a kilo, which is the highest I had seen it so far. Here, though, there is no market for herring as bait, although much does go to fishmeal.

But what do we have to remind us of the herring industry that once employed one in four people in parts of the country? The answer is not much. We have our herring, pilchards, sardines, sprats and whitebait to remind us of what they taste like, but not much tangible evidence of its relationship to the past. The Pickled Herring quay in London, where many a ship loaded up with barrels of fish, has long gone. Cannon Street Station hides the warehouses of the German merchants. Those hundreds of businesses relying upon the great fleets of drifters have all gone. Today the pelagic trawlers, unrecognisable from the rest of the ugly, modern fleet, pump their cargo into road tankers that whip it away like some unwanted commodity. Only a handful of smokehouses remain, and Brussels tries in vain to close those down, just like the vast majority of American canning factories that have disappeared. Herring nets decorate pubs. Quarter-cran baskets have been demoted to their new stations by the firesides of the houses that once hummed with fishermen, storing logs for the fires of the weekend holiday cottages. Wooden fishing boats are fast disappearing, being chopped up on the beaches where the sands were once kissed by fishermen's feet. The seas are almost empty where the herring once danced.

In the same way as it has across the Atlantic, the legacy of the herring industry in Britain has also survived in a few place-names. Herringfleet, already mentioned, is some miles inland from the sea nowadays. Herrington is a suburb of Sunderland while Herringwell lies at least forty miles inland. Whether the latter two have had an association with the fish is unclear. In Wales we have *Porth Sgadan* (the herring beach), where herring were landed, while in

Montgomeryshire there are bridges called *Pont-y-Sgaden* (bridge of the herring), denoting places where fish sellers met. Langton Herring is a small village close to Chesil beach, but its name comes from the local Herring family and not the sea.

Talking of the Herring family, I once met Mr and Mrs Herring in Penzance, with their three children. One year Mr Herring bought five copies of my book *The Herring Fishers and Other Vignettes*, and the following year five 'Herring boat' tea towels I designed. He couldn't resist one for each member of the family, he told me!

Herring pop up in many other strange places. One current West End opera is named after herring. I have a CD by the 'HKippers' entitled 'Gutted'! We have already seen the linguistic connection in the Greek word for herring – *regga* – so is there one between the French *hareng* and to 'harangue' someone? Or perhaps the Dutch *haring*? In Polish herring is *śledź*, in Swedish *silde*, in German *hering* (another hint that the word comes from the Teutonic *heer*) and in Finnish it is *silakka*. Throughout these countries – and Norway, Denmark, Belgium, Iceland, the Baltic States and Russia – herring remains a staple food. I was handed a tin of Russian herring just recently; they too add herring to pizza

There are various herring festivals today. The Baltic Herring Festival is held in Helsinki each year in the autumn. Dieppe has a festival of both mackerel and herring, while Yarmouth still has a herring festival. In Newcastle, County Down, they have a Herring Gutters' Festival. Bergen in Norway has a herring festival while in Stavanger there is a museum of, in part, the herring. And there is, of course, my own Herring Exhibition.

In Caernarfonshire, strings of herring were seen hanging outside the poorer cottages and this was deemed a sign of these folk being willing to eat the fish when they could get it. Those strings were then replaced by the sign of the three herring. John Knox was renowned for the sign of the three herring outside his Edinburgh bookshop. In Nefyn, one such sign survives today, presumably one of many around Europe.

But it is perhaps to the red herring that we must turn to understand the real epitaph of the herring. Agatha Christie is renowned for introducing more than one false scent into her books, and one well-known author used the cliché in the title of his book. Red herring, seemingly, appear everywhere: in books, on television, in politics. Politicians are perhaps the best at laying false trails in their endless desire to avoid too much truth. Yet, as I sit writing these final words, I cannot help but wonder at the irony of it. We began this journey with red herring in Greece and now end with today's red herring. To the British fishermen Europe is a red herring, in which their livelihood is just part of the game to gain access to the club. Their survival is of no interest in the higher matter of things to those that do not care. The world order is today's agenda, and the suppression of the people through fear of risk to their well-being and safety is promulgated by careful manipulation of world events. To the politicians this is a chance to appear strong, to retaliate and to control through power. To do this he has to lay his false trails, to lay down red herring. To the rest of us, though, herring are simply a reminder of a bygone age, a nostalgia yearned for, a sign of gentler times. But they also remind us of a 'stinking, putrefying, ungracious' fish with bones, the monotonous food of the poor. Two parallel sentiments, yet miles apart. How sad mankind has become! Perhaps, just perhaps, through progression we have forgotten how to live.

Bibliography

The following bibliography contains a fairly comprehensive list of books concerned with the herring fishery. Most of them are not entirely focused upon the herring but include more than a few paragraphs in that direction. In general, these various books cover all aspects of the fishery. The second list includes the works of the major visitors to the coasts of Scotland in the eighteenth and nineteenth centuries which themselves include observations upon the fisheries. There are, of course, many more books that mention the herring fishery and contain a limited amount of information on the fishery in specific areas. Space excludes their inclusion.

Anson, P.F., *Fishing Boats and Fisher Folk on the East Coast of Scotland*, London, 1930

— *Fishermen and Fishing Ways*, London, 1932

— *Scots Fisherfolk*, Banffshire, 1950

Beaujon, A., 'The History of Dutch Sea Fisheries' in *The Fisheries Exhibition Literature of 1883*, Vol. IX, Prize Essays, Part II, London, 1884

Bertram, J.G., *The Harvest of the Sea*, London, 1885

Bompas, G.C., *Life of Frank Buckland*, London, undated

Buckland, F., *The Natural History of Fishes*, London, 1880

Butcher, D., *The Driftermen*, Reading, 1979

— *Living from the Sea*, Sulhamstead, 1982

— *Following the Fishing*, Newton Abbot, 1987

Buckland, F. & Walpole, S., *Report on the Herring Fisheries of Scotland*, HMSO, 1878

Campbell, J., *A True and Exact Description of the Island of Shetland*, Edinburgh, 1753

Couch, J., *A History of the Fishes of the British Isles*, London, 1877

Coull, J.R., *The Sea Fisheries of Scotland*, Edinburgh, 1996

De Caux, J.W., *The Herring and the Herring Fishery*, London, 1881

Dunlop, J., *The British Fisheries Society 1786-1893*, Edinburgh, 1978

Duff, R.W., 'Herring Fisheries of Scotland' in *Papers of the International Fisheries Exhibition of 1883*, London, 1884

Dyson, J., *Business in Great Waters*, London, 1977

Elder, J., *The Royal Fishery Companies of the Seventeenth Century*, Glasgow, 1912

Finn, W., 'The Icelandic Herring-Fisheries' in *Report of the Commissioner of Fish and Fisheries (USA) for 1879*, Washington, 1880

Friele, M., 'An Account of the Fisheries of Norway in 1877' in *Report of the Commissioner of Fish and Fisheries (USA) for 1877*, Washington, 1879

Fraser Darling, F., *Island Farm*, London, 1943

Gibbs, W.E., *The Fishing Industry*, London, 1922

Gilman, J., *A History of the Sardine Industry*, Lambertville, 2001

Goode, G.B., *The Fisheries and Fishing Industries of the United States*, Washington, 1887

Gunn, N.M., *The Silver Darlings*, London, 1941

Hawkins, L.W., *The Prunier Herring Trophy*, Lowestoft, 1982

Heath, A., *Madame Prunier's Fish Cookery Book*, London, 1938

Hodgson, W.C., *The Natural History of the Herring in the Southern North Sea*, London, 1934

— *The Herring and its Fishery*, London, 1957

Jenkins, J.T., *The Sea Fisheries*, London, 1900

Johnstone, J., *British Fisheries*, London, 1905

Lewis, E.A., *The Welsh Port Books*, London, 1927

Ljungman, A.V., 'The Great Herring Fisheries considered from an economical point of view' in *Report of the Commissioner of Fish and Fisheries (USA) for 1883*, Washington, 1885

Lundberg, R., 'The Fisheries of Sweden' in *Report of the Commissioner of Fish and Fisheries (USA) for 1884*, Washington, 1886

March, E.J., *Sailing Drifters*, London, 1952

Martin, A., *The Ring-Net Fishermen*, Edinburgh, 1981

— *The North Herring Fishing*, Isle of Colonsay, 2001

Mathieson, C., *Wales and the Sea Fisheries*, Cardiff, 1929

Mitchell, J.M., *The Herring, its Natural History and National Importance*, Edinburgh, 1864

Mitchison, N. & Macintosh, D., *Men and Herring, a documentary*, Edinburgh, 1949

Preger, W., *The Humble Dutch Herring*, Melbourne, 1944

Samuel, A.M., *The Herring; its Effect upon the History of Britain*, London, 1918

Sinclair, J. (ed), *Statistical Account of Scotland* (OSA), Edinburgh, 1791-9

— *New Statistical Account of Scotland* (NSA), Edinburgh, 1845

Smith, P.,   *The Lammas Drave and the Winter Herrin'*, Edinburgh, 1985

Smylie, M., *The Herring Fishers of Wales*, Llanrwst, 1998

— *Traditional Fishing Boats of Britain and Ireland*, Shrewsbury, 1999

— *The Slopements* – unpublished MPhil dissertation, St Andrews University 2002

Sutherland, I., *Wick Harbour and the Herring Fishery*, Wick, undated

Washington, J., *Report on the Loss of Life and Damage to Fishing Boats on the East Coast of Scotland*, HMSO, 1849

Widegren, H., 'Short Introduction to the proper care and management of Baltic Fishery' in *Report of the Commissioner of Fish and Fisheries (USA) for 1878*, Washington, 1880

Government Papers

Annual Reports of the Herring Fishery Board

Books of Herring Acts

Registers of British Fishing Boats

Reports from the Select Committee appointed to enquire into the State of the British Fisheries 1786

Papers of the International Fisheries Exhibition, 1883

Reports from the Commissioners on the State of the British Herring Fisheries 1798, 1799 and 1800

Reports of the Commissioner of Fish and Fisheries of the United States of America

Tours In Scotland

Anderson, J., *An Account of the Present State of the Hebrides and Western Coasts and Scotland*, Edinburgh, 1785

Bowman, J.E., *The Highlands & Islands – a Nineteenth-century Tour*, Gloucester, 1986

Daniell, W. & Ayton, R., *A Voyage round Great Britain* (8 Vols), London, 1814-1825

Defoe, D., *A Tour thro' the whole island of Great Britain*, (2 Vols), London, 1927

Garnett, T., *Observations on a Tour through the Highlands of Scotland* (2 Vols), London, 1811

Johnson, S. & Boswell, J., *Journey to the Hebrides*, Edinburgh, 1996

Knox, J., *A View of the British Empire, more especially Scotland, with some Proposals for the Improvement of that Country, the Extension of the Fisheries and the Relief of the People*, London, 1784

— *Observations on the Northern Fisheries with a Discourse on the Expediency of Establishing Fishing Stations or Small Towns in the Highlands of Scotland and the Hebride Islands*, London, 1786

— *A Tour through the Highlands of Scotland and the Hebride Isles in 1786*, London, 1787

Leland, J., *The Itinerary of John Leland the Antiquary*, (9 Vols), edited by Thomas Hearne, Oxford, 1770

Martin, M., *A Description of the Western Isles of Scotland circa 1695*, Edinburgh, 1994

McCulloch, J., *The Highlands and Western Isles of Scotland* (3 Vols), London, 1824

Newte, T., *A Tour in England and Scotland in 1785 by an English Gentleman*, London, 1788

— *Prospects and Observations on a Tour in England and Scotland*, London, 1791

Pennant, T., *A Tour in Scotland*, third edition, London, 1774

— *A Tour in Scotland 1769*, new edition, Edinburgh, 2000

— *A Tour in Scotland and Voyage to the Hebrides*, new edition, Edinburgh, 1998

Southey, R., *Journal of a Tour in Scotland in 1819*, Edinburgh, 1972

Wilson, J., *A Voyage round the coasts of Scotland and the Isles* (2 Vols), Edinburgh, 1842

Wordsworth, D., *A Tour in Scotland in 1803*, Edinburgh, 1974

HERRINGS ARE "BARGAINS"

When herrings are at their best they are at their cheapest. That is not so surprising when you consider that herrings are only landed in big quantities when they are in prime condition. So a plentiful supply of fine fat herrings means a plentiful supply of *cheap* herrings—that's why they are such splendid value for money—such bargains.

A Measure of Herring

Terms used in the Counting of Fish

CAST:
tally fish; one per
two score (Isle of Man)
three fish (Devon)
twelve fish (East Coast of England)

CRAN:
37½ Imperial gallons, 28 stone (Cran Measures Act 1908)
26½ gallons (Whitby)
3½ cwt (Scottish Fishery Board 1899)

LAST:
100 Hundreds, nominally 2 tons of herring = 13,200 fish (East Coast of England)

LONG HUNDRED or HUNDRED:

no. of fish			
	120	40 cast	Devon (no tally)
	123	—	Whitby
	124	40 warps + 4 casts	Isle of Man
	132	One East Coast of England warp	

MAND:
Eight hundreds, nominally 1,000 herring i.e. 1 cran (or 1,056 on East Coast of England)

MAZE/MEIZE/MEASE:
5 Hundreds x 123 = 615 (Whitby)
5 Hundreds x 124 = 620 (Isle of Man)
5 Hundreds x 124 = 620 (Wales)
5 Hundreds x 120 = 600 (Devon) no tally

PAIR:
2, usually kippers

QUARTER–CRAN:
Standard basket size, about 7 stones, used to land fish

TALE:
1 fish thrown aside per Hundred (Wales)

TALLY:
1 fish thrown aside per 3 x 2 score (Isle of Man)

WARP:
1 fish thrown aside per 2 score (Wales)

The 1799 House of Commons Commissioners' Report on the British Fisheries

The reports of the Commissioners of the House of Commons on the British Fisheries sometimes make interesting reading when one is so inclined; some of them are so full of statistics that they are made unreadable. But to find part of the 1799 report in *The Sun* would seem unimaginable in these days of 'kiss-and-tell' journalism. Nevertheless, finding two successive copies of the ancient daily brought a very unusual article to my attention.

The issues were dated Thursday 21 August and Friday 22 August 1800. On the back of the first is an article simply entitled 'Fish Trade'. It notes that there was considerable interest in the country in the promotion of 'this valuable branch of our trade which is considered as the nursery of our navy'. The article highlights the examination by the committee of the Revd Herbert Marsh, and notes that his judgement is considerably reliable. While it might, in some respects, make tedious reading, this report does portray the international trade, within Europe anyway, of the herring industry.

The committee commences by asking Revd Marsh how long he resided in Germany: twelve years is the answer. Then he is asked what he knows of the herring trade and other salted fish; where they are sold and consumed; the sorts favoured; how they are transported and the various ways of preparing and eating the herring. From this point I copy the piece word for word, for it is fascinating reading:

'The quantity of white salted herring consumed during the last two or three years in Germany (including all the Dominions of the King of Prussia) may be estimated at about a hundred and thirty thousand barrels annually, which is much less, however, than used to be consumed in that Country, as complaints are continually heard at present in Germany about the scarcity of that article. The grounds on which I estimate the consumption of white salted herring in Germany during the last two or three years, are the following: In the year 1798, the exact number of barrels imported to Hamburgh was 12,674; and in 1799, they amounted to exactly 13,067, as appears from the printed lists which are annually published at Hamburgh. I do not know the exact number imported at Bremen within the last two years; but according to a list of the year 1790, the number of barrels of Herring brought to that part amounted to 10,205, and in the same year the number of barrels of Herring brought to Hamburgh amounted to 17,719. If we make therefore a proportional deduction for Bremen, we must estimate the present importation then at only 8,000. The Port of Altona, which is contiguous to Hamburgh, is supplied by the Busses, which are fitted out at Altona, and carry on the Herring Fishery from the Shetland Islands Southward, in the same manner as the Dutch used to do. The number of Busses, which sailed in 1799 from Altona, amounted to about 26, as I was lately informed there; and as it is a moderate estimate that each of these Busses caught a thousand barrels between 24 June and the end of the Fishing Season, we may assume that at least 26,000 barrels were brought to Altona in 1799. The exact number of Busses which sailed from Emden last year I do not know; but as 40 have sailed from that Port several years ago, and there is no reason to suppose that their number has diminished since the Dutch have been prevented from getting out, we shall hardly exceed the truth, if we suppose that at least 40,000 barrels were brought last year to Emden. According to the foregoing estimate then, to the four German ports on the North Sea, Hamburgh, Altona, Bremen, and Emden, were brought about 87,000 barrels of white salted herring. To determine the quantity brought to the German Ports on the Baltic, I have no other method than by comparing the number of vessels laden with herring which passed the Sound, with the probable share of them which went to German Ports on the Baltic: Now it appears, from the lists published at Elsineur, that the exact number of vessels laden with white salted herring, which passed the Sound in 1799, was 338, of which 287 were Swedish (from Gothenburg, Marstrand, Uddewalla, &c.) 43 Norwegian, five from Emden, one from Altona, one from Aalborg, and one from Leith. We shall hardly exceed the truth if we assume that one-third of these vessels were bound to German Ports on the Baltic, as Lubec, Rostock, Stralsund, Wolgast, Stettin, Dantzick, Pellan, Konningsberg, &c. and that each vessel held, on an average, 400 barrels. According to this computation, the German Ports on the Baltic received more than 45,000 barrels, which, added to those received by the German Ports on the North Sea, estimated at 87,000, make a total of 130,000; and I have been informed by several Merchants in Germany, who import herring, that before the Dutch were prevented by the War from sending out their Busses, the consumption of white salted herring in Germany was very greatly superior to the present consumption.

'Of the quality of other merchantable Fish, such as salted Cod, dried Cod, Tusk, Ling, &c. annually consumed in Germany, in general I am unable to form any particular estimate; but it appears, from the Hamburgh printed lists, that the importation of the preceding kinds of Fish to that Port is very considerable; and that the Country from which they are chiefly brought at present is Norway. It is probable also that Norway will continue to supply the German Market at all times with dried Cod, because in the Northern part of Norway, where the Cod Fishery is carried on in the middle of Winter, the cold is so severe, and the air at the same time so very serene, that the mere drying of the Cod in the open air, without the use of salt, is sufficient to preserve it, which is an advantage and a saving not to be had elsewhere. Besides, the Germans are more fond of the Norwegian unsalted dried Cod, than they are of the dried Cod which had been previously salted. The salted or pickled Cod, called by the Germans *Laberdan*, is less valued by them than the dried Cod, which they call *Stock Fish*, insomuch that in the year 1798, only 488 barrels of salted Cod (or *Laberdan*) were imported at Hamburgh, and in 1799 the importation was reduced to merely eight barrels, which were brought from Shetland. But salted Ling appears to have met with better success; it is highly probable that Scottish salted Ling, especially the Barra Ling, which is in great estimation, might be sent to Hamburgh with advantage. An attempt at exportation of salted Ling was made from Leith to Hamburgh in 1798, and the speculation must have been attended with some success, as in the following year, 1799, were imported from Leith to Hamburgh 140 cwt. of salted Ling, as appears from the Hamburgh printed lists. It is true that this quantity was very small in comparison with what was brought to Hamburgh in the same year from Bergen, Drontheim, and Christiana; but it may serve at least as an encouragement to future adventurers from North Britain.

'With respect to the places in Germany where herring are sold and consumed, it may be observed that, in addition to the above-mentioned Sea Ports, almost every Town in Germany exposes salted herring to sale, either wholesale or retail; and the adjacent villages are supplied by hawkers from the respective towns. The mode of carrying the Herring into the Interior of Germany is partly by means of the Rivers, and partly by land carriage. Herring sent to Leipzig, Dresden, and other parts of the Electorate of Saxony, are carried on the Elbe from Hamburgh to Magdeburg in Barges, and from Magdeburg to Leipzig, &c. they are brought by land. Those sent to Berlin have the whole way water carriage both from Hamburgh and Stettin; herring imported at Bremen are sent up the Weser, and formerly immense quantities used to be sent up the Rhine by the Dutch, to Cologne, Mayntz, Franckfort on the Mein, Manheim, &c. whence they were sent on the Mein and the Necker into the Interior of Franconia and Suabia. Herring destined for Bohemia and Austria are sent by sea to Stettin, and are thence conveyed in the Oder Barges, as high up as possible into Silesia, whence they are further carried by land.

'In regard to the value set on different kinds of herring, a decided preference is given in Germany to Dutch herring; insomuch that though Swedish herring were latterly sold at a third and even fourth of what Dutch herring were sold for, none but the poorest people would purchase Swedish herring, as long as they could get Dutch, or at least herring cured in the Dutch manner. The people of Emden and Altona have learnt from the Dutch their method, though they have not hitherto in every point the Dutch excellence; I have been told by persons in the trade, that herring cured by the People of Altona do not keep so well as the Dutch herring.

'Of all the prices of Dutch Herring, as sold per Barrel in the Dutch Ports, I have procured a list for ten successive years, from 1788 to 1797, which was the last year that Dutch Herring could be procured.

'These prices were as follows;

Years	Rix Dollars	Years	Rix Dollars
1788	13	1793	10?
1789	13	1794	17
1790	12	1795	16
1791	12	1796	19
1792	8½	1797	25

'When the Course of Exchange is at par, six Rix Dollars are equivalent to one Pound Sterling and five or six pence; so that in 1797 Dutch herring were sold, even in the Dutch Ports, for more than 4s per Barrel. Since that time the Altona and Emden Herring, which are the only substitutes at present for Dutch Herring, have borne a still greater price. Last year (1799) Altona Herring were sold at Altona for more than 30 dollars, or £5 per barrel; and I was assured last September by a Merchant who had lately been at Magdeburg, that though there was water carriage from Altona to Magdeburg, Altona herring were then sold at Magdeburg for 38 dollars per barrel, and that the Emden herring were sold there at a still higher price; yet in the very same Summer two cargoes of herring were sent from Leith to Hamburgh, and I was assured by the Merchant who shipped one of the cargoes, that though he bought the herring at Leith at about 20s per barrel, no Hamburgh Merchant would give him even prime cost for them. I afterwards tasted some of the Leith herring, and found that they had not only no resemblance to Dutch herring, but they were as badly cured as it was possible for herring to be. About the same time, however, a cargo of salted herring arrived at Hamburgh from Stornoway in the Island of Lewis; and though they did not fetch above half the price of the Altona herring, they were sold for three times the price of the Leith herring, the Stornoway cargo being sold for about 33 marks (about £2 of our money) per barrel. Swedish Herring [were] sold last year at Gothenburg (namely in March 1799, which is about two months after the Swedish Herring Fishery is ended) for 4½ Swedish Rix dollars, or about £1 2s of our money, which is the price that the North Highland herring bore last Summer at Greenock; being equal therefore in price, the Greenock herring would everywhere meet with a more rapid sale, even than the Gothenburg herring, if their quality was decidedly superior; but at present it is difficult to say on which side, upon the whole, preference lies. The great objection to the Greenock herring (of which I procured some barrels to be sent last October to Saxony) is their inequality in the very same barrel; for though many single herring had a good flavour, and were much superior to the Swedish, there were others again in the same barrel which were greatly inferior to the Swedish. Of the causes of this inequality, which can never take place according to the Dutch method, I shall offer a conjecture, in the answer to one of the following questions. The Norwegian herring brought from Bergen, Drontheim and Christiania are inferior even to the Swedish herring, one principal cause of which is that the herring casks in Norway are made of fir wood, which communicates a disagreeable taste to the herring, and affects the pickle throughout the whole barrel. The Swedes, on the contrary, though, on account of scarcity of oak in Sweden, do not make use of oaken casks, as we, as the Dutch, as the People of Emden and Altona do, make their casks of beech. The price of the Danish herring I do not know; but they must be made cheaper even than the Swedish, or they would not meet with a Sale. In 1799 were brought to Hamburgh 3,291 Barrels of Swedish, and 1,593 barrels of Norway herring.

'Lastly, in regard to the manner of eating white salted herring, the Germans always eat Dutch herring raw, like Anchovies, for which purpose it is necessary to be much more nice in the mode of curing them, than if they were cooked before they were eaten. But the want of Dutch herring at present in Germany, and the high price of the Altona herring, which obliges the Poor to use Swedish herring, has induced some persons to broil or roast them, though this custom is even now far from being common; but I know of no instance of any one's boiling them.

'As far as I know of Germany, white salted Herring, when good, are everywhere equally esteemed in that Country, and have been purchased partly because when cured according to the Dutch method, they are very agreeable to the palate of the Germans, and partly because, before they had risen to so great a price, they afforded, with a few Potatoes, not only a wholesome but a cheap meal. In the Roman Catholic part of Germany, the want of fish for the fast days occasions an additional demand for them; but, on the other hand, this additional demand is rendered less powerful in its operation, by the circumstance that the Roman Catholic part of Germany lies to the South, the consequence of which is, that the length of the land carriage greatly enhances the price of herring before they arrive there.

'Since I have been acquainted with Germany, I have not heard of any importation of British Herring into that Country before the latter end of 1798, when a vessel arrived from Isle Martin in Loch Broom, laden with 301 barrels; and about the same time a vessel arrived at Hamburgh from Greenock, with 30 barrels on board. Of the quality of the herring brought from Isle Martin or of the price which they fetched, I was not able to gain information; but as no vessel came from Isle Martin in the following year, 1799, it is probable that the Herring that were brought in 1798, were not cured in such a manner as to fetch a price which made it worth while to make a second voyage to Hamburgh. In 1799 were brought to Hamburgh from Leith 664 barrels, from Alloa 260, a lading from Stornoway, and some lading from Shetland, making together (namely, from Shetland) 1,208 barrels. These brought from the Firth of Forth, as well as those brought from Stornoway, I have mentioned above; of the rest I could get no account, other than that they were not suitable to the taste of the Germans. In addition to the preceding, twelve barrels of herring from Greenock were sent for on trial, by a Saxon Merchant; six of them were North Highland, and six were Loch Fyne herring; they were all large herring, but were far from being so fat as the best Dutch herring; the Loch Fyne herring were better cured than the North Highland, and bore a higher price; but both sorts were much inferior to Dutch-cured Herring: one grand objection to them was their great inequality of taste; many of them had a tolerable good flavour, while others in the same barrel had a very disagreeable flavour. This inequality arose probably from a circumstance which I will explain in the answer to the next question.

Do you know any reason which gives Dutch herring a preference to British, and if so, in what respects are they preferable?

'There are various causes which give Dutch herring a preference to the British: First, the Dutch are much more exact in regard to the quantity of the Salt, so as neither to render the Herring too salty, nor on the other hand to endanger their stinking from using too small a quantity. Secondly, in regard to the quality as well as quantity of Salt, whence the

Dutch herring derive their peculiar fine flavour. Thirdly, in regard to the sorting of herring before they are salted the second time. The second salting of the Herring is performed after the Herring are brought to Port, by a set of men called Fish Wardens; and it is the skill of these men which gives the Dutch Herring their peculiar excellence.

'Another material cause of the difference between British-cured and Dutch-cured Herring consists in the mode of treating them when they are first taken out of the water. It is well known that the sooner a Herring is gutted and salted after it is taken out of the water, the better it is, and that by being suffered to lie only a few hours in the open air, especially if the Sun shines, it is rendered less capable of receiving a fine flavour; hence the Dutch never expose their Herring uncovered to the open air, but the moment they draw the Herring out of the water, they throw them into brine or pickle; then they immediately gut and pack them; and if any remain, when they shoot their nets again, they are obliged by the laws of Holland to cast that remnant overboard as unfit for use; hence arises that equality observed in the Dutch Herring. But in North Britain, when the Herring are taken out of the net, they lie exposed till they have been gradually gutted, salted, and packed; those which are packed first, therefore, have a much better flavour than those which are packed last; and hence arises probably the inequality in the same barrel (tho' they are afterwards re-packed) which was observed above. Wherever the Boat-fishery is adopted, and the Herring are cured on shore, it might be difficult perhaps to adopt this part of the Dutch method, unless Curing-Houses were built on the different Lochs, as already on Loch Torridon, to which the Fishing-Boats might carry their draughts of Herring as soon as they get them; but as many Busses are sent out every year from Greenock and Campbeltown, no reason can be assigned why those Busses should not in all respects imitate the Dutch Busses; and if after the first curing on board the Busses had been regulated according to the Dutch method, Fish Wardens were established at Greenock and Campbeltown, or other places, to receive all the Herring which arrive, to arrange them in Fish-houses on the footing of Enkhuysen and Vlardingen, then to unpack, sort, and re-salt the Herring according to the different Markets for which they are intended, British-cured Herring might attain the excellence of Dutch Herring. It must be observed, however, that not even the Dutch mode of curing will do for the German Market, if the Herring themselves are meagre, whatever may be their size; the Herring must be round and fat, called by the Dutch Volehering, and such as they caught in the deep sea after the 24th of June from the Shetland Islands Southwards. Meagre Herring, caught late in the season, the Dutch send to the West Indies.

Do you think the sale of British Herring might be promoted in Germany; to what extent might it be carried; and what would be the best means of encouraging it?

'The sale of British Herring might certainly be promoted in Germany to a very considerable extent; but it is impossible, even to conjecture, with any probability at present, how many thousands of barrels might be disposed off annually. That the consumption of

Herring in Germany, which was estimated above at only 130,000 barrels annually, under the present circumstances might be more than double is evident, not only because with the present importation there is an universal complaint of scarcity, but because the Dutch alone, when their Herring Fishery was in its most flourishing state, and they used to employ above 2,000 Busses in it, are supposed to have furnished Germany with more than 300,000 barrels annually. With respect to the best means of encouraging the Herring Trade with Germany, the *sine qua non* is the immediate adoption of the Dutch mode of curing; and when that is adopted, the Herring Trade between North Britain and Germany will establish itself without any kind of difficulty, because the advantage of catching the Fish on our own coast will enable us to undersell the Dutch, the Emdeners, and the People of Altona, who have a long voyage to make before they get to the Fishing grounds: And as the Swedish Herring, which a few years ago were much cheaper than our Herring, have been gradually rising in price, till they have at length (I do not mean the present year 1800, after the failure of the Swedish Herring Fishery in November and December 1799, but I allude to the two preceding years, in which there had been no dearth) reached the Price of Herring at Greenock, it is evident, that as soon as our Herring have attained the excellence of Dutch Herring, not even the Swedish will be able to hold out the Markets against them.

'Those parts of the British Coast which lie the nearest to those Fishing Grounds, on which such fat Herring may be caught as are fit to be cured for the German Market, are undoubtedly best situated to carry on the Herring Fishery, with a view to supplying the German Market. Hence neither Yarmouth, nor any other Port on the Eastern side of South Britain, is to be recommended for this purpose; a very advantageous place appears to be Wick, in the County of Caithness, because it is to the North-East, East, and South-East of that Coast that the Dutch used to catch the best Herring. We might even establish there a Colony of Dutch seamen skilled in the Herring Fishery, of which we have now many hundreds serving partly on board our Ships of War, and partly on board our Merchantmen; but if such an establishment be made, it must not be forgotten to procure professed Fish-Curers like the Dutch Wardens, to put the finishing hand when the Busses return to Port; and these Fish Wardens should be subjected by Law to the same regulations, as those to which the Dutch Fish Wardens at Enkhuysen and Vlardingen are subject. The time for carrying on the Fishery, off the Coast of Caithness, is from the 20th of June to the end of July, when the Herring are in their highest season. An establishment might likewise be made on the Western Coast of Scotland for the purpose of catching and curing Herring for the German Market: For instance, a Colony of Dutch Fishermen might be settled in the neighbourhood of Loch Crinan, who, when they had given their Fish the first curing, according to the Dutch method, might send them through the Crinan Canal (which will soon be finished), to be sold to Merchants at Greenock; these Herring would then be brought to a Fish-house proposed above to be established there, and be rendered by a Fish-Curer fit for the German Market. The Clyde and Forth Canal affords them an easy method of transporting them to Hamburgh.

'N.B. I recommend the employment of Dutch Fishermen, because when the Scottish Fishermen and Curers once see how much it is to be got by the adoption of the Dutch

method, they will be more inclined to embrace it: Thus the Dutch method will be gradually adopted at Oban, Tobermory, Stein, Ullapool, and other Fishing establishments.

*Are Swedish or Pomeranian Herring consumed in Germany in large quantities; and if not, what
reasons impede their introduction?*

'Since the time that the usual supply of Dutch Herring has failed, on account of the
War, a very great quantity of Swedish Herring is consumed in Germany; for, though the
Germans do not relish Swedish Herring, yet the lower classes are obliged to purchase
them, or go without, because the Altona and Emden Herring bear at present so great a
price; but last year the Swedish Herring Fishery (which is carried on in November and
December, when a shoal of Herring from the North Sea usually fills all the bays and
creeks from Gothenburg to Stromstadt) was very defective, and therefore the
Exportation of salted Herring from Sweden is prohibited till November, 1800, that the
Swedes themselves may not have a too scanty supply. The reason of its failure was that a
part of the shoal, instead of going towards the Sound, entered the Elbe, and another part
again, instead of stopping before the Sound, entered the Baltic, and advanced to the
Island of Ruigen, and other parts of Swedish Pomerania, where no Herring had been
seen for a considerable time. Whether any of the Herring caught on the Coast of
Swedish Pomerania were salted, if they were, to what amount, and of what quality, are
questions which I am unable to answer.

'Swedish Herring are not agreeable to the palate of the Germans, because they are
not cured according to the Dutch method, and the peculiar mode of taking the
Herring on the Coast of Sweden, must render the adoption of the Dutch method
extremely difficult, if not impracticable.

'I have known so many Englishmen abroad who have had opportunities of tasting
Dutch Herring, and have thought their taste very agreeable, that if our Herring were
cured as well, I have no doubt that there would be a great demand for them, and that
they would be purchased as a cheap, wholesome, and palatable food, both in London
and other parts of England. But it is not surprising that the salted Herring, whether
Scotch or Irish, or Isle of Man Herring, which are at present exposed to sale by the
London Fishmongers, are not much sought after; for though they possess the first quality, that of cheapness, they are quite defective in the two last, being neither palatable nor
wholesome; they are either over-salted, and their flesh rendered hard, as well as briny, or,
on the other hand, they are cured in the contrary extreme, and taste as if they came out
of train oil.

'I have no other observations to make, than that which results from the preceding
statement, namely that the only method of promoting the sale of British salted Herring
at home, as well as at the German market, is to adopt the Dutch mode of curing, to
adopt it to its full extent wherever it is possible, and, where it is not, to adopt so much of
it as circumstances will permit. It would be likewise a great advantage, if measures were
taken, as soon as possible, to introduce the Dutch method in some parts of North
Britain, in order that the German Merchants may be convinced before the War is over,

and the Dutch vessels can get out again, that we are capable of furnishing them with good salted Herring; whereas, if we wait till the Dutch have regained the German market, the German Merchants, after the many bad specimens of British Herring, may then be less disposed to make new trials of them. It is said that the Dutch method, which is certainly unknown in Scotland, as appears from actual experience, as is acknowledged by the best judges in that country, (Mr Osborne, Solicitor of the Customs at Edinburgh, in a letter dated 18th October, 1799, used the following expression: 'the mode of curing Herring in Scotland is in general very exceptional;') is known to the Yarmouth Fishermen, though the distance of Yarmouth from those Fishing Grounds where the best fat Herring are taken, and the consequent expense of fitting out Busses, confines them to the Fishery on their own Coasts, where the Herring are meagre, and are unfit for the German market, except as red Herring; whether it would be proper to send Yarmouth Fish Curers into Scotland for the season, which is about to commence, or whether, if the Yarmouth Fish Curers should be deemed insufficient, it would be necessary to take other methods in order to introduce completely the Dutch method, the Committee, after the necessary information has been given on this subject, will be best able to determine.

In another paper from October the same year I noted the following:

'James McDowell observed a very big herring-hog in the River Comber (Ireland). A local blacksmith stripped off and jumped into the river with a pitchfork, but, although the herring-hog attacked him, it was killed. Once the tide had ebbed the hog was measured. It was 9¼ feet long and 13½ feet in circumference, with a broad fin on its back and five rows of teeth. Weighing 1,100 lbs, it produced 29 gallons of oil.'

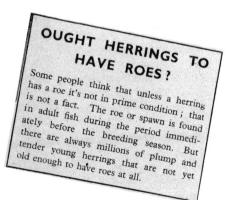

OUGHT HERRINGS TO HAVE ROES?

Some people think that unless a herring has a roe it's not in prime condition; that is not a fact. The roe or spawn is found in adult fish during the period immediately before the breeding season. But there are always millions of plump and tender young herrings that are not yet old enough to have roes at all.

Index

Places

General

If you are interested in purchasing other books published by Tempus,
or in case you have difficulty finding any Tempus books in your local bookshop,
you can also place orders directly through our website

www.tempus-publishing.com

or from

BOOKPOST, Freepost, PO Box 29, Douglas, Isle of Man IM99 1BQ
Tel 01624 836000   email bookshop@enterprise.net